RAGS TO RICHES

Motivating Stories of How Ordinary People Achieved Extraordinary Wealth!

Gail Liberman and Alan Lavine

Authors Choice Press
New York Lincoln Shanghai

Rags To Riches
Motivating Stories of How Ordinary People
Acheived Extraordinary Wealth

Authors Choice Press
an imprint of iUniverse, Inc.

For information address:
iUniverse, Inc.
2021 Pine Lake Road, Suite 100
Lincoln, NE 68512
www.iuniverse.com

Originally published by Dearborn

This publication is designed to provide accurate and authoritative information in
regard to the subject matter covered. It is sold with the understanding that the
publisher is not engaged in rendering legal, accounting, or other professional service. If legal advice or other expert assistance is required, the services of a competent professional person should be sought.

Senior Managing Editor: Jack Kiburz
Interior Design: Lucy Jenkins
Cover Design: Design Alliance, Inc.
Typesetting: the dotted i

ISBN: 0-595-30091-X

Printed in the United States of America

DEDICATION

This book is in memory of Robert Deitchman,
who devoted his life to helping people in rags.

ACKNOWLEDGMENTS

It's tough to talk about money.

For some reason, society puts a number of stigmas on how much money you have. Everybody seems to want it. Yet some—even those who have it—think it's evil. Others think it's not polite to talk about money. Moreover, many think that talking about money discolors their other worthwhile achievements.

The people described in this book represent only a fraction of those we contacted to learn how people can go from rags to riches. Most are extremely busy, but they wanted other people to learn from their experiences.

We wish to give the following people our heartfelt thanks for taking their valuable time to talk to us: Del Hedgepath; Chi Chi Rodriguez and Eric McClenaghan, president of Chi Chi Rodriguez Management Group Ltd., Stow, Ohio; Jay Thiessens; Fran Kelly; Judy Walker; Paul and Cheryl Jakubowski; Joe and Eunice Dudley; Dal La Magna; Lisa Renshaw; Marvin Roffman; Humberto and Georgina Cruz; Scott Oki; Dennis Lardon; Tim and Karen Faber; and Henry Lo Conti Sr.

These people bared their souls to us for one specific reason. They wanted you, the reader, to learn exactly what it takes to go from rags to riches.

We'd also like to give special thanks to Cynthia Zigmund, Dearborn associate publisher, for making this book possible.

CONTENTS

INTRODUCTION

Millionaires are viewed by many as mythical creatures who in some mysterious way managed to amass great fortunes. Some look on these people as local heroes who made it big with a brilliant business idea or from unusually savvy investments. Others, who have amassed several hundred million dollars or even billions of dollars, are national figures. In the 1920s through the 1940s, for example, presidents consulted with Bernard Baruch, a Wall Street guru and multimillionaire. Today, everyone wants to know what highly successful people have to say about our economy, world affairs, and government policies. After all, these people made it on their own in a dog-eat-dog world, right? Why wouldn't they have important things to say that would benefit and inspire all of us?

That's why we've written this book. You won't read too much about people you already know a lot about. Rather, the focus is about people—like you and us—who overcame poverty or, in some cases, middle-class lifestyles and single-handedly beat seemingly insurmountable odds to become financially successful. They may not be advisors to presidents, although perhaps some could be. But their stories can serve as an inspiration to all of us.

We think there's no better way to learn how to make money and hold onto it than to examine how other folks, who once had the same daily struggles we do, already have succeeded. In fact, we're willing to wager that many of these people had to struggle even more—people like Jay Thiessens (see Chapter 3), who grew up illiterate in Nevada but became a successful local businessman and millionaire. Or Judy Walker (see Chapter 5), who was among the first 20 black applicants ever admitted to Mercy College in Detroit. Now she's a successful real estate entrepreneur.

By reading about these people's strategies and the obstacles they overcame as well as the lessons they learned and mistakes they made—told, in most cases, firsthand—we're hoping you'll gain the information you need to mold a better life for yourself. Take David Geffen (see Chapter 6), a billionaire who grew up sleeping on the couch and wore hand-me-down clothes in Brooklyn. He was made fun of and beaten up by his childhood peers because of his appearance. Geffen, though, never gave up.

By studying these people's suggestions, you can figure out what in your own life you can change to get out of your rut and get yourself onto the right track—whether a financial or moral one. Look at "Chi Chi" Rodriguez (see Chapter 2), Maya Angelou (see Chapter 16), or Dal La Magna (see Chapter 9). Each had unique talents and took advantage of the opportunities that arose, although in some cases a little tweaking was needed. They all had difficult times growing up. But they believed strongly in themselves—even in the face of failures.

This book is not your traditional book about how to make money in the stock market, although you're apt to find some great ideas on its pages. It's not focused on the hi-tech boom of Silicon Valley, although, we admit, we did interview one former Microsoft techie, Scott Oki (see Chapter 14). Oki's parents had been in a Japanese interment camp during World War II.

Nor will you find stories about how the great discount stores—such as Wal-Mart or Home Depot—got off the ground. Those are two massive success stories, but they're also isolated incidents. Nor are we striving to paint a rose-colored picture of the ultimate goal of so many—financial success. Sometimes, financial success just "ain't" that great. Other times, there are obstacles—even though you have reams of money—to overcome. We show you how others have done that too. But if you are inspired and learn how the people in this book improved themselves, it could pay off. You might find yourself working a little harder, getting a promotion at work, starting your own business, or just maybe becoming a little more financially secure.

We do prove one thing: There's nothing magical about accumulating wealth; even though you'll read about magician David Copperfield (see Chapter 12). Nor, you'll see, does having money require you to be any particular age, speak any specific language, or have unique knowledge. We've proven, though, that knowledge, in many cases, helps! We have included some people who never graduated college or even, in at least one case, high school. You can get rich by having a skill or a creative idea, by investing wisely, or, with the right know-how, find success in a field that most people consider low-paying. In fact, you'll learn that merely getting your debts under control could give you the single jump-start you need.

This book is full of one-on-one interviews. Not only will you learn specifics about how people accumulated riches, but you'll also discover the impact money has on people and how they dealt with it. We searched the country to bring you the most varied group of millionaires that we could find.

Exactly how much money constitutes extraordinary wealth? That depends on who it is you talk to. Recent magazine reports have put the figure at $5 million. However, we set the threshold lower—a net worth of $1 million. That's because current statistics indicate there are a mere 4.6 million households with a net worth of at least $1 million out of a U.S. population of more than 274 million!

The median household net worth, according to the Federal Reserve Board, is $71,600. So to the majority of people, it seems, $1 million sounds like an attractive net worth. Besides, once you learn how to build a net worth of $1 million, it's that much easier to grow it even more.

In our efforts to find a varied group—including people in fields you'd never expect could earn $1 million—we include some you probably already know. You'll see an interview with golf great "Chi Chi" Rodriguez, for example, and syndicated Tribune Media Services columnist Humberto Cruz (see Chapter 13). Unfortunately, though, not everyone we tried to talk with would agree to an interview. Business mogul David Geffen was too busy with his company, DreamWorks SKG, his assistant said. Poet-author-actress Maya Angelou didn't consider an interview in good taste, according to an assistant to her literary agent. Although illusionist David Copperfield agreed through his new publicist, Amanda Laurence of Polaris PR, to fax back answers to some written questions we provided, his answers (presto-chango?) never appeared.

We thought these people, though, illustrated success stories important enough for us to analyze how they succeeded. So we scoured published reports to find out everything we possibly could that would reveal what they did differently from the majority of people who haven't quite made it yet. We wanted to know exactly how they overcame the odds.

We hope that by reading their stories and heeding their advice, you obtain the financial information and inspiration you need to reach both your financial and personal goals. Tell us what you think!

—Gail Liberman and Alan Lavine
  <MWliblav@aol.com>

CHAPTER 1

DEL HEDGEPATH

Real Estate Millionaire
Ignores Financial Planner

Del Hedgepath of Kansas City had a crystal clear goal. He aimed to be a millionaire within five years. This was 1995, and his published net worth was $590,000, largely in real estate investments. So when a local newspaper offered to have a financial planner review his finances for free, Hedgepath figured, why not?

Hedgepath, a 35-year-old Kansas City bachelor, achieved his $1 million goal, not in five years, but in two. By May 1999, he reported that a bank financial statement had pegged his net worth at "a little over $2 million."

He completely ignored the financial planner's advice. Diversify and put some assets into growth and, to a lesser extent, aggressive growth categories, the financial planner had advised.

Hedgepath, instead, listened to his gut instinct and common sense. "I know what I've been doing works," he bluntly told the *Kansas City Star* during the makeover attempt. "I don't know if I should take the risk of getting into something I don't know as well." He never did.

You might not think that Hedgepath is the millionaire type. He dropped out of Johnson County Community College, Overland, after one and a half years. Nevertheless, at this writing he was just beginning to change his understated lifestyle thanks to his newfound wealth. He had bought a 3,500 square-foot house for

$500,000—a lot of money in the Kansas City market—and began driving a 1997 Chevrolet Camaro convertible in addition to his pickup truck. An admitted tightwad who used to go so far as to reuse tea bags, he stopped that habit when its mention in a newspaper article drew teases from friends. He has splurged on a housekeeper, and instead of mowing his own lawn, he has a maintenance person from one of his apartment buildings do the mowing. "I don't have time," he explains. He also spends more for his haircuts—$15 instead of the $9 he had spent a few years earlier, although he still does his shopping at Kmart. "If I can save money by taking the red eye flight, I'll do it."

The financial planner who examined Hedgepath's finances had offered what seemed to have been sound advice. The largest share of Hedgepath's assets—80 percent at the time—represented equity in real estate holdings. And his real estate was mostly near the University of Kansas campus. The planner warned that Hedgepath's current holdings could be threatened by such events as an unforeseen zoning change, population shift, overbuilding, or declining values. In addition, the planner told the *Kansas City Star* that "a thoughtfully chosen variety of investments almost always will outperform one solid one. That's often true even if part of the diversified portfolio doesn't do very well."

At this writing, none of the potential threats had occurred, Hedgepath noted. Instead, he had increased his holdings from about 80 units to a whopping 240—representing individual apartments in the building he owns as well as single family homes. The income from these units comfortably covers his living expenses and he expects will ultimately fund his retirement.

"I might be sorry for it," Hedgepath said of his decision to ignore the professional advice. "The planner was suggesting that I diversify into the stock market. To me, that sounds like no fun whatsoever. You're giving your money to someone else."

Hedgepath is not worried. He admits that the few hundred thousand dollars he keeps in a bank to secure a credit line could disappear shortly with his next real estate purchase. Yes, he says, even the real estate market could move against him.

"If I did get into trouble, I would sell or refinance and get my money back out," he said. People, he believes, always will need someplace to live. "If worst comes to worst, I might have to go a year or two without raising the rent." Meanwhile, he is free to tap the large amount of equity he has built up in his buildings, which he has owned for 10 to 14 years.

"All my properties are in good locations—either around Lawrence or the University of Kansas." The University of Kansas is a strong draw, he believes, and should continue to attract plenty of students.

Hedgepath does not own a company. He answers his own phone from a home office, and fax attempts interrupt his phone conversations on a single phone line. Although his workweek generally runs longer than 40 hours, he loves the challenge of what he does and doesn't envision retiring anytime soon. The longest vacation he ever takes—by design—is three days, typically over a weekend.

Born in McLouth, a farming community of 700, Hedgepath had no father to guide him. His father left home when he was a child. His mother, who remarried when he was in high school, worked as a government secretary. She raised him along with his three sisters while they all shared his grandmother's three-bedroom, one-bath home. "When I was smaller, we struggled. We never went hungry and we never had dirty clothes. But there were no vacations, movies, or restaurants."

One thing, though, that his mother emphasized to her children was that there were other ways to live. Particularly with his sisters, he said, she often stressed the importance of looking for men with higher incomes.

"From the 'get-go,' I always knew I wanted to do something I enjoyed and something I made money at," he said. No one in Hedgepath's family was in real estate. Nor was there anyone, other than his mother, who inspired him to succeed. He happened to notice, though, that "most of the wealthier people around had been involved in real estate at some time."

Often, he added, he heard people around town saying that they wished they would have bought real estate years ago. He took those words to heart.

As Hedgepath grew up, he developed an interest in saving money. He chuckles at the thought of how he surprised his mother when she asked what he would like for his tenth birthday. His response: not a bicycle or a toy, as a typical ten-year-old might have answered, but a savings bond.

Unlike many who have succeeded financially, Hedgepath does not consider school or education an overriding factor in his success. Perhaps it's because he had been a below-average student. "I didn't apply myself," he admitted. "I was into being a troublemaker. I was more interested in having a good time."

In fact, he remembers taking a field trip one time with the student council. "For some reason, the whole group of us were late getting back to school." The punishment: the students were required to start copying the dictionary. Hedgepath said he refused and was suspended for three days as a result. His refusal, he confided, was because he really didn't want to be in school in the first place. His mother, he says, spoiled a good time by calling the school and insisting that he be readmitted.

Hedgepath often worked 15 to 20 hours a week while in school so that he would have extra spending money. Initially, he mowed lawns. He remembers working at a gas station; cleaning up slaughtered cows at a butcherhouse; housekeeping in a nursing home; and working as a cook in a fast-food restaurant. He saved enough money to buy a car when he was 16—old enough to drive. It wasn't exactly a shiny new Corvette designed to impress, he stressed. "I would get a car that would get me by and save the rest."

On graduating high school, he took the brazen step of buying his first house in his hometown of McLouth for $12,500 and over his mother's objections. It wasn't hard, he says. McLouth was such a small town that if something was for sale, everyone knew it. Hedgepath bought a three-bedroom, one-and-one-half-bath fixer-upper. "The people who were living there when I bought it had gotten a job transfer.

"I went to the bank for a loan and sold a motorcycle to get a down payment of $1,000 to $1,500." The interest rate, as he recalls, was 20 percent from Bank of McLouth. Hedgepath admits that throughout his career it has always been a challenge to get attractive financing in his market for non–owner-occupied property. Often, the ability to obtain seller financing helped. So did an effort to obtain bank cooperation on a property that was going into foreclosure.

Despite the high rate of interest, Hedgepath was confident he could generate a positive cash flow. He worked his fingers to the bone during every spare minute for at least a month during the heat of the summer on that first house. People kept coming by and asking what he was doing. He painted and made repairs. Then he put a sign out front to rent it. "I rented it for $275 a month, which was pretty high compared with the value of the house." Although he sold the house after eight years for $32,000 in 1995, he managed refinancing it at least two or three times before its sale. "It paid for itself."

Despite his distaste for school, Hedgepath found he enjoyed business subjects and did especially well in business law. Wanting to learn more about real estate, he often borrowed books on the subject from the library. Although he doesn't recall any specific books that influenced him, he says that titles were along the line of *How I Turned $1,000 into $1 Million*. It was not uncommon for him to read a single book as many as three times to make certain he absorbed the information.

Johnson County Community College, where he paid for himself through a student loan before dropping out, provided him the most important connection of his life—the contact that helped him realize his dream of success in real estate.

Hedgepath had befriended one of his business professors, who doubled as a builder. Hedgepath approached the professor about a job and began work for him on construction projects. "I would pick up after the carpenters and paint or mow the lawn." By Hedgepath's standards, he was a "gopher." He found the whole real estate process interesting. Occasionally, he did work at the professor's mansion. "It was the nicest home I had ever seen." Today, he admits, "it wouldn't have turned my head." The job put him closer to his dream of being in real estate. He worked hard at his menial chores, and his efforts drew favorable comments from neighbors.

The professor owned an apartment complex that was just four or five years old, "but he was the type that had too much going on," Hedgepath said. "He'd open his briefcase and paperwork would fall out. He would always lose his keys. He was juggling careers as a builder, professor, and an owner of rental property. Meanwhile, he had a family. It was all just too much for one person."

The complex the professor owned was a 40-unit building in Olathe, a suburb of Kansas City. Hedgepath, who had built up a friendship with the professor, talked him into letting him live there and run the property himself. The agreement was that Hedgepath could have an apartment and earn a "couple hundred dollars a month" for running the building.

"It was a newer building but hadn't had any attention. Tenants were tearing it apart. Nobody was paying rent. The rents weren't as high as they should have been." Some of the apartments had too many people living in them.

Hedgepath started out by serving eviction notices. "I don't think I even went to an attorney." As he recalls, he simply went to the courthouse and picked up an eviction package that was available with forms to fill out. Because the building was relatively new, it didn't need major improvements. Hedgepath painted, did cleanup work, and exterminated.

That building, which he managed for about two years—even after it was sold to new owners—gave him invaluable experience in managing property. It was through managing the building that Hedgepath learned valuable lessons on getting along with tenants. Among the most important: Express interest in the tenants.

If a tenant had a plumbing problem—perhaps no hot water— and the complaint came in on a Friday night, Hedgepath learned to handle the situation very delicately. Getting a plumber on Saturday, when plumbers charge overtime, would cost extra. So Hedgepath would immediately call the tenant back, express sympathy and concern, and promise that the plumber would be there on Monday, when rates reverted to standard prices.

Avoiding a Saturday job, yet calling immediately, saved on the building's bottom line yet showed Hedgepath was a caring manager quick to respond.

After buying his first home in McLouth, Hedgepath bought a duplex, giving him a total of three rental properties. Then the purchases snowballed.

As he amassed his real estate holdings, each purchase was made with an important goal in mind. Hedgepath not only tried to buy the property with no out-of-pocket money, but he actually tried to finance his deals and still come out with cash in his own pocket. Anytime you buy an apartment building, he notes, there is an opportunity to come out of the deal with money, including credit for a tenant's deposit, taxes, and deferred maintenance. Plus, he says, on larger projects he tries to get the seller to carry back a mortgage. The more cash he emerges with and the more liberal the terms he can get, the more cash he has on hand for his next deal, which may be just around the corner.

Although he considered taking courses on buying property with no money down, Hedgepath decided that reading and hands-on experience already had taught him more than he likely could learn elsewhere. He recalls that one professor in a night class made each student stand up and tell the class what each was doing and why he or she was taking the course. The professor was so impressed with Hedgepath's real estate success that he sat back and remarked that Hedgepath should be teaching.

Hedgepath was particularly proud of a deal he did on a seven-unit building in Lawrence, a college town 30 miles west of Kansas City. "The guy had it for sale and was losing it in foreclosure because he wasn't giving the house enough attention," he said. Nearly half the units were vacant and many of the others had tenants who weren't paying rent. It was listed through a real estate company. "I paid $69,000." The owner had been buying it on a contract for a deed from the original seller, who was foreclosing. "I took over the balance from the original seller."

The real estate company needed a 7 percent commission. Hedgepath convinced the Realtor not to take it in cash but to let him pay it over the next seven months.

Meanwhile, Hedgepath came out of the deal with extra cash from deposits, rent, and taxes in addition to several thousand dollars for deferred maintenance on the building. Total: $3,000 to $4,000. Not only was the house in a great location—walking distance to campus—but the house he bought for $69,000 was appraised at $180,000 some five years later. Instead of selling it, he used the property to borrow against. "It's tax-free money when you do that," he said.

Hedgepath acknowledged it was tough going when he was starting out. He didn't have much money. If he got involved in a huge renovation project, he wasn't getting income from it because it was being remodeled. "A lot I tried to do myself. A lot of times, I had no idea what I was doing." On the other hand, he also had little to lose. Luck and a good real estate market played a hand in the positive results, he admits.

One rueful note emerged in his real estate career though. Hedgepath had worked at a night club for about three months and thought it would be a fun business to get into. He bought a bar and grill on contract but found he had made a bad move.

He owned the business for two years. "It was strictly a type of college hangout," Hedgepath reflected. "In the first year, it was the hot place to be." Then came summer break, and it never got busy again.

"I pretty much gave it back to the guy I bought it from—with some extra money. He ended up settling for $10,000, and I made $666 monthly payments for 15 months. It was a lot of money." He admits that was a low point in his life. He owned three to four other properties at the time and was threatened with court action. The property never was foreclosed on because Hedgepath was successful in negotiating with the mortgagee.

"It was kind of an embarrassing time in my life," he said. The bills for utilities and rent were coming, and there just wasn't enough income to cover them. Nevertheless, he says if he could go back and erase the experience, he wouldn't.

The experience taught him he could bounce back—no matter what. It also taught him a key to financial success that he continued to use despite contrary financial planning advice: "I'll stick with what I know." From then on, he was determined to stick with owning real estate and residential properties.

Besides avoiding use of his own money, Hedgepath had some other unconventional strategies to get where he is today. For one thing, when he was starting out in real estate, he never used a real estate agent. "I would look for a drive-by property for sale. I'd look for a house that was in disrepair with cars on the front lawn and broken windows. This told me the person needed to sell."

Then he would call the county to find out who owned the property, and he'd either call or write a letter to the owner. "If I had easy access to the owner's phone, I'd call to introduce myself and say I noticed your house at such and such an address, and was wondering if you want to sell it."

He'd specifically target the homes with the cars and refrigerators in the front yard, staying clear of the nicer homes on the block.

Sure, the houses needed repairs, but Hedgepath was unafraid. Occasionally, if he thought an inspector could help him in the negotiations, he'd hire one and pick his or her brains in the process. Eventually, he learned how to spot problems on his own. A wall in the basement with a big horizontal crack down the middle was a sure sign of a foundation problem. "I've never known a problem that couldn't be remedied."

Hedgepath says he has sold only three or four properties in his life. He still rarely uses an agent. Nor has he had any liquidity problems, which are typical of owning real estate. He admits, though, that "a couple properties lack a positive cash flow." But cash flow is not always the most important factor when it comes to real estate, he stresses. "There are other ways investors are making money. You're building up equity every month. You get a tax break. Inflation is increasing the value of your property."

Hedgepath says he now can look at a property and immediately run the numbers through his head. He figures he can buy a four-bedroom house across from a campus and dramatically increase rental income by putting in a dishwasher for $500 or $600 or by spending $400 to $600 on a washer and dryer or paying another $100 for ceiling fans. Other factors that allow you to collect more rent, he notes, are central air-conditioning and the landscaping in front of the house.

For the majority of the property he wished to sell, he merely would stick a For Sale sign in the front lawn and sell it for top dollar within a month. He says he is able to do that because he buys his property in prime locations. "I wouldn't buy a property that was in a very distressed area. I wouldn't want to deal with the type of tenant such an area might tend to attract. I wouldn't be attracted to a building that had a bad foundation. I wouldn't buy a building where I wouldn't live myself—next to a railroad track."

For a large building, he looks at the rent roll and projects what he can have it up to in another 12 months. Then he subtracts the mortgage, insurance, taxes, utilities, and the cost of a maintenance person and manager. And now, on occasion he does use a real estate agent to buy some larger properties.

Another key to Hedgepath's success is negotiation. Hedgepath is careful to shun a suit and tie for important negotiations. "Right now, I have on a pair of shorts and tennis shoes. Even though I may be looking at a $1 million deal, I want them to think it's just little 'ole' me. It puts us on more of a personal level. The sellers might relax a little bit more. They don't think they're going up against someone tough trying to squeeze them and get every last concession." He follows that rule—whether he's negotiating with one of his own property managers, a seller, or a contractor.

Another rule of thumb: Never be the person to mention the first price. Instead, always get the other person to say what he or she needs. "I always try to find out exactly what the other person needs—not what they want. I never give anything more than what they need."

Hedgepath also tries to find out exactly what a seller is going to do with the money he gives them. "It tells me what I need to come up with. If he's selling because he's getting married and the bride doesn't like rental property, it tells me he doesn't need money at closing and might be willing to carry a second mortgage. If he tells me he's getting foreclosed on by a bank, that tells me I can contact the bank and maybe take over the second mortgage."

Or if a seller says that he or she is a couple of months behind on payments and the bank is urging the seller to get rid of the property, Hedgepath might suggest that the seller provide him a name so he can contact the bank directly. Perhaps he could have the seller contact the bank to notify it that he has a strong buyer. The bank might be more willing to come up with favorable financing.

Hedgepath says he never deals with a person who doesn't have to sell a building. Instead, he seeks out people that he knows he is doing a favor by buying the building at a reduced cost.

Learning a seller's motivation is critical. "If a seller's going to pay a real estate agent, I can pay the real estate agent myself over time. I can negotiate with the agent and get that reduced down." Hedgepath doesn't necessarily need to give extra money to the seller to do the job.

Now, he admits, he doesn't knock himself out paying Realtors over time or negotiating lower commissions, because he doesn't have to. But when he was starting out, these strategies were valuable ways to increase the cash he had on hand to save for his next deal.

Hedgepath is a firm believer in periodically writing down his goals. "It helps me to know where I'm at and where I want to be. When I started, I had the goal of buying two properties a year."

His goal to make a $1 million in five years was firm and in writing. Right now, he says, a personal goal is to get to the gym daily, and he is in a buy mode property-wise.

Hedgepath also is firm with his tenants—another factor that distinguishes him from other landlords. He doesn't screen tenants but has managers who do that. But when anyone owes him money, he does whatever he can to collect, no matter how small the amount. His property managers know that they at least must send a letter or make a phone call to collect from the tenant.

While most landlords are apt to ignore a broken lease, Hedgepath maintains it's well worth a 33-cent stamp and perhaps a few phone calls—no matter how small the amount—to claim what's owed him.

Hedgepath, perhaps based on his own experience, does not give much credit to formal education for his financial success. "If I had a kid, I wouldn't stress that on him," he said. "I don't think it's really been a major factor. Certainly, there's tons of stuff I don't know, but for the business I'm in, I feel like I know a lot."

Whether a formal education is worthwhile, he believes, largely depends on a person's goal. If the goal is to be a teacher or doctor, education is a necessity. In Hedgepath's case, though, it wasn't. "For the career I chose, I didn't need an education." In fact, Hedgepath doesn't even have a real estate license.

Hedgepath warns anyone considering a formal higher education to weigh the pros and cons carefully. "You're going to be spending four to six years in class," he says. "There's a good chance you'll be out of the workforce and losing potential income for those years. Add that to the money you're spending or borrowing to obtain your education. Then, ask yourself how worthwhile it is.

"When people my age were in school, I was out making money," he says. "It was kind of a compounded advantage."

It's not that Hedgepath didn't learn anything. For what he does, it's important to know a little about everything—finances, negotiating, taxes, advertising, painting. "Sometimes you have to be a psychiatrist to your tenants." He learned largely through reading and hands-on experience.

In his new house, Hedgepath has two big-screen television sets. There is a hot tub and pond with rocks. French doors open onto the patio, and his office lies just off the living room. Much of his work is handled by three property managers and four maintenance people. In screening property managers, he looks for someone with a friendly appearance who can get new tenants in and make current tenants happy. "I don't look for someone who has experience, because I like to train managers myself."

When a newspaper article in 1997 christened him a millionaire, about half a dozen strangers approached him for money, and there was a little ribbing from his family.

Hedgepath says that once in a while, either at tax time or when he's working on a financial statement, he'll say to himself, "Hey Del, you've done good." But apart from that, he doesn't think much about the money. If he needs something, he buys it.

"Maybe people expect more of me," he says. "They might expect me to pull up in a fancy car, or they might be looking at my watch to see what brand it is. I try to turn that around to be a positive."

Often, Hedgepath said, people mistakenly assume the reason he is doing so well is the result of help from his parents. "For me, that definitely was not the case."

He clearly sees a major difference between people who have earned money and people who have inherited their wealth. "There's a huge difference from the way they spend the money to their work habits—even in their overall happiness. The people who made money are so much happier with themselves. They're not necessarily out to prove or impress anyone." People who get money from their parents, he says, are "out there trying to buy friends a little bit." And, he believes, lottery winners tend to take cruises and buy fancy cars and houses.

Hedgepath says he took advantage of the *Kansas City Star*'s free offer to have a financial planner look over his holdings because it cost him nothing. "Before I met him, I had no idea what he was going to suggest." When he heard the outcome, "I just didn't want to part with money to put in stocks. I wanted to keep it and still do my little game."

CHAPTER 2

JUAN "CHI CHI" RODRIGUEZ

Golfs His Way to Millions

A great skill, a unique sense of humor, and the right agent may have been the keys to financial success for Juan "Chi Chi" Rodriguez.

One of six children, the famed golfer grew up so poor in Puerto Rico that he went without food at times and nearly died from two ailments attributable to vitamin deficiencies.

Today, Rodriguez at 64 has won more than $7 million combined on the Professional Golf Association (PGA) and the senior PGA tours, and he's moved to tears remembering those early days. As an adult, his fingers have remained crippled.

In the manner that has endeared Rodriguez to fans, however, he publicly downplays the impact of his ailments. "The crookedness makes for a perfect golf grip," he has quipped.

Rodriguez was instrumental in revolutionizing the sport of golf away from the stodgy, quiet upscale game that actually had turned off a portion of the nation's population. He brought his brightly colored hats with ribbons to the greens, along with a trademark Zorro-like sword dance.

Whenever it's time to putt, he draws his golf club as if it were a sword, aims it at the ball as if readying for a duel, appears to wipe the blood off the blade, and then ceremoniously returns it to an imaginary holder on his side. "There's an art to doing this sword," he once very seriously told a commentator on TV's Golf Channel who tried to copy this legendary antic using a golf club. "Do it wrong," Rodriguez warned, "and you can break your thumb. [Golfer Lee] Trevino puts it here," Rodriguez explained, holding the golf club out to the right. "The bull is going to get him." The correct way, he demonstrated, is to hold the club straight in front of you—directly at the imaginary bull.

Rodriguez never arrives at a golf course without a slew of one-liners that have lent a unique brand of vaudeville to the sport.

This five-foot-seven golfer says he was brought up to always put others ahead of himself. And many published reports actually have speculated whether Rodriguez, in the early days of his popularity, actually had as much money as you'd expect before his joining the senior tour in 1985. He made $1,037,105 in 25 years on the regular PGA tour and was reported to be concerned about taking care of his family as well as the disadvantaged.

Eric McClenaghan, Rodriguez's agent and president of Chi Chi Rodriguez Management Group Ltd., Stow, Ohio, in which Rodriguez is a partner, cites a comment made by Eddie Elias, Rodriguez's late agent: "He's an agent's dream and a financial manager's nightmare." "He's very marketable and very salable," McClenaghan explains. "He has a tendency to give away all of his money." Nevertheless, Rodriguez, he confirms, is a multimillionaire who definitely dislikes debt. "He has very little of it."

Today Rodriguez, though, seems puzzled when queried about his past finances. "On my first tournament, I made $465. It was the Buick Open in Grand Blanc, Michigan. I shot a 77 the first day. With nine holes to go, I was tied for the lead. I shot a 42 and lost out. It was the most money I've ever seen in my life! Then, in the Eastern Open, played in Baltimore, Maryland, I shot 67, 67, 76, 67. I won $1,400 and finished fourth. I thought that was the most money I'd ever seen. Then I won $5,300 at the Denver Open in 1963. That was the best money I ever made. I bought my mother a home in Puerto Rico and took her out of the Bronx."

Although he averaged about $40,000 a year in winnings in the PGA, in those days, Rodriguez says, that was nothing to sneeze at.

"Life was a struggle when we started," he notes. "But then as it got better, I never looked back. Now it's very, very good—especially since the senior's tour. For the past 20 years, I knew I would never starve."

14

With career winnings of more than $7 million, lifetime spon-sorship deals, and some 50 speeches and golf clinics he often jets to annually, Rodriguez lives comfortably. He owns a condo on the beach in Puerto Rico, a home in Palm City, Florida, and a home and condo in Hawaii. He also owns a private jet and five vehicles, four of which, he says, are Lexuses. Two Lexuses, he reports, are kept at his Palm City home, which he bought after selling a home in Naples, Florida. Naples, he said, was getting too crowded—"too much road rage."

"My wife thinks I'm Rockefeller," Rodriguez tells us. "I'm re-ally oysters Rockefeller." As for the private jet, "this is a necessity. I live with my needs and not with my wants. I need the airplane. I'm always going different places. I don't have it for ego purposes."

McClenaghan agrees. "He couldn't keep the schedule he has without his jet. He's all over the place—especially the past two or three years. This year [1999], he's started to slow down a little bit."

Rodriguez's inspiration for his well-known giving, he has said, came directly from his late father, Juan, who never earned more than $18 a week for his minimum six-day-a-week job toiling under the steamy heat in sugarcane fields.

His father, Rodriguez has reported, never missed a day of work and thought nothing of giving up meals for the unusually frail Rodriguez—or even others, for that matter.

"The man never complained," Rodriguez said of his father. "He'd come home and take off his boots. My sister cut his corns. My daddy never kissed any one of us. My dad used to shake hands and look us in the eyes. He was a serious man. He'd say, 'Hello, son. I've got to sit down with you.' He would give every child 15 to 30 minutes at night to see what we did. There were six of us. He wouldn't go to bed until he talked to every one of us."

Rodriguez acknowledges it was quite a bit different from today's world. "People don't have time for kids. Kids don't have time for parents."

When Rodriguez's father looked at his children and said the lights were going off at 7 PM, the children knew he meant business. If he ordered them up when the roosters crowed, they were up at 4 AM. Showers were mandatory. Never mind that hot water was nonexistent.

Rodriguez says his father encouraged him to be a leader. The training began when he was around 12. "I had a fight with a kid one time. The kid beat the heck out of me. When I came home, my dad said, 'What happened?' I said, 'I fought this kid and I lost.' He said, 'Did you back off?' I said, 'No.' Then, he said, 'You didn't lose. Why you lost was you were not prepared. I'm going to teach you how to fight.'" He did.

He advised Rodriguez to call the challenge the next time and fight again. "I said, 'This time, I did all right,'" Rodriguez reflected. "That's when he and I knew I was going to be a leader. I never backed away from an argument."

As a child, Rodriguez grew up hungry. He suffered from rickets and tropical sprue. "There was no such thing as fried eggs for breakfast; I had black coffee. I used to drink seven cups of coffee a day." After suffering a heart attack and undergoing angioplasty in 1998, he says he switched to decaffeinated tea—doctor's orders. He also halted trips for alternative medicine that he used to swear by. In the past, he had admitted to trying lamb embryo injections, intravenous chelation therapy to get plaque out of his arteries, and homeopathic dentistry to remove mercury-filled silver fillings. "The doctor says your body will tell you when you need them," he says. Rodriguez blames his smoking three packs of cigarettes daily since childhood for his heart attack.

He was born in Rio Piedras and grew up not far from the then-popular Berwind Country Club, which since has moved and come under different ownership. Much like his laborer father, Rodriguez started plowing the sugarcane fields at a wage of $1 a day. He used to admire the club's golf pro. "He made $3 for one-half hour. I wanted to dress like the pro. I wanted to make what he was making. He was always very well dressed, with pressed pants and a shirt. His shoes were polished. I only had one pair of shoes when I was 15 years old." Rodriguez figured a job as a caddy could provide a way for him to make more money. "They used to pay me 10¢ to tee up the balls."

As a child, Rodriguez and others noticed he had a unique skill for hitting balls. He swung a broom at bats and rarely missed. His family also observed his ambitiousness. His father called him "El Millonario" and "Don Juan." His golf game started with a guava tree branch as a golf club and a tin can as his ball. He began sneaking onto the golf course to practice, often with the other caddies.

"One morning we were playing for 5¢ a hole," he told *People* magazine. Although he made a 40-foot putt, there was a frog in the hole that took the ball with it when it leaped out. That, he claims, is how another of his trademarks originated. Now, anytime he gets the ball in the hole, he throws his hat over it so the ball can't "jump" out.

It wasn't only golf that intrigued Rodriguez, though. He played other sports, including baseball. In fact, he hit the semipros with Hall of Fame Puerto Rican Roberto Clemente. And he was said to have boxed until age 15 for sodas. He coined the name "Chi Chi" from a baseball player, Chi Chi Flores, who, Rodriguez once reported, might not have been the greatest but tried harder than anyone. Rodriguez is not the only pro golf star in his family either. His brother Jesus, he says, "has won over 100 tournaments worldwide."

Chi Chi Rodriguez joined the army at 19 for two years and captured a post championship at Fort Still, Oklahoma. He sent most of his earnings home to his family. He subsequently worked as an orderly in a psychiatric clinic feeding and showering the mentally ill at night while practicing golf during the day. At the hospital, which he says was the best job he had ever had, he was earning $80 a month. Trying to better himself, he took a job in 1957 as the new caddie master at the Dorado Beach Resort in Puerto Rico. His salary, he said, quickly skyrocketed from $80 a month to $300 a month.

"I went there with a friend in his car," Rodriguez recalled. "The car broke down five times." Fortunately, his friend knew how to fix it. "We got there." Ed Dudley, president of the PGA for eight years, was the one who hired him.

Peter Cooper, winner of ten PGA events, trained him. Cooper immediately changed Rodriguez's grip and ordered him to practice 50-yard wedge shots until the ball hit the green and stopped. In addition, Cooper ensured that the green was barely watered, making the task even more difficult. Rodriguez, nonetheless, stayed away from tournaments while in Puerto Rico and concentrated on trying to beat his instructor. Once he did, Laurance Rockefeller, one of the Dorado Beach owners, put up a stake so Rodriguez, taking Cooper with him, was able to join the PGA tour.

"Laurance Rockefeller was the reason I have everything I have," Rodriguez said. "He built Dorado Beach in Puerto Rico. At the time it was the best resort in the world."

Not only had Rodriguez worked as an assistant pro and caddymaster but also as a waiter and bartender. "If you were a kid and you could mix rum and coke, and scotch and water, you could be a bartender," he reflected. "In those days, they didn't have the laws they have now. Sometimes, if you didn't get a job as a caddy, they would pay you $1 to tend bar at the golf course."

Rockefeller, a member of a family known for its generosity, gave Chi Chi $15,000 a year to go on the PGA tour. "He liked me and knew I needed help." To qualify for the tour, he had to be a Class A member, which required spending five years working as an assistant pro in the club. "Then you go on tour and have to qualify to be in the tournament." In 1960, it was reported that, at the age of 25, Rodriguez played that first tournament in a long-sleeved white shirt, cuff links, and a necktie.

His first PGA victory came in 1963 at the Denver Open. Seven other victories followed. By the mid-1970s, Rodriguez was reported to be getting as much as $200,000 annually, largely from exhibitions and corporate outings. At this writing, he has won 22 tournaments on the PGA senior tour.

Although it looks like a lot of fun to observers, golf isn't always an easy sport. Earnings are unstable. Unlike baseball, there are no contracts, and it's influenced to a great extent by the player's mind-set. At times, the media reported that Rodriguez had lost his touch. He was supporting his wife, Iwalani, a native Hawaiian, and her daughter from a previous marriage. "I love her as much as I could love my own," he says of his stepdaughter. Sometimes there were crises, such as the death of Rodriguez's father in 1963. Media speculation off and on indicated that the golfer sometimes tried too hard at the game and lost confidence.

Rodriguez, though, who remembers his early hungry days, doesn't consider those days to have been so bad. Nevertheless, he does say the chief catalyst in his financial life came in 1964, when he signed his agent, Eddie Elias Enterprises, Akron, Ohio, just after he won the Western Open. Elias, who died in 1998, had been a lawyer who founded the Professional Bowlers Association. His agency also has represented Phil Donahue, Marlo Thomas, and Phyllis George. "That was the best move I ever made in my life. Eddie and I were like brothers. He made me a very, very successful businessman."

The deal, he says, was that Rodriguez would give Elias 25 percent of everything he could line up. "He said, 'I'd take 20 percent if you do your own taxes,'" Rodriguez said. No thank you. Rodriguez preferred the 25 percent arrangement. "In 1964, 1965, and 1966, I was a mental millionaire," Rodriguez said. "Forty thousand dollars a year was a lot of money then. We used to run out of the woods to play a $50,000 tournament. Now we run back in the woods when it's only $1 million."

Yes, golf, he says today, has changed quite a bit over the years. "In the old days, we didn't play golf for money. You used to play to get a big name for yourself so you could be a head pro at a club. Now we play golf so we can buy the club."

Things started changing, Rodriguez says, when his friend, Jack Nicklaus, got his first jet, a Sabreliner, around 1960. "We saw the money he was making," Rodriguez said. "We thought, hey, maybe we can start making money. We figured when Nicklaus had his jet that he was doing extremely well. He only played 15 tournaments a year! That was tremendous."

Nicklaus, "who's so modest," Rodriguez commented, had his own management company. "The purses went up," he said, noting that television fueled further interest in the sport. "Arnie [Palmer] kept winning. Arnie's the reason golf is so big."

Once Rodriguez signed with Eddie Elias, Elias made several smart moves. One involved investing the golfer's money in about seven buildings in the Akron, Ohio, area. The two aggressively sought properties in which they could claim depreciation. "He was the most brilliant man I ever met in my life," Rodriguez says of Elias. "It takes a genius to recognize another! Eddie Elias was a big believer in real estate property," acknowledges McClenaghan, who had worked with Elias for many years before Elias's death and now is independent of the agency, which continues to exist but represents mostly television commentators. McClenaghan and Rodriguez's agency, by contrast, represents Rodriguez along with other golfers.

"Eddie Elias invested heavily in real estate—not only in Ohio but around the country," McClenaghan said. Elias took Chi Chi with him, and together they owned office buildings, homes, and raw land. He [Rodriguez] still owns some of the properties."

While earning more than $7 million in golf tournaments is nothing to sneeze at, it is personal appearances at golf clinics and speaking engagements, Rodriguez notes today, that account for the overwhelming bulk of his earnings. In fact, almost every Monday of the year, McClenaghan says that Rodriguez has something scheduled.

Rodriguez typically earns $40,000 a day for appearances, McClenaghan says. "And some events are two or three days long." Nevertheless, Rodriguez says he has never felt wealthy: "What Mr. [Sam] Walton [founder of Wal-Mart] says is that any man who knows how much he's worth ain't worth much."

Now that he has plenty of money, though, he is careful not to throw it around, although he says he is a "very, very big tipper." "Even if I go to a restaurant and don't get good service, I still tip the same," he said. "We all have off days."

Too many people, though, use money as a weapon, he believes. "Money should never be used as a weapon. If you buy a nice car because you can afford it, that is wonderful. If you buy a nice car to impress your neighbors, now you're using money as a weapon. It might come back to haunt you."

Rodriguez's sense of humor has become his calling card. "Golf is a kind of stuck-up sport," he told the *Saturday Evening Post* in 1989. "Therefore, it's tough to be a golf fan, because a golf fan has to go there and be a deaf mute. He can't speak, he can't even cough when a guy is hitting a shot. Fans have to be quiet all the time, but they pay their money and they work hard to get there; and when they come to watch, I'm going to make sure that I do something to make them laugh or make them enjoy themselves. What is life without a laugh?"

Although many now say Rodriguez's showmanship was ahead of its time, it initially spawned complaints of distraction from fellow golfers. Even Arnold Palmer issued a warning to him after they played in the 1964 Masters. Dave Hill in the early 1970s went so far as to complain about Rodriguez to tournament officials. Rodriguez offered to punch Hill in the nose for his trouble, according to the *New York Times*. "Now," Rodriguez told the newspaper, "if I do anything on the green, I do it only when I'm the last to putt . . . I want them to know I love them all."

Rodriguez is known as a diehard, failing to cancel games even when ill. In fact, he continued playing a bit too long, he since has admitted, when he suffered his heart attack.

McClenaghan, though, says that after his heart attack, Rodriguez cut back somewhat on his schedule. The cutbacks are in tournaments rather than in exhibitions. "He's playing 24 or 25 [tournaments], tops, versus 30 to 32," McClenaghan said, "so that's another four to six weeks he's kind of laying low."

After his last PGA victory in 1979 at the Tallahassee Open, Rodriguez was reported to have lost his putting stroke and couldn't swing. He actually had thought about retiring when he reached 50 but credited Jack Nicklaus for setting him on the right path when he started to peter out while the two were at Pebble Beach in 1984.

Nicklaus invited Rodriguez to endorse a line of golf clubs for MacGregor Golf Company, which Nicklaus co-owned. "Jack told me I could still play," Rodriguez told the *New York Times*. "That meant a lot."

That contract was the start of a renewed momentum for his career. The following year he joined the senior tour, which stunned the nation with its success, and his playing improved.

The senior tour, which spotlighted well-known names that baby boomers had grown up with, began attracting the attention of corporate blue chip sponsors. After all, sponsoring the senior tour was cheaper than sponsoring the regular PGA Tour.

Yet a National Golf Foundation study commissioned by McKinsey & Co. pegged golf as growing from a $20 billion industry in 1988 to a $40 billion industry in 1998. The National Golf Foundation reports those projections have been realized. Sponsors have been attracted by the game's ability to reach a high-income market of top executives, who were about the same age as the participating senior golfers and often fanatical about the sport.

Performance Research, a consultant firm, in 1991 released a study that said 70 percent of golf fans recognize Cadillac, Buick, and Toyota as major golf sponsors. Forty-seven percent of those fans said they would buy a vehicle from a golf sponsor if everything were equal.

The National Golf Foundation has said more recently that golfers spend $30 billion annually to play golf. Attracting more and more sponsors to the upscale demographic market, the senior tour grew and grew. In 1978, *Business Week* reported there had been only one tournament for pros over 50. In 1989, seniors were to participate in 41 tournaments; by 1999, that number had swelled to 45.

After Rodriguez lined up what was reported to be a "lifetime" contract with MacGregor, a deal with Toyota and other endorsement arrangements followed. Rodriguez initially had tried to get contracts with the Big Three U.S. automakers, reported the *Dallas Morning News,* but each turned him down. By contrast, Toyota, which had begun competing aggressively in the United States and recognized the importance of the Hispanic market in its competitive sales arena, offered him a deal.

The Toyota contract along with the MacGregor deal, Rodriguez had said, made him "secure for life." Financial security certainly helps to eliminate worries that might impede your golf game.

Meanwhile, Rodriguez's advertising deals helped increase his visibility, securing more offers. A slew of subsequent endorsement and spokesmen contracts followed. One that attracted much media attention was his endorsement contract with Callaway Golf. The company was trying to influence wealthier golfers able to afford its clubs' steep $300-plus price tag. The deal gave Rodriguez 75,000 shares in stock in 1992. In 1994, after two splits, those shares were said to be worth $10 million.

A 1998 article in the *Tulsa World* credits Rodriguez's use of the clubs for improved play and tournament victory as one factor that made Callaway the hottest seller in golf shops. "Today, the once-small company has become a major player in the golf industry," the newspaper said. Rodriguez says today that he has no affiliation with Callaway or MacGregor.

Along with the popularity of the senior golf tour, casual clothes too gained popularity. In fact, Rodriguez has a clothing line with Block Sportswear, New York, consisting of Chi Chi Rodriguez signature shirts; and Block "could get into other apparel," McClenaghan said. Sponsors began realizing that a company's logo televised on a T-shirt or hat during an event could actually have a greater impact than a commercial.

"When Chi Chi Rodriguez is wearing Toyota and it's an Oldsmobile-sponsored event, they [the viewers] think about that," Robert Cotman, chairman of Joyce Julius & Associates, a sports marketing and consulting company in Ann Arbor, Michigan, told *Advertising Age* in 1992. Besides, it is during the commercials, he had noted, that people "go to the john or get some chips."

McClenaghan says now that despite published reports, the original Callaway and MacGregor deals never actually were for a lifetime. Rodriguez's relationship with Callaway had been a five-year agreement that ended, he said, because "Callaway was asking for things that Chi Chi couldn't commit to." MacGregor, he added, fell on hard times so it was deemed in the best interest of all parties to end the relationship.

McClenaghan says that most deals with golfers are not for life, although many assume they will be; in fact, Rodriguez's current deal with Orlimar Golf is for life. Under the arrangement, Rodriguez has agreed to use Orlimar's golf clubs and be a spokesman for the company. At this writing, McClenaghan reported, Rodriguez also had a deal with Toyota. While it's not written that it is for life, McClenaghan said, "He has such good rapport with the executives, I can't see that ever lapsing." He also has had a long-term deal with CertainTeed Corporation, a company based in Valley Forge, Pennsylvania, that makes insulation, roofing, shingles, siding, and vinyl windows, in addition to having a "small deal" with Liberty Mutual.

"Chi Chi is very fortunate," McClenaghan said. "Most of the contracts he's signed are long term. Once he signs a deal, he's usually with that company for a long time because he does a great job."

Rodriguez is very outspoken about how he handles his endorsements. "I have turned down more commercials than most athletes ever have," he said. "I just don't want to be prostituted. I never put a logo on my hat. My father said my head is the highest part on earth and I must never sell it. I carry things from my shoulders. I don't carry things on my head. I've probably turned down as much as $1 million a year."

He says he also only endorses products he uses. It is unethical, he says, to endorse more than two products at one time. "I used to be at Spalding too. Also Northwestern. A lot of athletes make a lot of money and they never use it (the product). The government ought to make a law that you can't do that."

Federal Trade Commission Guidelines on Endorsements and Testimonials suggest that if an advertiser represents that the endorser uses the endorsed product, the endorser must have been a bona fide user of it at the time the endorsement was given.

Besides endorsements, sponsorships, golf clinics, and speaking engagements, Rodriguez says he has designed about eight golf courses. "I never put money in anything that eats or grows," he says. He also has a book, *101 Super Shots* (HarperCollins, 1991), and a video, *Chi Chi's Bag of Tricks* (ABC).

Rodriguez provides his own take on the growth in golf's popularity and the senior tour. He believes golf has grown at the expense of some other sports—especially tennis. "Tennis did so well with a bunch of great role models," he said, citing people like Arthur Ashe and Chris Evert in earlier days.

"You take tennis and the role models are guys 15 to 25. After that, they're gone. They don't have the experience and savvy that golfers have. In golf, the role models are guys that are 30 and older. I also think that every time—and I'm not going to pick just on tennis—every time an athlete in baseball or football gets into trouble, that makes golf even better!" Women's tennis, though, he observes, might well be making a comeback.

Sometimes, Rodriguez acknowledges, his endorsement deals include obtaining shares of stock, as in the Callaway Golf deal. But Rodriguez offers a warning about stock to potential investors. He cites the time when he lost $8 million to $10 million on a stock investment he simply held too long. "I became a hog," Rodriguez said. "Hogs get slaughtered."

He also criticizes the capital gains tax. "Capital gains ought to be taken away," he declares. "There should be no capital gains. If you buy a stock for $800 and it grows to $1,000 and you sell it, you've got to pay $200 in capital gains. Take that $800 and reinvest it and sell it again, you've got to pay tax again. They tax you and tax you and tax you.

"If you go into the market and double your money," he says, "get out! Where else can you make a 100 percent profit? I became a hog. I just kept it too long instead of dumping it."

Reports had hinted that Rodriguez was having trouble making ends meet in the early 1980s. "I could have used the money," the *Dallas Morning News* quoted Rodriguez as saying on writing a check to help finance a school. "The IRS sent me a get-well card. I'd make $37,000 and spend $200,000."

Meanwhile, in 1979 he cofounded the Chi Chi Rodriguez Youth Foundation for troubled youths in Clearwater, Florida, with Bill Hayes, a teacher, golfer, and part-time detention officer. The foundation, a 501(c)(3) nonprofit organization, now runs four different programs for children with low self-esteem and poor interpersonal skills and grades; it serves 450 children. It has two golf courses and a voluntary minischool designed to provide an interactive program for fifth and sixth graders who are having trouble adjusting in public school.

Rodriguez himself left high school in 11th grade. "I got a little tired of hearing my teacher say there is life on Mars. . . . If you questioned teachers, they threw you out."

Even though he dropped out of school, he considers higher education essential in today's society and says he provided 14 children scholarships to go to college. "It used to be that 99 percent of millionaires never went to college," he said. "That's really changed.

"Every kid should try to go to college because they can take away your citizenship, passport, ticket, and your money, but they can't take away your diploma.

"When you're educated and you're working for a corporation, your goal should be to buy the corporation some day; if you're intelligent, you can do that." He also suggests, though, that teachers "ought to listen a little more to kids when they bring up an argument."

Although Rodriguez didn't finish high school, "I've always read quite a bit. My daddy always used to tell me, 'Son, when you read something, make up your own mind with it. Don't let whatever you read influence your mind.' My daddy was a brilliant man. He never wanted anybody to control your brain."

Rodriguez advises that another key to success is to maintain confidence. He cites the case of Abraham Lincoln, who repeatedly failed the bar. Yet he ran for the Senate. "He lost twice and ran again." People, he said, always put him down. Even when he became president, his Gettysburg address was panned as the worst speech ever. "Now," he says, "it's the most famous speech."

He also advises that you set goals and picture yourself achieving them. "No matter what happens, go forward. Give it your best shot.

If you give it your best shot, it's just as good as if you had conquered it. Pick a role model like me or Lee Trevino or Arnold Palmer. Say 'Hey, if these guys can do it, I can do it too.' Don't look back."

Rodriguez has been hailed for his humanitarian efforts and has won the U.S. Golf Association's Bob Jones Award. Often, many say, he is the instigator behind getting his corporate sponsors to promote events to raise money for charities. Rodriguez repeatedly has said his idol is the late Mother Teresa, known for her work with the unfortunate and whom he once met in the Philippines.

Besides raising more than $5 million for his Chi Chi Rodriguez Youth Foundation, Rodriguez was named to the Horatio Alger Association in 1986 and the World Humanitarian Sports Hall of Fame in 1994. In 1992 he was inducted into the PGA World Golf Hall of Fame. In 1993 he received the Civilian Meritorious Service Medal, the highest award given by the U.S. Department of Defense. And in 1995 he was grand marshal for the 106th Tournament of Roses Parade in Pasadena, California.

"I have an orphanage in Mexico I just finished. There's a bed for every kid—137. When I go back in November [1999], we're going to raise more money and go do another orphanage. I give money to kids," Rodriguez maintains. "Adults had their chance. Kids haven't had their chance. I don't believe much in giving money to some organizations that don't show me their books. I have organizations that send me letters to raise money. I call them back and say, 'Send me a dry sheet.' They never send it.

"We have the books of my foundation open to everybody. We have nothing to hide. It bothers me when some organizations collect money and as much as 80 percent of the money goes to administration. I give money to kids."

In fact, he says, a chief goal of his is to keep his Chi Chi Rodriguez Youth Foundation running through an endowment when he dies. Although he already has raised $1.5 million, his goal is to raise $10 million.

McClenaghan says that Rodriguez never has trouble getting his sponsors involved in his charitable work. "When he's doing exhibitions for sponsors, he has a tendency to start talking about them [his charitable projects] because it's the love of his life. He doesn't go out there looking for them to donate. But after they're around him, they start jumping on the boat.

"I'm trying to slow him down," McClenaghan admitted. "He's always trying to help people. I have to say let's step back here and make sure everything's taken care of. Then we'll move on."

Rodriguez says that he currently has no plans to retire. "Most people pay to do what I do. I get paid, so why retire? I need something to do. At our age, guys like us, we don't have nothing to do—except maybe Lee Trevino. He's lucky. He got married to a young lady and has two young kids." Rodriguez, during this interview, explained that his own wife was in Hawaii hosting a junior masters world tournament.

If there is any downside to wealth, Rodriguez says it has been some of the repercussions of celebrity that come along with it. Fans sometimes get insulted when he is forced to turn down requests for autographs. "Two or three guys say, 'And I thought he was a nice guy.'"

If Rodriguez turns anybody down, he says, there is a very good reason. "Sometimes I will sit on a golf cart and sign autographs for one hour. After a while, your shoulder hurts." In fact, he says, sometimes it hurts so much he has to go to a trailer so that therapists can massage it.

Also, he notes, he risks a $300 fine if he signs autographs on the golf course. Rodriguez says that in one hour he typically signs 500 autographs nonstop, and it hurts to have fans think he's being rude just because he stops. "Sometimes I have to leave. I'm hurting. Or sometimes I'm just walking fast," he says. "They don't know I'm going to the bathroom."

CHAPTER 3

JAY THIESSENS

Despite Illiteracy, Builds $5 Million-a-Year Business

For nearly 56 years, Jay Thiessens was unable to read, but he faked it. In restaurants, he ordered what he heard others order from the menu, and he laughed at written jokes—without really knowing what they said. Nevertheless, illiteracy didn't stop him from parlaying a $200 check into his own $5 million-a-year company. Fortunately, Thiessens was strong in math and smart enough to negotiate an unusual deal. He convinced a former employer to rent him equipment but hold off collecting the rent until Thiessens was able to generate enough business to cover it. As a result, B&J Machine & Tool Inc., Sparks, Nevada, was born. Living frugally and steadily plowing virtually all earnings back into the company, Thiessens implemented what he could learn from area seminars. Once he became a success, Thiessens admitted his illiteracy to the company's 48 employees. When he was appointed a bishop of the Mormon Church, he finally hired a personal tutor to teach him the one skill that had eluded him for years so he could read the mail coming from Salt Lake City.

Despite the ultimate success of his business, its day-to-day goings-on have always been traumatic. They required him to involve another party—often his wife of 37 years, Bonnie, and owner of all his company's stock. Bonnie is the reason for the B in his company name, B&J Machine & Tool. But needing assistance was only part of the problem of not knowing how to read. "Part of not reading is you've got low self-esteem," Thiessens says. "You consider yourself not as good as other people."

It's when the going gets particularly tough and you want to give up, Thiessens added, that the handicap of illiteracy really slams you over the head. And Thiessens's life had a ton of difficult moments! "I would say to my wife that it's no wonder I can't accomplish this because I'm stupid. It doesn't matter what I accomplished in my life. What mattered is I was not able to read.

"It's still an issue," Thiessens, 56, admits, adding that it's only recently that he has started saying what's on his mind. For most of his life, his handicap made him quiet and withdrawn. Only his wife, close church associates, and his accountant knew.

Now, Thiessens says, "I'm to where I can read practically anything that comes across my desk. I'm a slow reader—my tutor says about fifth-grade level. Because I still lack confidence in myself, any legal documents, even if I read them, I have my wife read them over to me to make sure I didn't miss something important."

In 1999 the U.S. Chamber of Commerce and MassMutual thought enough of Thiessens's accomplishments to award him a Blue Chip Enterprise Initiative National Award. The award initially stemmed not from being unable to read but from overcoming adversity—including a flood in 1997 that almost closed the doors of his company. It was the unusually open way he ran his business that attracted the national attention.

Thiessens and his wife live comfortably in comparison with many in his fast-growing industrial sister town to gambling mecca Reno. Besides their four-bedroom, 2,600 square-foot home, they own a fishing boat and motor home. A father of two, Thiessens, unlike many in this book, doesn't necessarily keep workaholic hours. He is careful to work 8:30 AM to 5 PM five days a week. He is a firm believer, he says, in one of Stephen Covey's *Seven Habits of Highly Effective People*. Take time out to refresh and renew, he firmly believes, and you'll be more productive. He became a Covey fan, incidentally, by listening to the book on an audiotape, the way he has accomplished much of his learning.

Fortunately for Thiessens, money is basically math. Math, along with anything logical or mechanical, happens to be his strong suit. It started when he used to pull toys apart and put them back together as a child. Then he enjoyed driving to school on the bus with a chess set on his lap. He'd use those chess pieces that fit in little holes so he could resume a game on the way home on the 13-mile trip. Chess, he believes, is very similar to business. His favorite toy: an Erector set.

Thiessens grew up largely in McGill, Nevada, one of seven children. His father worked as a welder; his mother was a housewife. "We struggled," he said. "You know, I wore a lot of hand-me-down clothes because I was the youngest boy. But I know there was love in my house. That makes up for a lot of material things."

School was tough. When he was five years old, he had rheumatic fever, so he missed kindergarten. But he stops short of blaming his inability to read on the illness. He places at least some blame on the lack of logic of the English language.

"I figured out I'm a very logical person," he said. "Since I went back and went through the relearning process, to me the letters having two sounds is logical. It's when they have three or four different sounds that I have trouble—like when the *ph* is silent. That makes no sense at all to me!"

The straw that broke the camel's back, though, came around second grade when a teacher told him he was stupid because he was unable to read. "The other kids would call me stupid also and made fun of me because I couldn't read," he says. That incident branded him for life. He began to believe it. He was left back in grammar school one year. "Up until recently I was in my own little shell. I withdrew to keep the hurt out as much as possible. I never let people know I couldn't read." He'd take job applications home for his wife to help him fill out. He'd slough off questions of how to spell something by saying, "I'm the world's worst speller." If forced to read, he would make up words.

Thiessens graduated from White Pines High School, Ely, Nevada, in 1963. High school took five years rather than four because of a bout with rheumatic fever in his freshman year. How did he finally make it through the school system without being able to read? Good question.

A May 1999 letter from Nevada Governor Kenny C. Guinn states that Thiessens is not alone. In his county alone, 12 percent of the adults cannot read. Statewide, the rate is 15 percent; nationwide, 21 to 23 percent of Americans are unable to locate an intersection on a street map, enter background information on a Social

Security card application, or calculate the total cost of a purchase on an order form.

"All I can say is I wasn't a disruptive child," Thiessens said. "I didn't create problems. They just passed me."

Thiessens said that if there were written tests, he wouldn't take them. "The written tests were horrible! I used to love true-false tests because there was a 50–50 chance of getting the answer." He didn't mind the multiple-choice tests either because with four options, he knew he'd stand a 25 percent chance of guessing right. His sense of logic could help him through. "If I got a C, that was the exception. Usually, it was Ds or Fs."

Believe it or not, Thiessens made the honor roll in his last year of high school. He credits that to the fact he was able to take two electives to complete high school, choosing a three-hour course in auto mechanics in the morning and a three-hour course in machine shop in the afternoon, for which reading is not essential.

Although neither of his parents read well enough to help him out through his younger years, Thiessens says his mother inspired him to succeed in many other ways. She always seemed to have the most practical sayings for whatever problem he had.

"If you were pitying yourself, she would say, 'I thought I was bad off because I had no shoes until I met a man who had no feet.'" Thiessens recalled her saying, "Jay, you can have anything you want in this world if you want it bad enough." And, Thiessens said, "That's what convinced me to do my own business." In fact, he admits that he owes completing high school, which he obviously hated, largely to his mother. "She sort of begged me to finish."

His father, who had been a welder, also played a significant role. Thiessens desperately wanted to drive. So at age 17, after his brother taught him how, his father bought him a clunker he had picked up for $50—a 1949 Mercury. Because it was in such bad shape that Thiessens always had to repair something, the car was a major challenge. His father helped and encouraged him. "We overhauled the motor," he said. "We got into the transmission. We even changed the body. Once I tore it apart, I had the motivation to get it put back together so I could drive again."

A year earlier, when Thiessens had finished driver's ed and it was time to take the test for a driver's license, illiteracy reared its ugly head. "I told the driver's ed teacher I couldn't read. He arranged to have the driver's test given to me orally." Then, of course, Thiessens was able to pass.

Thiessens remembers that one of his lifelong fears was having to take the driver's test again. He doubts that he'd be able to get away with an oral version a second time.

Ironically, Thiessens met his wife, Bonnie, in English class. "My cousin was out cruisin' one night and I told him I was looking for a date. He said, 'I've got the girl,' and drove me to her house. She was living with her mother and grandparents. Her parents had divorced. I asked her out."

Because the two were in English class together, Bonnie discovered Thiessens's inability to read, but it didn't stop the relationship from blooming. The couple married in high school, and the day after Thiessens graduated, they moved to Reno to live with his older brother. Thiessens took a job working with machines, only to get fired six months later because his wife called the shop looking for him on a Saturday. The business shop owner, according to Thiessens, was angry that anyone would dare call his shop on Saturday, and he told Thiessens's wife on the spot that her husband was fired. The young groom then went to work at Saunders Machine Shop, a one-man shop, and was there for nine months before he was laid off. Out of work for three days, he found another job at a Reno machine shop, Hankell Manumatics Company. Thiessens recalls that shortly after starting there, he was ordered by a foreman to work on a screw machine. "I'd never seen one of those things before in my life!" he said. "I was working there only a short time, and they fired the guy who was running the screw machine and basically said this is your department."

Thiessens would bring home books and have Bonnie read them. After about two years, he was promoted to foreman, but he didn't make much money. His wife had to work on and off driving a bus and ultimately operating machines in the shop to help support the family. Thiessens says he even taught her how to run the screw machine. Although being in management didn't pay much, his job was worth its weight in gold. It put Thiessens in a position to absorb almost everything there was to know about machines.

"I'm the type of person that if I see something done once, I know how to do it," he said. "I grasp it. I had a lot of older guys working underneath me, so I was able to see a lot of stuff done.

There was a die maker there. I got into making die. This was very critical . . . to getting me to do my own business.

"I learned a lot of management skills," he said. "Even though they paid me poorly, they rewarded me very well by giving me the skills to be successful in this business."

After about nine years, Hankell Manumatics filed for bankruptcy, and Thiessens was laid off just before Christmas. He then found a job with a company that restored antique cars. With the new job, though, his pay dropped—from $5 an hour to $3 an hour. That just wouldn't do. Thiessens had three children to support. (His oldest son, Ronald, subsequently was killed in a motorcycle accident in 1987 when he was 23.) To make up some of the difference in pay, he made a deal with the manager to pay the company $1.50 an hour to use its equipment after hours.

Thiessens started building up business on his own. Meanwhile, another company had bought the building and equipment of his former bankrupt employer and offered him a job for slightly more money. Thiessens left the antique car company. But this time, he successfully insisted on some conditions before agreeing to work there for $3.50 an hour. "I went under the condition that I got to use their machines after hours for free," he said.

The business he drummed up on his own continued to grow. "I worked there for nine months and got enough work that I went in one day and told the boss I could only work four days a week for him. I needed the other day to do my own thing."

Thiessens subsequently tried to cut his time with the company to three days a week but was refused, so he quit. He found a financial partner to buy the equipment he needed and formed Standard Machine & Tool, but that arrangement failed to pan out. "I became a slave to the person who invested the money," he said. In a business, the person who fronts the money tends to have all the power. Thiessens said he, in effect, was on salary as the company's hard-working employee. "That lasted nine months, so I broke up the partnership."

Once his partnership split, he was prohibited from spending any of the money involved in it because it was tied up with an attorney in a trust account. When Thiessens collected the last $200 paycheck from Standard Machine & Tool, his options appeared limited. It's pretty tough to start a business on your own while supporting a family. Thiessens had to be resourceful. He returned to the very employer he had left before forming his partnership and negotiated a deal to rent that company's equipment and space for $500 a month so he could work on his own. Of course, Thiessens had only $200, and his mortgage alone was $105 monthly.

By 1972, though, he was back in business with his new start-up company. Thiessens had talked his former employer into not collecting the $500 a month until he was able to complete enough work to cover the bill.

He, his wife, and their children were forced to live on that piddling $200 check for five weeks. "I had the work. I just had to get it out." Fortunately, he did. He already had a great reputation from his long stint as a foreman. So lining up his old clients—printing press companies and casinos—was not hard. "Anytime I would knock on doors, I would automatically get work," he said.

Although Thiessens still couldn't read, he always listened carefully. He attended seminars to learn as much as he could and was able to retain what he learned. One seminar, sponsored by Ralston Foods, dealt with a team concept of management. Realizing its advantages, Thiessens implemented it in his own shop. "What they said is if you get employees complaining about something, start a committee and allow employees to fix what they're complaining about." Now, he says, his company has an office team, management team, machine shop team, sheet metals team, production support team, and a team that covers employees in his other building, Laser Stamping Specialties. He was planning, at the end of 1999, to move into another 54,000-square-foot facility. He had purchased 11 and a half acres in a total deal of $6.5 million. Already, he's anticipating another 50,000-square-foot expansion he hopes to accomplish in three to five years.

It was a good thing Thiessens took the team concept to heart. It actually bailed out his business in January 1997, when his main office flooded. Thiessens will never forget the day. While he might have trouble grasping *ph,* he easily recalls the exact amount of water that gutted his equipment that day: three feet, five inches. "They didn't like that," he chuckles, referring to his machines. In other words, he translated, his equipment was ruined. Had that same flood occurred four years earlier—before he implemented his team concept—he probably would have closed his doors. "Due to the team concept, everybody felt they were part of the business." All the employees came in, tore apart all the equipment, and worked hard to fix it. B&J Machine & Tools was back shipping products three days after the flood.

"I used to have an attitude if you worked here and would say anything bad about B&J, I'd point and say there's the door," Thiessens said. The team concept taught him not to say things like that but rather allow employees to say what they feel.

"Once they found out they could say anything without being afraid of being fired, they barraged me about everything they thought was wrong with the place." His learned team techniques actually wound up taking a big load off his shoulders. "I don't have to fix it," he says. "*We* have to fix it. Anytime somebody comes to me with a problem, I listen to what they have to say. If I consider it valid, the first thing I say is 'O.K., what are we going to do about it?' It's a company effort."

Hawley MacLean, district manager for MassMutual in Reno, the state's award coordinator for the Blue Chip Enterprise Award, said team concepts are not unusual. "Everybody talks about team management," he said. "The difference is that a lot of people will talk about it and have meetings. But whoever's running the company does whatever they're going to do anyway."

The teams, when truly implemented, according to MacLean, release the owner to accomplish more. "It's a major culture change. Sometimes they're going to have some turnover because some employees may not want to go along with that."

Thiessens's team concept might be among the few success stories. To start, Thiessens says he gave employees some control over their own areas. "If you think about it, traditional management dictates how things are going to be done. To allow the working person to have control over his own job is kind of incredible. That right there gives them the incentive to do it."

Since then, he says, the concept has developed as he attended more seminars. Now, there are team reps that lead weekly one-hour meetings for each team. Team reps are rewarded for taking the responsibility by earning either a dining-out package—dinner at one of three award-winning restaurants and a show with big-name entertainment during the week at a local casino, valued at about $60—or a B&J jacket, which costs about the same. Each team rep has an assistant in case the team rep can't make the meeting. There are also rewards for serving on different task committees. Take the committee charged with planning the company picnic; in exchange for planning the agenda and games and arranging for food over a period of six months, committee members get a $40 gift certificate at their choice of local stores.

"Last month, we had the best month we ever had," Thiessens said. "Also, we had the best quarter we ever had. We bought everybody a gift certificate of $40 as a reward for us hitting our goal. The gift certificate was for two at a really nice seafood restaurant. We also got a reward program where anybody who works here can give anybody else here a reward."

Meanwhile, an awards committee, comprised of one person from each team, but not Thiessens, determines the awards. It's each team's responsibility to let its rep know what kind of award it wants. Too often, management determines the award and the people on the floor don't necessarily consider it a reward. "I once went to a seminar," Thiessens explained. "The gal talking said she did something good one time so the boss rewarded her by taking her out to lunch. She said that was the last person she ever wanted to eat lunch with!"

The team concept, in fostering openness among employees, also helped Thiessens open up. "I went through a lot of changes. I started believing in further education." Ultimately, he read a book along with one of his teams.

Besides the annual revenue he pulls in, Thiessens says he owns his 18,000-square-foot headquarters. He made the last payment in December 1996—just before the flood hit. The headquarters was appraised at just over $1 million, but Thiessens says the machinery is probably worth about $3 million. In addition, he owns another 7,000-square-foot building that lodges a portion of his business, Laser Stamping Specialties, appraised at $300,000. He's particularly proud of that deal. He bought the building around 1973 because he needed more space. "The guy who owned the building walked in my door and says, 'Do you want to buy the building?' I said I'd love to but I can't afford it." "You wanna bet?" the owner responded. He was right.

The deal wound up costing Thiessens $676 out-of-pocket to cover closing costs on the building worth $105,000. "He let me assume the original note. He financed one-third for me. We told the bank I'd put $10,000 down on it. After the escrow closed, I signed a fourth for $10,000. It was appraised at $105,000." The fourth note, he said, actually covered the amount he originally told the bank he'd use as a down payment.

Meanwhile, Thiessens's company is able to use 4,000 square feet in that building and lease out 3,000 square feet. "There's enough income from the tenants to make a payment on the building without Laser Stamping Specialties' money."

MassMutual's MacLean also praises Thiessens's move to computerize his business operations: "They know how much time each person's spending on each component. They know whether a client or product is profitable."

"We're all bar coded," Thiessens explained. "It's called a data collection system." It uses "DCD software" on an IBM AS/400 computer and runs everything from estimates to accounts receivable to accounts payable, he says. Each employee is responsible for scanning the bar code into a computer when he or she comes in. "If anybody's time is wrong, it's their own fault," he said. The same system is used on every work order. "If we lose money on an operation, I can tell you what operation, who did it, and what time of the day it was done. The cost of the system is probably nil, but it pays to implement it."

The difficulty and high cost lie in the implementation. He estimates it took eight years and upgrades of software and hardware to get it properly used; the last upgrade cost $70,000. "Even though it's a really neat thing, the people on the floor don't necessarily view it that way. You don't have to keep an eye on them because the computer does it for you. They don't like that." Getting employees to use the system required Thiessens to get tough and reiterate that usage was a mandatory part of the job. The system, he explained, has a statistical process control that allows employees to chart the quality of their parts making. "Again, I got a lot of flack. They were going to prove it was going to take too long. I said this is not an option."

Now, through the team concept, employees are using the system to gather data on incorrect parts and to track how many people make mistakes clocking in and out. "They're doing it instead of us."

Through the data collection system, he is able to review every job and examine where the company made or lost money. Then, affected people can come to a planning meeting and figure out a better, faster, and easier way to do a job so it doesn't lose money the next time.

"The last thing we do is raise prices. At least 80 percent of the jobs we raise prices on go away. They send them out for bid."

Thiessens says that he doesn't yet feel wealthy, although he admits he's definitely a millionaire. He has no real investments because he puts all his money back into the company. He shuns charities that he says perpetually knock on his door.

"Charities drive you nuts. It's not just me. Businesses are looked at as having money—you've got all this extra money so you can just give it away. I've got one answer for them all. It's no." He believes that very little of the money solicited actually goes to help the person you think you're helping. "There are too many presidents of these charities lining their own pockets." He is generous, though, to his own employees.

His company has a 401(k) plan and an employee stock option program, which provides employees stock in the company out of its profits, although they are unable to take it until retirement. He also has life insurance through a living trust "because we're planning on passing the business through to our daughter and son-in-law. Everything we buy is in the trust. The insurance policy is being paid for by the children so that when we die, there's no inheritance tax on the insurance money. Otherwise, the children would be forced to sell the business to pay the inheritance tax."

Since his business started, he drew $200 a week out of the company and reinvested everything back in. "I'm a great believer that it takes money to make money," he said. "If you take it out personally, then you don't have money to make your business grow."

Even though he lives in a 2,600-square-foot home with his wife and granddaughter, he only paid $130,000 for it. "If the house would have been over here where the rich houses are in the Southwest, it would be a $400,000 house."

Thiessens said that one key to becoming wealthy that he learned the hard way is to never give up. "I've got a brother two years older than me. I remember he brought home As and Bs in high school. High school was easy for him. High school was a struggle for me. Life, I believe, is a struggle.

"Even though I was a bad student, I was more prepared for life than he was. I learned that in order to get anything, you had to kick, scream, fight, and dig. The one thing I have not done is give up."

Success boils down to believing in yourself. "When I went into business for myself, I could see that if the work stopped, we'd be filing bankruptcy in a couple of months." Today, he feels, there is no security—whether you work for someone else or you're on your own. So positive thinking and being secure in yourself is important. "I think I'm very wealthy because I'm happy. I'm doing what I want, and I'm satisfied within myself. Money can't buy that. Money can only buy certain things."

Thiessens says if you were to ask him to draw a picture of his company, he'd draw a steam locomotive going down the track with money in the coal car that you throw into a steam locomotive so you can go further down the track. In other words, he says, "money is good to get you from one place to another."

One of the greatest lessons he learned, and one accounting for a chief flaw in too many businesses today, he says, is that money sometimes is weighed too heavily in important company decisions. "There's a gentleman here managing a very large business. I mentioned to him that I don't allow money to come into my decision making. He was astounded. Everything the main office governs *him* by is bottom line, which is money. They consider him to be a success depending on how much money he makes for the company. He's totally money driven."

Thiessens now believes that this type of thinking—all too common in business today—is completely flawed. You're better off, he believes, not to consider money in your corporate decision making at all. Rather, consider what's right for the company, what's right for the employees, and what's right for the customers. It doesn't do much good if you use cheap parts to fix something if the customer is ultimately dissatisfied.

Thiessens once considered paying employees to take a 20-hour course. Had he operated like most businesses today, he would have backed off immediately after adding up the numbers. The instructor charged $9,000. "I took a look at our lost production. Sending everybody to the class was going to cost us $58,000 in lost production hours. If I would have been looking at the money, I'd never have done that. To make that kind of an investment, that's huge!"

The course wound up being one of the better things his company ever did. It educated his employees to monitor their own progress and the speed at which they produced parts. It taught them to figure out ways to correct problems and how to collect and process data.

Once, after his employees began collecting their own data, the building became short on space. They figured out that just moving parts outside so they had room to work was costing $34,000 annually. "Without putting them through this course, we would never have known that. Therefore, we never would have done anything about it." Once they realized the high cost of moving parts outside, they started looking at alternate steps they could take. They invested money in additional shelving and storage space—a small expense by comparison.

The other important lesson Thiessens has learned is to seek help if you need it. When he finally hired a tutor to teach him to read, it wound up being a simple solution to what had been a lifelong obstacle. "My fear was that if I ever went for help, I'd have fun poked at me, so I never even went to look for any help until now."

Thiessens is not angry at the school system that failed to identify his inability to read. "I believe definitely back then, teachers had to probably know I had a problem. I think they were lacking or just didn't want to take the time to correct it, or didn't know how to correct it.

"The reason I had the problem is I was told I was stupid. Teachers back then believed if you couldn't read, you were stupid. I don't hold any resentment, but I do know they're still doing some of the same stuff in the school system today. I'm going to tackle it from a different angle."

Now he is working with the state of Nevada. "My ultimate goal, if I were to look a long way down the road is, I would love to have one school that we could use as a site to prove the theories."

He'd like to run data—which he has been able to do so well in his business—to determine more exactly what works and what doesn't when it comes to combating illiteracy. While some theories on how to correct illiteracy have been offered, not all might work for all people. Also, he says, many people who have potentially valid theories lack the data to prove them. Data are the only thing governments want to hear about. "I want to find out how to get to practically everybody," he said. "My situation is different from somebody else's. I want to do a beta program that will prove what does work." Data, he believes, are key.

CHAPTER 4

FRANCIS "FRAN" J. KELLY III

Advertising Marketer
Selects Right Career

When Francis "Fran" J. Kelly III, 43, was growing up, it was a struggle to afford the 50¢ per game and the rented shoes he needed to participate in one of his favorite sports: bowling. But his father, who had been in the Army, was the first in his family to become college educated—thanks largely to financial assistance from the GI bill. He slowly kept improving his family's financial situation. Kelly, who now lives in Weston, one of the wealthiest communities in Massachusetts, has followed suit. He has grown his own family's fortune to "between $3 million and $4 million."

Kelly in 1997 had been close to the million-dollar threshold, scribbling his assets on the back of envelopes before the visits he and his wife, Heather Mayfield, made to their financial planner. What threw him substantially over that seven-figure mark, though, was the sale of the ad agency he worked for, Arnold Communications, in 1998 to Snyder Communications, Bethesda, Maryland. Kelly, Arnold's managing partner and chief marketing officer, held 39,638 shares of stock, reported *Adweek* in 1998. That alone became worth $1,744,072.

The sale of the ad agency was a twist of fate in a lifelong struggle for Kelly. He has been torn in his quest to obtain enough money to live comfortably and, at the same time, doing what he wanted to do for a living. The largest amount of money he earned came directly out of his passion: advertising.

Kelly prefers to think of himself as part of a typical American family that has slowly improved its financial situation. He is quick to admit, though, that choosing the right people to work for and coming up with a niche—new business marketing—were keys. He would not necessarily encourage everyone to sit idly by and wait for a shower of wealth to fall upon them.

For Kelly, born in a Chicago walk-up, aiming to succeed started at a young age. His mother drummed into him that no matter how little he had, he had a lot more than most. When he wanted a $150 set of golf clubs, for example, she would tell him about the ice skates she always wanted but never got. She also talked about how, when she was growing up, her family had only enough money to eat meat two nights a week. Her father, because he worked so hard, would get first stab at the meat. The rest of the family ate meat only if any was left.

Meanwhile, Kelly's father, who had worked in marketing for Aetna, the insurance company, also taught him a valuable lesson by often remarking that he was too nice for the business he was in. "I remember thinking in my career, I've got to find a road where just being myself will get me to the top," Kelly said.

Kelly, the oldest of three boys, moved around a lot. In fact, the first house that his parents bought, in New Brunswick, New Jersey, was a major stretch, costing $14,995 in the late 1950s. His father kept getting transferred, and the family moved to the New York City area; Maine; Scotch Plains, New Jersey; and then to Reading, Pennsylvania.

All of his grandparents, though, lived in the Hartford, Connecticut, area, so when his mother's father unexpectedly died from a heart ailment, the family moved to Simsbury, Connecticut, to be nearer the family. Kelly's father wound up working at Aetna's headquarters.

When Kelly was growing up, he was aware of how lucky he was compared with others. Frequently, he thought about how well his upwardly mobile parents had done in comparison with their own parents. "But I remember thinking it sure would be nice to have a lot more money around," but there simply was nothing extra. Vacations were typically short excursions to places like the Poconos. "I remember the first time I heard about somebody going to Harvard Business School," he said. "I was a sophomore in high school, and there was a senior girl I liked who was dating a guy going to Harvard. She was very impressed with this." Another friend of his had a summer home. "I remember thinking that's about as much as you could ever have in the world."

Kelly got good grades at Simsbury High School and was in the top 20 of a class of 450. He chose Amherst College because it was a good small school in New England. He liked the idea of a small school—someplace where he could make a difference. And it was close to home—less than a one-and-a-half-hour drive—but far enough to live away from home yet close enough in case he wished to return.

Initially, life at Amherst was difficult, and the first year was a major struggle. Kelly had been getting As at Simsbury High School but at Amherst, where many classmates had come from prep schools, he found it tough to get Bs. Fellow students were simply better prepared than he was. "I definitely felt like a naïve sheltered public school guy stepping up into a wealthier private school world. I had enough confidence to believe I could be very successful there, but it wasn't easy finding the right places to succeed."

He spent the first two and a half years of his college life attempting to be a doctor, figuring it was a respectable career that paid well. Many of the students had more lab experience than he did. "I was a little Irish Catholic kid," he explained. "I wanted to make a lot of money but still be able to go to heaven." The problem with that strategy is that he hadn't realized he was going to have to take physics, biology, and advanced chemistry to reach his goal. "I was horrible at lab courses!" he said, noting he broke beakers. "I dissected a frog and made such a mess that when I went back to get another frog, the professor suggested I pureed the frog."

Then he found his way onto the golf team and did so well that he became captain of the team. In two of his years on the team, the team won the New England championship. Kelly began gravitating to English and psychology courses and broadcast the Amherst football games on the radio.

Although Kelly felt out of place at first, "I found a group of people who wanted to do well in school but loved sports and had an interest in dating. We liked going to Smith and Mount Holyoke," he said. "We were a minority group at Amherst." For two years, he lived in his Theta Delta fraternity along with a sports-loving crew that included hockey players, golfers, and baseball players. "Half were prep school guys. Half were public school guys like myself." Kelly finally began fitting in as part of a small but accepting group.

Kelly majored in psychology, but his career path had a fortuitous turnaround. Amherst, one of the last colleges to remain all male, was following the path that many others had adopted by going coed. The college was having problems, though, being accepted as a coed institution by its largest donors and alumni. Kelly was asked, along with a few other students, to give speeches before the Sabrina Club, the college's exclusive club of large alumni donors. The speeches were aimed at convincing these donors that the college was on the right track by taking the historic step of admitting women. The speech was after a big fraternity party the night before. "Some idiot had moved all the furniture into the front yard." The day of the speech, "I lay in front of the fraternity, closing my eyes and trying to pretend I was one of the wealthy alumni who hated the fact that the school was going coed. I tried to imagine myself in the same shoes."

Kelly always preferred to give his speeches extemporaneously. He figured out that the donors were thinking that Amherst had done very well for them by being all male, which helped him focus his talk.

The world was dominated by males when the donors grew up, he acknowledged to that elite group. "For Amherst to train you to be the best, it had to be all male." But the world that Kelly is growing up in and the world that their kids are going to grow up in is going to be half male and half female dominated. If Amherst was going to be as good as it was in the past, it *had* to become coed. They *had* to let it go 50–50 and pledge their support, he told them.

The speech attracted the attention of Edward Ney, the chairman of one of the nation's most prestigious New York–based ad agencies, Young & Rubicam, an Amherst alumnus. Ney felt that anybody who could sell him on the idea of Amherst's going coed should be great in advertising. So he sent Kelly a letter inviting him to New York to visit the ad agency.

"I was wearing a powder blue sport coat with checked slacks," he recalled. "Everybody around me was wearing designer Brooks Brothers suits and a lot of black." However, although Kelly's outfit might have been out of place, he found he knew quite a bit about advertising. "I knew the history of every campaign just because I had always watched them."

Kelly had been unusually close to the advertising world and, in effect, viewed the world through an advertising filter. An avid reader and writer as well as the first generation of children who had grown up constantly watching television, Kelly truly had his attention captured by advertising. Of course, his father had been in marketing, and his mother had worked in advertising for a Reading, Pennsylvania, department store chain, Boscov's, as well as for Westledge Associates, a Simsbury, Connecticut, real estate agency. Her philosophy, Kelly said, was to write herself into the advertising campaigns, so he frequently would find his baseball games at night interrupted by his mother's voice. "I found it mortifying," he laughed.

Kelly used to get mad at his father because Aetna never spent money on advertising. His father would say, "I'm in marketing. We don't need to advertise." The company, after all, already had a large sales force. But Kelly often disagreed.

While making the long drives to his grandmother's home, Kelly would manufacture games based on advertising. Those drives "felt like a year," so on the way he would count the number of cars on the road. He would pit Camaros from Chevrolet against the number of cars from Ford. "I was rooting for Chevrolet to win because I liked the Chevy ads better than Ford ads," he said. "I've always rooted for Coke against Pepsi because I liked the Coke ads."

Kelly said he knew he didn't want to be a salesperson for an insurance company. Nor did he wish to work for a bank. So when the letter arrived from Ney inviting him to work in a summer job at his agency, "bells started going off and the sun started to shine."

"I really wanted to do that," Kelly said. "But I needed to make money in the summer. I had the chutzpa to say to Ed Ney that I would like to work at Young & Rubicam, but I'd like to make good money, and I can't spend money looking for a place to live in New York." Ney found him a free place to live with a senior vice president at Young & Rubicam, who had been a good friend of Kelly's family and volunteered his home.

It was like a dream come true. The executive he stayed with happened to have an extra car—a Chrysler New Yorker, "which he let me use quite often." The executive also belonged to an exclusive country club—an old Rockefeller estate that had been turned into a golf club. Through another Amherst connection who had been fascinated with Kelly's role as captain of his college golf team, Kelly was invited to become a full member of the club.

The experience was new and exciting. A day consisted of riding on the train to New York and then coming home and driving a fancy car to his fancy country club. "It was an easy decision to accept Young & Rubicam's offer to join its assistant account executive training program. "I thought if I followed my heart, I would probably be more successful," Kelly said.

He started working at Young & Rubicam in the fall of 1978 as a regular employee. "I might have had $7.95 in my savings account," he reflected of his move to the big city. "A good apartment in New York cost $1,000. I had two friends starting in New York at the same time, so we went apartment hunting together."

When it came time to rent the apartment, he needed to supply a check up front. "I turned to the other two and asked if they could loan me $1,000 for six months." It actually took him one year—between buying rugs and suits and all his other necessities—to repay that money.

His starting salary in the fall of 1978 was a mere $13,000 compared with some friends who were making $15,000 to $20,000. "I remember the difference," Kelly said. "I had one job offer from a major hospital supply company, where I could have earned $17,500 annually with a car and an allowance for the move and furnishing the apartment." But he turned it down. "Going with $13,000 was giving up quite a lot of money," he said. Nevertheless, "I felt I would make more by doing what I loved."

After three years at Young & Rubicam, Kelly thought he should make more money. Some friends had introduced him to his future wife, Heather, who had gone to school at Dartmouth while he had been at Amherst. They had started dating in 1979. In 1981 she had decided to get her masters degree in business administration (MBA) at Harvard Business School. This worried Kelly because he feared that once she was in that environment, she probably would start dating other potentially wealthier men. "I ran the numbers," he said. "At the time, I was making $20-something-thousand as a junior account guy. Harvard business school grads were making $50,000 plus." It seemed like a losing proposition.

Fortunately, the stock market had started a long bull run, and the ad industry was in the heat of an MBA craze. Many firms were starting to go out of their way to attract employees with MBAs, and their clients were also hiring MBAs. So Kelly had no difficulty hammering out an attractive deal from Young & Rubicam that allowed him to go to Harvard for an MBA. Chairman Ney arranged for him to borrow $25,000 a year for the two-year program. If Kelly did not return to work at the ad agency on graduation, he had to pay back the money.

Kelly and his fiancée went through the two-year program together starting in the fall of 1981. In the summer between his first and second year, he decided to test out another career by working at investment banking firm Goldman Sachs.

"It never occurred to me that I could be bored stiff and hate a great job like that," he said. After the first couple of weeks, though, "every 8-hour day felt like 24 hours. Every week felt like a month."

The work, Kelly said, was too transaction oriented. "Get a deal done, get a deal done, get a deal done," he said. "There was no talk about the future. I'm a relationship kind of person. I had a lot of long-term relationships in life. That whole atmosphere was very push-push-push. And push-push was the personality most respected at Goldman."

Also, Kelly noted, while his work had been admired at Young & Rubicam, he did not feel like the same kind of star at Goldman Sachs. He decided he was not ready to change who he was to be successful there.

After graduation in 1983, he and his fiancée invited their friends to stay on through the weekend to attend their wedding. After they were married, they stayed in New England, where Heather had her roots. One year later, they were contacted by a former classmate who worked at Warner Books and enticed them to cowrite a book, *What They Really Teach You at Harvard Business School*. The book, which had a ten-year run, was translated into at least seven languages.

Kelly decided to stick with his first love, advertising, strengthened by a renewed sense of what was important in his career. "I wanted reassurance that I could have an accelerated career path were I to stay," he said.

Toward that goal, he interviewed only with the two top Boston-based agencies, which were Hill Holliday and HBM. HBM had been run by Harvard Business School graduate Ed Eskanderian. "I wouldn't have gone into marketing if I couldn't have gotten some reassurance that if I did a great job and brought with me a Harvard MBA, I could have an accelerated career path and could close the gap on my peers that had gone into higher-paying industries." He joined HBM/Creamer, the ad agency run by Eskanderian.

On graduating Harvard Business School in 1983, Kelly's net worth was minus $50,000 as a result of his outstanding loan from Young & Rubicam. Because he failed to return to Young & Rubicam, Kelly was forced to repay the loan. The newlyweds spent their first five years after business school getting out of debt and trying to get ahead.

Kelly, however, made a smart move. Although he knew he would have to pay off the loan, he was careful to propose his own terms. It was Kelly who proposed a plan of $5,000 a year for ten years—the fastest he felt he could pay it off. The agency agreed to charge him no interest, and to this day, Kelly considers that loan one of his greatest gifts.

Kelly created a Young & Rubicam file and worked out a 20-payment, ten-year timeline and kept it in his bottom right-hand drawer. "At first, I said, 'God, I'll never pay this off.'" But he wrote the final check to the ad agency in 1993.

While at HBM/Creamer, Kelly developed his skills in attracting new business, a part of the business that most found difficult. It required work on nights and weekends—just when most employees want to be home with their families—and running accounts during the day. Kelly, however, loved the job. He had to be at work at 8 AM and didn't get home until 8 PM or 9 PM. Fortunately, the 12-hour or 13-hour days didn't conflict with his marriage. His wife was in management consulting and worked from 8 AM until midnight. "It doesn't do a lot for your love life or your social life," he admitted, "but it's a good way to get a fast start in your career!"

One key to Kelly's success was that he always talked to his employers about his future and how he could improve his position, including a talk he initiated with Ed Eskanderian about a five-year plan. "At the end of four or five years, I could feel I was doing as well in advertising as I might have done in higher-paying industries. We laid out a plan. I did my part by working hard. He did his part."

In 1984, while at HBM, for example, he succeeded in capturing the business of a Canadian beer company, Molsen. "We hired set designers and turned the conference room into Molsen Golden Bar and Grill," he said. "We had waitresses serving hamburgers and wound up winning a chunk of business. The whole agency had a great time."

As Kelly climbed to senior vice president-management supervisor at HBM, he became a major player in the new business arena for ad agencies. In 1989 he was offered a partnership in what came to be known as Leonard Monahan Lubars & Kelly, a small, prestigious ad agency in Providence, Rhode Island. "I have to say during that period, my salary had more than doubled from where it had been three or four years earlier," he said. Among the agency's clients were Keds and Polaroid.

Kelly contends that the chief force behind his wealth has been putting his faith in good people and careful planning. He stuck with a business he loved and found a niche within it. He specialized in getting new business for the ad agency—one of the most crucial jobs yet one that most people shunned. "I not only found a business I loved, but I also found a part that became very difficult to succeed in. That was part of the reason I was asked to join Leonard Monahan." In that company's attempt to woo him, it made him a partner.

Then, Ed Eskanderian, the person who initially hired Kelly out of Harvard Business school at HBM, was building Arnold Communications in Boston. He was looking for someone to pitch new business, run the big accounts, and publicize the agency—all the things Kelly already had been doing successfully. "In fact, my agency had beaten his agency three or four times in a row," Kelly said. At the time Kelly joined Arnold in 1994, it was still a regional firm with the goal to build a national reputation.

Among the accounts he helped win for Arnold was Kinney Shoes, a $15-million account that was unusually large for a New England–based ad agency.

Kelly was named a managing partner in 1996 and feels his success at new business marketing probably is driven by the fact that unlike most new business marketing pros, he is both an idea person and a team leader. "I always had a desire to not only be part of a team but to be a leader. I brought that desire to every team or job we took on. It's a skill that's very valued in business. A client is looking for a new agency to guide it to the promised land. It's half knowing what you want people to do and half getting your whole team to work well together to solve a problem."

According to Kelly, most people in advertising tend to be either a good idea person or a good team leader (that is, a good process person) but not both. "The best advertising people blend ideas with action plans really well."

With Kelly's Harvard Business School background, he was able to create a strategic and creative model, dubbed "Brand Essence," which became the guiding philosophy internally at the ad agency. The model borrows techniques of top consulting firms to help generate new business. Inside the agency, it helps organize ideas and get people to work together as a team.

Although consulting firms normally use similar models, most ad agencies don't. "So it made Arnold [Communications] feel like half McKinsey [the consulting firm] and half a great creative agency. A lot of clients really liked the combination."

They started using the model in 1994 to pitch a Hood Milk account in New England, garnering a few million dollars in business. "It was very exciting," Kelly said. "But a couple months later, it won the $100 million Volkswagen account. That was the biggest account ever won by a New England ad agency. It really put our company, Arnold Communications, on the map nationally."

At this writing, the company was moving aggressively to take advantage of the Internet. "Every client has to decide whether to ignore the Internet or make it a part or base of their marketing plan. We believe marketing is more important in the Internet world than ever before."

The agency helped Volkswagen set up its <VW.com> program and is picking up new clients, such as <theWallStreetJournal.com> and <Toysmart.com>.

In the ad business there is typically a base salary and a year-end performance bonus. That combination, Kelly says, let him almost become a millionaire by 1997. "My deal allowed me to accumulate stock in Arnold based on performance. So when Snyder came in and acquired our company, the stock I had built up allowed me to become a multimillionaire."

Kelly since sold a little over 50 percent of his stock to deal with taxes that were coming due, but he retained the rest as a long-term investment in the company. Since that time, he has been picking up stock in the form of options.

"I have to be honest," he says. "The good thing is I did a great job and was rewarded. I never really negotiated anything. I don't think I did a particularly good job as a negotiator. I've always put my heart and soul into doing a great job and assumed the people at the top would take care of me."

Fortunately, in Kelly's case, that's what happened. But he admits it's not necessarily the technique he would recommend. Not everyone is likely to be as generous as Ed Ney, who secured an interest-free loan for him, or Ed Eskanderian, who gave him stock in his agency.

Kelly made some good professional choices. "I worked for Ed Ney (Young & Rubicam chairman), who was about the most prominent man in the advertising business. He really delivered for me." Ed Eskanderian also took care of him. "Every year, they said here's what we hope we can accomplish. Fran, if you do, here's the kind of money you can make. I met the goals."

Kelly advises that if you want to make money in a business you love, it is important to have a plan. You can't get to the top unless you work long hours and perform exceptionally well. "If you don't think you'll ever do that, somebody else will blow by you if you're only doing it for money. I identified a new business route as a way to get to the top."

Also, he advises, it's critical to find a company that gives you the opportunity to make a lot of money. "I loved being at Leonard Monahan," he admitted. "It's a small, very creative, very respected company in Providence. But there wasn't a lot of upside potential. It was a hard decision for me to leave and join Ed, but Ed had such a great track record for making money." Kelly saw the potential of the move and is several million dollars ahead as a result of his insight.

It was important to his family that Kelly choose the right path. His wife had been the primary breadwinner initially, bringing in more money than he did. Although she had expected to return to work after giving birth to twins in 1987, she never did. The twins were a surprise because for a long time, the doctor maintained she was not going to have twins despite her friends' observation of her size. Once the Kelly's knew that twins were on the way, they needed a larger house and moved in Massachusetts from Wellesley to Weston.

Kelly assumed an active role in building his wealth. He and his wife began seeing a financial planner. When he was a partner at Leonard Monahan, he had some financial questions. Initially, he had some terrible experiences with financial advisors. "We didn't trust them," he said. Not only did advisors charge more than they said they would, but they put the couple into investments that were not what they wanted. Finally, Kelly went to a highly recommended financial planner, David Simmer of Wellesley, a lawyer, accountant, and financial advisor. "He's roughly our age and very understated. He doesn't 'bullshit.' He clicked—particularly with my wife who's very conservative and suspicious."

Simmer was a fee-only planner but Kelly didn't yet have a lot of money. "I think you're going to be worth a lot of money some day," Simmer had advised him. Simmer in 1992 laid out a 20-year financial plan for the couple. "I remember his goal was to get us to have $3 million in the bank by age 55 so we could retire comfortably."

The couple had more than reached that goal in their early forties. Now, Kelly says, he is able to concentrate on doing great ad campaigns for his clients and growing the agency but leaving his finances totally in Simmer's hands.

Since he became wealthy, Kelly has indulged in some luxuries. He is a member of the Essex County Club, an exclusive 100-year-old club on the North Shore of Boston. He admits he drives a $40,000 car, and the couple was able to negotiate a little less vigorously the last time his wife bought a minivan. "Usually, I take a lot more time and do a lot more negotiating," he reflected. But this time, he just decided to order all the extras and get the car immediately.

Kelly and his wife have spent two years looking for a larger house in Weston. It's a cautious search because something is holding Kelly back. "Having not had as much money as I would have liked for a long time, I don't spend my money as easily as some people might," Kelly said. "I hope I will some day."

He warns, though, that there is at least one major issue to contend with once you finally get the money you've always wanted. If you're not careful, you can find yourself on an escalator. The more money you have, the more you want. "A perfect example is that the house I could buy today is twice as big as the house I could have afforded five years ago," he said. "But it's half as big as the guy's down the street.

"If you're not careful, I don't think you ever feel wealthy. I very much want to enjoy what we've achieved, and I do, because I have perspective. I remember the times when I couldn't get $5 to spend a day at the golf course. It's a sin if you don't enjoy what you've achieved."

Kelly, at this writing, had no plans to retire. "I can envision writing or teaching advertising until they put me in the ground. Hopefully, I'll make some more millions along the way." He stresses that he's not the only multimillionaire in the advertising business. Many of his former coworkers at Young & Rubicam have had similar fates.

Kelly also believes there is a tremendous amount of money to be made in the next decade by getting into "leveraged situations where you not only get a salary but also a piece of the company or the sale of stocks. Anyone going out to get a job today is crazy not to get a job in a company that gives you leverage opportunities! That's where the big bucks are.

"Have a plan well ahead of time for how you're going to bene- fit when the leverage event takes place. If there is stock that is going to be given out, make sure you know how much you're going to get. If you don't think it's enough, speak up early. If there are options to be had and you're sure a leverage event is going to occur, pile up as many as you can. If you're very confident of a leverage opportunity, consider leverage to up yourself in the organization."

At one point, Kelly was encouraged to buy an even greater stake in Arnold Communications and regrets that he didn't. "I would do it next time," he declared.

His money challenges him to consider how he can help his young twins. "What I'm hoping to do is give them some of the things I really wanted when I was growing up so they can have more fun than I had," he said. "But at the same time, instill in them that you only get as much as you earn in life. If you don't work hard and you're not passionate about what you're doing, you're never going to achieve great success."

As for the most successful path in life? "On the one hand, I would advise them to follow my road. If you're doing what you love to do, you have a much better chance of being successful," he said. "On the other hand, there definitely are places in the world where you can make money and places where you can't."

CHAPTER 5

JUDY WALKER

*From Abject Poverty to
Detroit Real Estate Wealth*

Judy Walker doesn't flaunt her wealth. How can she? She grew up in abject poverty in Detroit's north end. She knows what it's like to go without things that most people take for granted. She also knows the bitter taste of discrimination. Rather than use her early misfortunes as an excuse, she became motivated to educate herself and succeed in a high-risk, treacherous real estate market.

You need ice water in your veins to buy foreclosed property and turn it around for a quick profit. One false move and you could be stuck with all its expenses and no income! Walker knows what it takes to get ahead in this fast-paced real estate game. She has accumulated a net worth of more than $2 million, largely through the purchase of foreclosures she typically turns over within six months.

Walker, 50, drives a Lexus, but her car and traveling with her ten-year-old son may be among the few visible signs of her wealth. Her home is a modest 2,700-square-foot four-bedroom, four-bath home in the North Rosedale Park section of Detroit. She is owner of the Riverpointe Realty, Southfield, Michigan; one-half owner of its Detroit office; one-third owner of Renaissance Mortgage in Southfield; and one-third owner of a 30,000-square-foot commercial property that lodges her mortgage company. She has 57 real estate sales agents in both offices and 4 employees as well as 20 loan officers and 9 employees.

"I hope very soon to get into a subdivision development," Walker confided. "I've got my eyes on a couple of scenarios now

54

that may pan out to be very good. If it works out, thank God, I will ascend to another level." She was also hoping to get into major rehabilitation projects.

Yes, she says, she is among the happy. But life wasn't always this good. Walker, a divorcee, grew up in the north end of Detroit, largely inhabited by blacks and Jews. She was raised by her mother and grandmother and lived with, at times, as many as 25 people in their wooden farm colonial home. In her early years, she slept in a baby bed and shared a room with three others, including one uncle in a single bed; one uncle in an army cot; and her grandmother in a double bed. Everyone in the house shared a single bathroom, which, she says, was a much easier task for the men than it was for her. Often, there were a few extra boarders, and her father, whom she terms "a rolling stone," didn't live with her. Times were tough in Detroit for the large population of Afro-Americans. Detroit was a factory town, dominated by the nation's largest automobile manufacturers. Young black men frequently enlisted in the military and sent money home to their wives. When they returned, many were employed by one of the Big Three automakers for less than $2 an hour. Certainly, it didn't buy a very comfortable existence.

But Walker had considerable support on her side. Her grandmother, though blind and crippled in one leg, was the matriarch. Her grandfather's wages from his factory job helped to support the household.

There always was food on the table. That was a start. Walker got her first job when she was 11 years old, cleaning a neighborhood clothing store. She swept, took out the garbage, and dusted before getting to the point of being able to use the cash register. At the store, she fraternized with the Jewish employees who worked there, and she picked up a few Yiddish words. *Ganev*, she learned, was the Yiddish word for thief.

Her grandmother, born just after the end of slavery, always pushed Walker to succeed. Walker had been one of the first blacks to attend a boarding school, to which she wore uniforms and fully absorbed everything she was taught.

"My grandma was a pretty smart cookie," Walker reflected. To both her grandmother and mother, education was constantly stressed as the only way for someone in her shoes to get ahead.

"My grandmother instilled upon me something that has always remained with me," she said. "It was her philosophy that being an individual of dark-skinned color, the most effective way to open up doors for upward mobility was to master the king's English. Once you've mastered the king's English, people will be so in awe of your intellectual level that color will then in some instances take a back seat."

Walker's grandmother made the grandchildren familiarize themselves with *Webster's Dictionary*. Each child had to learn ten new words every day, including how to spell the word, how to define it, and how to properly use it in a sentence.

Making reams of money was never an overwhelming objective for Walker. "I wanted to be a physician until I came to the realization that I wouldn't deal with the dying of my clients well," she said. Of the four brothers and sisters she knows of, she clearly is the most financially successful, pointing to the fact that her brothers and sisters had a different mother than she did as most likely the chief reason.

Fortunately, just as Walker was finishing high school, the Civil Rights movement had begun generating momentum. The Civil Rights Act of 1964 prohibited discrimination in voting, education, and the use of public facilities. Another Civil Rights Act in 1968 extended the protections to housing rentals or sales. Walker, with all the prodding of her mother and grandmother, was quick to take advantage of the new environment. After considering several colleges, she settled on Detroit's Mercy College (now University of Detroit Mercy) and became one of the first 20 blacks to be admitted in 1967. Her counselors and principals had suggested several options to her for furthering her education so that she could take advantage of what had previously been nonexistent opportunities. Nevertheless, after careful discussions with her mother, she opted to choose a Detroit-based school. Her family knew that being among the first to test the new racial environment wasn't going to be easy. So it was smart to attend a school close to home—just in case things didn't work out. Their prognosis proved correct: she left the school in her second year.

Walker didn't have an easy time being among the "chosen" few. Religious and racial differences at Mercy College made life uncomfortable. "It was different because of the Catholic influence," she said of her initial college experience. "I'm a Baptist. Becoming acclimated to college life was difficult in itself."

In her first year of college, on April 5, 1968, Martin Luther King Jr. was shot to death and school immediately closed. Walker was forced to deal with ignorant questions from some of her white peers that, she admitted, "pissed you off. They would ask if we had tails. They would ask if we had shoeshine polish on our faces. Back 30 plus years ago, what they were accustomed to in terms of watching TV was white people with black-faced paint."

Add to the barbs a grueling schedule. At the beginning of her sophomore year, Walker took a full-time job working at the post office. "I went to school 8 AM to 4 PM and worked at the post office 5 PM until 2 AM. After one year, my body went into a physical exhaustion shutdown." Forced to choose between survival and education, she left the unpleasantness of Mercy College but continued working at the post office before taking a full-time job at Blue Cross-Blue Shield. Today, when Walker talks about those difficult early days in college, she expresses understanding of her white classmates. "Any rational mind could discern that these people certainly knew no better," she says. "This misinformation still exists and has been passed on by parents. Now, as they're embarking on adulthood, they find all this crap that they had been spoon-fed was not true."

Walker, though, did not have it much easier when she worked in the group billing department of Blue Cross-Blue Shield in Detroit. Employed there for about four years, she left as a senior account clerk before finally resuming her education at Wayne State University, where she graduated with a bachelor's degree in business administration with an emphasis on marketing and psychology.

Her experience with corporate life had been a turnoff. Although civil rights had made some progress, progress went only so far. Walker took written tests in math or psychology and often scored in the 90 percent range, yet was frequently bypassed for a promotion in favor of white male candidates. Frustrated, she took a leave of absence from the job, although she was permitted to retain job benefits during that period. When her medical benefits and reimbursement of one year of her college education expired, however, she left the job permanently.

By the time she had graduated from Wayne State University, Walker was totally fed up with white corporate America. So she decided to head to Los Angeles in pursuit of a less structured career in the record business. Five hundred résumés later, she gave up on that idea. "I wouldn't put that in the genre of racism," she stressed. You could get into the record industry quickly if you could sing, dance, or write music, but "other jobs came via nepotism."

Dejected after trying for a sales job, Walker's eye was caught by a television commercial for Tarbell Realtors in Torrance, California, which was offering free training in real estate to people wishing to go into sales. The idea of a field in which she could be her own boss attracted her. She took the free course, obtained her real estate license, and raked in a mere $6,500 in her first year while renting a town house in a predominantly white neighborhood.

Walker found Torrance, a middle-class suburb of Los Angeles, much different from culturally diverse Detroit. Less than 2 percent of the community's 130,000 residents were black. It was tough going that first year. To add to her income, she was forced to work for a temporary agency and was placed handling accounts receivable for a small manufacturer.

The problem as she saw it: She was in an entirely new locale that was predominantly white in her first year in the real estate business. Nevertheless, her efforts finally paid off. She had continued to contact a couple—both psychologists—who had a For Sale by Owner sign in front of their home. Having studied psychology in school, Walker had much in common with them. "I continued to go to their home each and every day. They rewarded me with a listing because of my diligence and persistence."

The couple became her first deal and gave her the confidence she so desperately needed to continue. After she found them another property, she kept going and going. She stayed with the company one and a half years before joining Real Estate Merchants, Carson, California. By the end of her second year in the real estate business, she had almost quadrupled her earnings but still only earned $24,000.

It's normal in the early days of selling houses for income to be scarce. The National Association of Realtors has reported that in 1998, the median income for a Realtor was $30,300. A real estate agent generally earns a commission that is typically about 5 to 7 percent, or $5,000 to $7,000 on a $100,000 home. The commission often gets split between two brokers—one that lists the property for sale and another that represents the buyer. The brokers then deduct their overhead office expenses from their share of the commission before splitting the difference with the real estate agent or agents that participated in the sale.

Because persistence and further education can pay off, each year things improved for Walker. "I was a lot more knowledgeable," she explained of her second year. Also, her new community, Carson, located just south of Los Angeles, was more racially diverse. It was a more positive environment where she could grow as a business person. She then resolved that if she wished to get ahead, she needed to start specializing so she decided to focus on foreclosed properties.

Walker, who colleagues say has succeeded in impressing people with her eloquent speech, at this writing served on the board of directors of the Southfield (Michigan) Chamber of Commerce. She won the distinguished award of the National Association of Women Business Owners and has served as president-elect of the South Oakland Board of Realtors.

She had realized earlier in California just how important to her business networking is. In Carson she began religiously attending social functions, seminars, and business meetings. They not only gave her an opportunity to stay in touch with people socially and keep tabs on her profession, but also put her in touch with people who owned small mortgage companies or investment companies. Soon she was rewarded with their business.

People were impressed with Walker's attitude and zeal. Once a relationship was solidified, people began turning to her as the real estate agent they wanted to sell their foreclosed properties. It also gave her easy access to data about the properties. Although in Torrance she had been renting her town house, she finally bought her own home in Carson in 1980 for $63,000, selling it three years later for more than $90,000. Now she was her own boss. Nothing was dictated to her. It was up to her to impose her own inner challenges, and she had complete freedom to make as little or as much money as she wished.

Unfortunately, the road to success is often pitted with mine fields. Walker was faced with one obstacle she was unable to overcome in California. A friend, who had been almost like an uncle to her in Detroit, had been struck by a car and was paralyzed and alone. She left California in 1984 to care for him in the home she currently lives in until he died in 1991.

The good news was that Walker now was not only in familiar territory with people she knew, but the Detroit market was unaffected by the real estate recession that engulfed much of the country in the late 1980s to early 1990s. Detroit has one of the highest ratios of single-family homes in the country—70 percent. The metro Detroit housing market has remained the nation's most robust.

Walker had to relicense herself in Detroit and worked for Earl Keim Realty in her own neighborhood for three years until she obtained her broker's license. In May 1988, she opened her first office, Red Carpet Keim Realty, in Southfield, Michigan. Part of a nationwide franchise like Century 21, the office cost her entire life savings and two insurance policies, she told *Essence* magazine, noting she put down $30,000 to buy the office. "For the first six months, the only one who got paid was the secretary."

Walker was among 18 of Keim's franchised owners who didn't see eye to eye with the bank that owned the company, Colonial Central Bank in Mount Clemons, Michigan. Under the whole master franchise umbrella, there were 67 offices. "We had filed a class action suit against the bank. Rather than everybody going broke by involving attorneys, the bank and company opted to sell the master franchise to the group in 1994." Each owner put up $20,000 and controlled and operated the company before it was sold for a profit to Home Life Inc., Toronto, in 1996.

The arrangement taught Walker one major lesson: It is almost impossible to be among the brokers running a company at the same time that you're a broker under that same company's umbrella. After all, as a broker, you're impacted directly by those decisions. "I think we all learned how impossible it is," she said. As committee members, the brokers met regularly to run the company along with an executive officer.

In retrospect, Walker, along with others, believes they should have hired an executive officer to handle the company exclusively. By taking such an active role, "we in effect had to make decisions that were not in the best interest of us as independent brokers under that umbrella." When the company was sold, the deal's terms were placed under a court gag order. However, *Essence* reported that Walker received more than 100 percent profit on her investment.

Walker remained a franchise owner under the umbrella until 1998, when she severed the relationship and went into an independent partnership with Willie Nabers Jr. She changed the name of the Southfield office to Riverpointe Realty.

Walker says she was unable to single out one transaction that has contributed to the bulk of her wealth. "I always have something cooking," noting her workdays often range from 12 to 14 hours.

One key mistake she thinks most people make when it comes to buying foreclosures, though, is buying into the no-money-down infomercials. "What these gentlemen are doing is selling videos and cassettes. I've never bought one of those deals." In fact, she gets telephone calls from people who have bought deals from infomercials without understanding that the only people making money from them are those conducting them.

Walker is not the only one advising against buying into no-money-down infomercials. Both the Federal Trade Commission and North American Securities Administrators Association also have issued stern warnings about attending high-cost seminars and buying expensive books sold via paid infomercials that resemble real television programs. Experts who endorse these promotions and persons offering testimonials are often paid by the advertiser, the two agencies caution. As a rule, free money or low-interest government loans are available only in limited circumstances.

Although Walker says she's a firm believer in holding mortgages on a property and using other people's money where possible, buying property with no money down is unrealistic. "I simply don't know of any scenarios where people who are in trouble are going to deal with no money down. They're coming to me because they want and need money."

If you want to be successful in real estate, she suggests, understand the science. It includes marketing, conducting a thorough investigation of the property; getting the property quickly into condition to sell; and having the available capital to offer cash. The price a property has sold for is a public record, often available at no cost through the local tax collector.

Walker says she runs advertisements, including billboards, flyers distributed in supermarkets, and mail-outs advising people that she purchases homes for cash. These help flush out private individuals who have tax or drug problems or who have gotten behind in their property payments.

She thoroughly researches the registry of deeds, investigating the chain of title, checking for any hidden liens over and above the primary liability of mortgages. "You want to make sure there are no other skeletons or ghosts that may arise."

Also, she is very careful to eliminate one of the chief hazards of real estate investing: its illiquidity. "I deal with a six-month turnaround program. From the point of acquisition through rehabilitation and resale, you should not be sitting on any property for more than six months. If you're talking about how to keep your cash flow moving, this is how. You need to know the exact schedule for turnaround of repairs and your marketing efforts."

So far, she has not made one unprofitable deal. She opts to buy single-family homes as rental properties rather than apartment buildings because they are easier to manage. "My philosophy is that you deal the hand you're dealt." When she was in her second year of real estate in California, she met a potential obstacle—the onset of the oil embargo when interest rates went from 17 percent to 22 percent. "I still made money in that market," she said.

The only change Walker has made in her program is adjusting her mind-set on financing. "In that market I used 75 methodologies for financing property when most people had traditional FHA, VA, and conventional loans or cash."

Creating the financing largely involved going to sellers and encouraging them to help with the deals. Often, she was able to knock down the mortgage interest rate as much as 5 percent simply through creative financing. For example, she might negotiate a wraparound mortgage in which the buyer makes a single monthly payment on two loans "wrapped" together, one of which typically is an existing loan assumed from the seller.

"You're only limited by your lack of imagination."

Walker says there are no hard rules. Many of her decisions are fueled by instincts and concrete research. Take the colonial house she bought a few years back that nobody was interested in, for example. "As you walked into the entryway, you could see above you clear into the upstairs bathroom. The ceiling collapsed. Paint was peeling off the walls. You had to step over things to get through. Looking at it through the lay eye, it was a horrendous set of circumstances!"

But Walker was able to see the potential. The house was in the Grandmont subdivision—one of the more desirable middle-class communities in the city. "It was the type of area that was constantly improving. I acquired it for $23,000, shelled out $15,000 and sold it for $100,000."

A key, she says, is knowing the right contractors and learning about the project yourself. "I'm a licensed contractor and builder," she explained. "That Grandmont house, though, was a major challenge. With any home that has been vacant for a long period, plumbing problems can develop. You think everything's all right and you may have some piping that has a fine hairline crack that doesn't show up right away. Then you bring in people to install drywall, and you go there one day and find a big puddle. The stress from constant water pressure could make that hairline crack split wider. Then you have to rip up the entire wall."

How much extra this is going to cost you, she notes, often depends on how much control you have over the crew doing the repairs. "If you have contracted this out to Mr. Belvedere or Father and Sons, then you become dependent on the information they give back to you."

Bad move. A situation could have been as simple as replacing a three-foot section of horizontal piping. Yet an outside company may try to convince you that you need to do a $3,000 or $4,000 plumbing job. "That's what they're in business to do if you don't know the base cost of the project."

Sometimes, she admits, there can be quick turnarounds that require all cash, but you can't always fund a purchase yourself. "At that point, call some friends. Don't let the opportunity go by. If an individual can make $10,000, $15,000, or $20,000 in six months by signing a contract, that's the thing you should do."

It's important to be prepared to share in the profits. "Say, you ran into some people and they're horrendously behind in taxes. They can't afford to pay. The home is suffering in its maintenance. They say, 'We're $20,900 behind in taxes. The house needs some tender loving care. We'll sell it to you for $23,000.'"

That is definitely an all-cash deal. But say you only have $15,000. Eyeballing the house, you figure it will take $10,000 to get it back into shape, which brings your cost to $33,000.

"On the backside, you can sell it for $70,000. I would not hesitate to go to a friend or business partner and say, 'Look, I found this great opportunity. I can't afford it totally myself and would like for you to take a look at the house. Sit down with me and do the Xs and Os.'"

In seeking financial assistance, Walker thinks it's important to couch the request as a great opportunity rather than a loan. "Generally, when it's presented in that way, people receive it in that way. Sometimes, it's virtually impossible to do the whole thing yourself. If you have to share or divide the proceeds on your first four or five homes, keep in mind that each time you knock down one, you're amassing more capital. Now you get to six. You've sold five others." The next one may be one you can do yourself—without any outside financing.

Walker admits that with her wealth, family members have asked her for money. But then again, she says, family always begs. When a family member asks for money, she treats it as a business request. The strategy has succeeded in making her one of the last people family members now come to. "I ask, 'What kind of collateral do you have? Have you gotten a second job? Have you looked for a second job? Did you know this was coming upon you? If you knew, why didn't you prepare yourself?'"

Walker stresses that she has not always been so comfortable financially as she is now. "If I saw situations coming, I'd get a second job. There have been times when I worked in an office building during the day and was a bartender at night."

Despite tough times, she has never aspired to be as rich as Rockefeller. "I see that as having a whole menu of problems in and of itself. You have heightened concern about your children. I don't have the biggest diamond or the most dazzling furs. These things don't drive my life."

She'd prefer to spend her time traveling. "I enjoy the experiences we have going places—particularly where the tour guides tell you don't go into the village." Walker says that if she's come that far, she wants to make certain she meets the real people. "I don't want to be on the strip buying all the poopla. I want to see how people live, the attitudes of people, what the country is all about."

One of her biggest challenges has been making it in a male-dominated industry. In 1995 Walker became the first black woman to serve on the board of directors of the Michigan National Association of Realtors. "As a female who is very assertive and very aggressive, that's the best posture for me. Sellers don't believe gals who are CEOs or presidents of a company and have mild mannerisms. Certainly, you have to be strong and firm in your commitments. You have to be a visionary and dedicated to what you're doing.

CHAPTER 6

DAVID GEFFEN

Brooklyn Slums Spawn
Billionaire Record Mogul

To surpass the $1 million mark once you've been poor is a wonderful accomplishment for anybody but to make more than $1 billion?

David Geffen, 56, with a whopping net worth of $2.3 billion in 1999, according to the *Los Angeles Business Journal,* certainly has passed that milestone. This, despite the fact that he grew up sleeping on the living-room couch of a one-bedroom apartment and wearing poorly fitting secondhand clothes.

Pegged by the *Journal* as the fourth richest man in Los Angeles, Geffen helped wheel and deal his way to give us such outstanding entertainers as Crosby, Stills and Nash; Joni Mitchell; Janis Joplin; Laura Nyro; Jackson Browne; and the Eagles. He was a millionaire by the time he was 26.

Even when you come from poverty, once you reach a certain threshold, according to Geffen, making more money isn't necessarily the important issue in life that it once was.

With $2 million, Geffen told *Playboy* magazine in 1994 that he didn't quite feel rich. "I didn't feel rich until 1972. . . . But when I had more than $10 million, I no longer could tell myself it was about money, which was a blow, by the way. It was difficult because as long as I believed money was the answer, I could work harder and make more, and I'd get to the answer. So when I had all this money and still didn't feel quite right, I crashed. I thought, Oh shit, money isn't the answer. This is a revelation when you grow up poor and assume money will solve everything."

Feeling jealous? It hasn't been so easy for Geffen, nor has there always been success. Geffen admits publicly that he is gay and has been in therapy, and that he had a mere 66 grade point average in high school and dropped out of college. But he subsequently taught classes at Yale Business School briefly after successfully capitalizing on his ability to spot and cultivate the talent that wooed the baby boom generation. Fortunately, Geffen's nose for talent seemed to strike just when television and stereos had pushed music to the forefront of the nation's culture.

Then, with his 1994 announcement that he would form an independent company, DreamWorks SKG, alongside film titan Steven Spielberg and animation czar Jeffrey Katzenberg, Geffen became a national symbol. The triumvirate, also backed financially by Paul Allen, cofounder of Microsoft, signified to many the triumph of creative artistry over corporate bureaucracy in a society that was beginning to breed job indifference.

It was an alliance born out of deep and loyal friendships. In fact, Geffen so values loyalty that it has been reported he gave a retiring secretary a gift of $5 million. "I'm a stand-up guy," he told *The New Yorker* in 1998, noting that his formation of DreamWorks was partly the result of his friendship with partner Jeffrey Katzenberg. "I can be counted on by my friends. And I'm proud of that and I feel good about that."

On the other hand, it's also been said that you don't want to be on the bad side of Geffen. Jeffrey Katzenberg himself admitted to the *New York Times* that "when [Geffen] sees a movie he doesn't like, he massacres me." Geffen has waged long-term feuds with other Hollywood players, including Disney's Michael Eisner, Barry Diller, and Michael Ovitz, as reported by *The New Yorker.*

"In Hollywood people lie to each other and cheat each other and then go and play tennis," Geffen stated in *The New Yorker* article. "But I don't want to be a tennis player. . . . I'm not going to go play tennis with people who lie to me or fuck me over in some way."

Geffen was raised in the Borough Park section of Brooklyn. David, his brother, Mitchell, and their parents lived in a one-bedroom apartment. The family got by largely on Mrs. Geffen's income from her sewing. Later on, the family increased its income slightly when she opened her own corset and brassiere shop. David's father, however, often didn't work and died when Geffen was 18. Considering himself an intellectual, he spoke several languages and was widely read.

Fortunately, David's parents fled Russia and Poland right after the Russian Revolution in 1917. They met and married in Palestine, now Israel, and immigrated to the United States. The more than six million Jews exterminated by the Nazis included Mrs. Geffen's entire family, except for her sister. They were reported to have been shot and their remains thrown down wells in the Ukraine. On hearing about the executions, David's mother had a nervous breakdown and was institutionalized for six months when Geffen was just six. She picked herself up, though, and went back to running her business.

A small, frail child who grew up in a tough neighborhood, Geffen frequently was made fun of and beaten up by neighborhood children. His mother, who affectionately called him "King David," would calm him down. "You never have to get revenge," she told him, according to *Playboy*. "All you have to do is live long enough."

Unfortunate as his early years were, they molded his character. Geffen first learned about business by listening to his mother handle customers and deal with suppliers at her small sewing shop, where he frequently went for his meals. He learned to understand what customers wanted and how he could get what he wanted.

A favorite story, recounted to *Forbes* in 1990, detailed how his mother realized she inadvertently quoted the price of a garment cheaper than the one a woman had tried on. Yet she offered to stand by the price, provided that the woman buy it right then and there. Instead, the woman left to shop around. When she returned to buy the garment at the lower quoted price, Geffen's mother refused. The price, she reaffirmed, had only been effective at the time it was offered. It was an experience that helped Geffen learn how not to be hustled, he told *Forbes*.

In 1999 Geffen's negotiating skills were highlighted by *The Wall Street Journal* as a force in the settlement of a long dispute that his DreamWorks partner Jeffrey Katzenberg had with Disney.

Geffen learned to follow his own drumbeat and not worry what other people thought. The fact that others didn't like him early on made him realize that he had to get by on his own. He moved in a totally different direction from his childhood friends. While most kids were into sports and macho activities, Geffen spent most of his time going to the movies and reading reviews. He was attracted to films and excited about the lives on the screen. Sometimes he'd spend an entire day at the movies. When he was young, he picked up *Hollywood Rajah,* the biography of Louis B. Mayer by Bosley Crowther, a book that fascinated him for years to come.

What was on Geffen's mind from a young age was money. Money, he figured, was a way out of poverty and a way to command respect he often didn't get as a child. Hollywood, to him, looked like a fun way to get it.

After Geffen graduated from high school, he spent one semester at the University of Texas and then returned to Brooklyn College. He preferred visiting his brother, who was attending UCLA Law School in the very city whose entertainment industry had so fascinated him.

Geffen's interest in Hollywood was heightened when he got a small role in a B movie. Added to that, his brother married the sister-in-law of Phil Spector, a top record producer responsible for such hits as "Be My Baby" by the Ronettes, according to *The Rise and Rise of David Geffen,* by Stephen Singular (Birchlane Press). Geffen, on returning home, was fired from his job as an usher for the Judy Garland Show and Red Skelton Show for allegedly being too nosy.

Out of work and looking for something in the entertainment business, he lacked one critical element—a college degree. In a bold move, he applied for a job at William Morris, a major talent agency, telling them he was a college graduate.

Geffen started at $55 a week in the mail room with plans to work his way up in the organization. He knew his employer would be checking with UCLA to verify that he was a graduate. As the story, which some accounts have altered slightly, goes, he went to work at dawn each morning to watch for the letter from UCLA. When it finally arrived, Geffen intercepted it and steamed it open. He obtained a new UCLA letterhead and wrote his own letter verifying that he was a graduate.

William Morris, New York, was a formidable training ground, being at the time the leading talent agency in the country. William Morris was a far cry from the statement in his high school yearbook that he wanted to be a dentist. He attributed the statement largely to a need to say something and to appease his mother, who "would have liked me to be a dentist, doctor, or lawyer," as he told *Playboy.*

At William Morris, Geffen listened to the people on the phone as he delivered the mail and quickly realized he was in the right place. "I can do that," he said. "They just bullshit on the phone." By contrast, he lacked the discipline to be a doctor or dentist.

Geffen spent a year in the mail room, moving up to a job as secretary to an agent and then assistant to another agent. He learned that the most successful people were the ones who brought in talent to the agency. The trick was to spot the talent, convince them they wanted him, and then convince those at the agency that they wanted the artists. "You have to be realistic," *Playboy* quoted him as saying. "You're certainly not going to be able to go after a major star when you're 21 years old. I went after people who were brand-new and who I thought were talented."

By the time Geffen became an agent, he had signed Jesse Colin Young, Joni Mitchell, and the Association. He hung out at places like Cafe à Go-Go and the Bitter End, where much of the talent played. It was easy then. He just followed his instincts about what he liked.

On his own, he met and signed such groups as the Youngbloods and Laura Nyro to record contracts. He lived with singer-songwriter Laura Nyro, who died of cancer in 1997 at the age of 49. Together they formed Tuna Fish Music, a publishing company they owned equally. Geffen was first attracted to Nyro after she had been booed out of the Monterey Pop Festival in 1967, and he became her manager. He succeeded in getting her a recording contract with Columbia Records from 1968 to 1971. He sold her hits—"Stoned Soul Picnic" to the Fifth Dimension and "Eli's Coming" to Three Dog Night, among others.

Geffen became a force in developing the talent in what was becoming a landmark California rock scene. The five-foot-seven-inch agent, known for being unshaven in a trademark attire of jeans, T-shirt, and sneakers, met many people during his early years in the record business who were mentors: such people as Nat Lefkowitz, head of the New York office of William Morris, and Steve Ross, head of Ashley-Steiner Famous Artists, where Geffen worked upon leaving William Morris. Ross, who eventually became head of Warner

Records and later a top executive with Time Warner, backed Geffen through the years when he started his own record companies.

These people provided him business opportunities and taught him the tricks of the trade: cut deals, don't give up, and be persistent. In addition, have faith in yourself. Geffen was famous for being on the telephone from 6 AM to midnight. It wasn't uncommon to find him casually dressed in heavy negotiations at Jewish delis, passing out knishes to rock stars on his private jet, or attending art auctions with a baseball cap propped backwards on his head.

Geffen met Ahmet Ertegun, the head of Atlantic Records in 1968. Ertegun, who recorded such greats as Ray Charles, John Coltrain, and Aretha Franklin, had a tremendous influence on Geffen's life and became his role model. It was Geffen who signed Crosby, Stills and Nash to a contract at Atlantic Records and set up their first performance at Woodstock.

In 1969, at the age of 26, Geffen sold Tuna Fish Music to CBS for $4.9 million and pocketed his share of $2.5 million. A year later, in 1970, he formed Asylum Records, giving it the name because "it was all craziness." He formed the company at the suggestion of Atlantic Records chief Ertegun. Geffen couldn't get a record company—even Ertegun's—to sign Jackson Browne, whom he managed at the time and had been placing as the opening act for Laura Nyro. At his own company, Asylum Records, he also became responsible for managing Joni Mitchell, Linda Ronstadt, and the Eagles. The challenge was unique; the stars he signed often had quirky personalities. Laura Nyro, for example, was known to develop paralyzing stage fright after her experience at Monterey. Geffen gave the stars encouragement to do their own thing.

Geffen, who never married and has no children, gave more than 100 percent to his job. But he wasn't a dictator. It's been said that he let his employees speak their minds, make their own decisions, and follow their instincts. Sometimes, a lack of structure and much sensitivity can be what it takes. He clearly paid attention to the money, though, and published reports indicate that while at William Morris, he recognized the importance of getting control of his clients' publishing, management, and record contracts to maximize profits. His business relationships, implied by the book *Mansion on the Hill* by Fred Goodman, were occasionally challenged as conflicts of interest.

Goodman's book quotes John Hartmann, who took over the management of Crosby, Stills and Nash, as noting two principal changes between the group's existing contract and the original contract negotiated by Geffen. "One was that Geffen had his commission written in to pay direct. And the other was that Atlantic got more product."

Meanwhile, Geffen got ahead by keeping his eyes peeled to what the book terms "significant artists." He focused his attention on "artists who create their own music, record and produce it." Geffen, the book continues, "was smart enough to know that his best contribution was to make the ground ready and fertilize it and then step away."

Nevertheless, Geffen is known for working as much as 18 hours a day. Over the years, he has kept a couch in his office but no desk. Everything is stored in his head; he shuns paper and memos. At this writing, his DreamWorks SKG office at Universal Studios did have a desk.

Steve Ross, one of Geffen's mentors at the William Morris Agency, moved on to Warner Communications and offered Geffen $7 million for his Asylum Records in 1972. Geffen accepted, but subsequently admitted that might have been the greatest financial blunder of his life. "Selling it was a stupid mistake by the way—a mind-boggling idiotic decision," he told *Playboy*. A year later Asylum was worth $50 million. Albums by Linda Ronstadt and the Eagles alone earned more than his take from that sale. But the sale, along with the money he already had, resulted in an impressive worth of more than $10 million.

Ross also purchased other companies and formed a new record label called WEA. Geffen was asked to run Electra-Asylum-Nonesuch label by Ross.

Geffen endured tough times in his personal life. One of the greatest disappointments of his early life was his breakup with Cher, who left him for Greg Allman. Cher, who claims to have remained friendly with Geffen, had been married to the late Sonny Bono at 16. When they parted—she was 27—Geffen took care of her. The two stayed together for two years, and published reports have indicated that Geffen wanted to marry her. They parted when she became involved with Greg Allman.

In 1975 Geffen moved from the record company to become vice chairman of Warner Bros Inc., but he left after a year even though he was held to his contract, which he has characterized as a noncompete agreement. Geffen was an entrepreneur, while the movie business was conservative. He felt stifled in corporate bureaucracy and spent his time teaching at Yale and UCLA.

Geffen was diagnosed with bladder cancer in 1976, just after he and Cher broke up. Four years later he found out he had been misdiagnosed, but the cancer scare changed his outlook on life. "When someone tells you that you have cancer, it changes your life in a profound way," he told *Playboy*. Geffen went into therapy at the EST Institute in California. He learned to feel good about himself as well as about others, realizing he was not responsible for how other people feel.

"I thought, 'I'm going to live my life and see who I really am and what I really like because I don't know.' I had been trying to be something else, but from that point on I had to be who I was. Cancer made it imperative not to waste any more time."

Geffen has said he is willing to try anything that makes him feel a little better. Freud, Jung, est, Life Spring, a Course in Miracles, and Twelve Steps are some of the spiritual paths he has followed. Although he acknowledges he has smoked marijuana, published reports indicate he stayed away from the heavy drug scene that ruined the life of so many in his business.

He came to yet another realization: his homosexuality. He announced that he was gay at a Commitment to Life AIDS benefit in Los Angeles in November 1992. In fact, Geffen in 1999 was listed by *Worth* magazine as having contributed $45 million in total donations to civil liberties, Jewish causes, AIDS organizations, and the arts. He ranked 84th nationally on *Worth's* list of the most generous philanthropists, and an AIDS foundation in New York has been named after him.

"Right now, I'm completely, 100 percent gay," he told *Playboy* in 1994. "But I'd be lying if I said that it's inconceivable to me that I might meet a woman and fall in love with her. I might. I'm not looking to, and I'm not planning on it." His announcement that he was gay was not intended to be as big a deal as the media made it out to be, he added.

While he was getting his personal life together, Geffen still had plenty of business to take care of. On the advice of singer Paul Simon, he decided to get back into the business he knew. So by 1980, Steve Ross and Geffen agreed to start a new record company; Geffen would own half of the company—Geffen Records—and Warner the other half. If it made money, Warner and Geffen would split profits; but if the company lost money, Warner would pick up the tab. After five years, they'd renegotiate. It sounded like a utopian deal in which Geffen couldn't lose.

Even though at the time the music business was faced with sluggish sales, Geffen used his skills to sign some big names and sold millions of records. The business was profitable after one year.

As with his other ventures, Geffen ran a sparse ship. But he did hire creative people and let them do their thing. Over the next several years, Geffen signed such legends as Bob Dylan, John Lennon, and Elton John as well as Peter Gabriel, Asia, Neil Young, Cher, Motley Crew, Aerosmith, and Guns N' Roses.

Geffen wasn't afraid to take risks because he felt he could bargain and run things properly. As if records weren't enough, Geffen also began producing such hit Broadway shows as *Dreamgirls*. He owned 33 percent of *Cats*—the longest-running show on Broadway —and a piece of the action of *M. Butterfly* and *Miss Saigon* several years later. He also bought some prime real estate in California.

In 1982 Steve Ross offered Geffen a deal to start a film company to be called the David Geffen Film Company. Again, Geffen produced profitable hits. Among them were *Risky Business, After Hours, Little Shop of Horrors, Lost in America,* and *Beetlejuice.*

By 1983 Geffen was getting a bit too old to hang out in rock clubs and pick talent on his own. He realized he had to hire others to do it, which was one of his smartest moves. In 1984 Ross refused Geffen's request for a $5 million advance against future profits. Instead, he offered Geffen 100 percent of the equity in return for signing another six-year contract with Warner, according to *Forbes.* By 1987 Geffen Records had captured 8 percent of the record market. The company had 110 employees and $225 million in sales, and Geffen was worth even more millions.

If a recording artist sells a gold album, it means there were at least 500,000 records sold; a platinum album indicates 1 million sold. By 1989 Geffen Records had 50 gold albums and 22 platinum.

Geffen was trying to sell. After Time merged with Warner, the resulting Time Warner failed to offer him what he wanted, nor was Disney interested. He turned down one lucrative offer because of foreign tax laws. So Geffen accepted an offer from MCA, the largest record company in America, of 10 million shares of MCA stock for his company, making him a 12 percent owner of MCA. His stock was worth $525 million.

As luck would have it, Matsushita Electric Company of Tokyo bought MCA and its subsidiary television station for $66 per share just after Geffen accepted MCA's deal. He made $660 million on the deal. Now Geffen's security holdings and other assets made him a billionaire, and it was reported that Geffen in 1991 had one of the nation's largest personal tax assessments.

Geffen was a billionaire by the time he was 50. He flies a DreamWorks jet and owns at least two homes—one in Malibu and a ten-acre, five-bedroom estate in Hollywood, which he bought after the MCA deal. The estate has gardens, a tennis court and golf course, a swimming pool, maids' quarters, and an esplanade.

Besides starting and selling his record companies over the years, Geffen also invested in real estate (he has owned several office buildings in California), stock (with a partner he owned a large stake in Honeywell Corporation), movies, and Broadway shows; but, for the most part, he has invested in art. His interest in art began in the early 1970s. Through the years he always rewarded himself by buying an art work after he made a big business deal.

Geffen's first art purchase was a Picasso he bought for under $50,000. Unfortunately, it was stolen but he collected enough from the insurance company to make a tidy profit of more than $20,000 as a result of the painting's appreciation in value. He also purchased Tiffany lamps and a number of valuable modern paintings in the 1970s. In the mid-1980s, he sold the Tiffany collection for over $1 million and purchased works of more modern artists, such as David Hockney. In the 1990s he bought more than $90 million of contemporary art, paying $3 million for one piece.

His biggest purchase was the Jack Warner estate that he bought for $47.5 million following MCA's purchase of Geffen Records; the ten-acre estate is on a hilltop in Hollywood and includes rare furniture, antiques, and valuable art. Geffen sold several million dollars worth of art and antiques just after he bought the estate.

He has admitted he leads the hectic life of a workaholic but has learned to take weekends off. Also, he doesn't encourage phone calls outside of business hours, and he does take vacations. "I have good friends and lots of interests." He has, he says, finally realized happiness, although "you constantly have to work out issues in your life."

Today, DreamWorks employees draw blanks when questioned about Geffen's work hours. There are no titles at the company. Geffen's responsibility is largely with DreamWorks Records. Among the artists now on its label are country superstar Randy Travis, alternative rock band Propellerheads, and solo artist Rufus Wainwright.

DreamWorks' motion picture *Saving Private Ryan,* a coproduction with Paramount, received five Academy awards and its film *The Prince of Egypt* won an Oscar for having the best original song. The movie's soundtrack, featuring the first duet by Whitney Houston and Mariah Carey—"When You Believe"—was released as one of three albums in association with the movie.

While many worry about losing business due to the far-reaching impact of the Internet and other technology, Geffen has said he is unconcerned.

"If there are new ways to deliver movies, Broadway shows, and albums, great!" he told *Playboy.* "It doesn't matter to me whether I deliver them on CD, record, videocassette, or by some cable system with 500 channels. Everybody claims to have a crystal ball about this stuff in the future. I don't have a crystal ball."

CHAPTER 7

PAUL AND CHERYL JAKUBOWSKI

Couple Uses Software to Cut Debt and Invest Wisely

For Paul and Cheryl Jakubowski, the rags part of their rags-to-riches story started later in life when they were in their mid-30s and living in Dallas with two young children.

Unlike others in this book, they didn't grow up in poverty with many people sharing a single home. They hadn't even experienced severe deprivation. In fact, they only realized the extent of their financial troubles when Paul decided in 1985 to enter into a computer the amount of the family's assets and liabilities. The results were startling: they were $20,000 in the hole. "That was including profit-sharing money I couldn't put my hands on," said Paul, 48. "The rub was it was probably more like $35,000 to $40,000 by the time you totaled all the short-term debt." Many of the month's bills hadn't even arrived.

There is nothing worse than having your financial security threatened when you have a family to support. From Paul's perspective, money is one of the most critical areas of a marriage, and theirs was spinning out of control. "I was concerned that my perception was going to be different from Cheryl's," he said. "That was why I thought it was so important to deal with it and do it in an objective sort of way that wouldn't cause undue strain on our marriage."

Sometimes, it's a lot harder to fall from the top than it is to start out at rock bottom. But, fortunately, the Jakubowskis, who both hailed from Nebraska, were raised with a strong midwestern work ethic, and both their parents were hard workers. Failure isn't in the cards when you know that you can bite the bullet and work your way out of a situation.

About 14 years later, in 1999, Paul carefully checked his computer program to find his current net worth: $1.52 million. Rich? "I don't feel wealthy," he said, but he supplies the documentation. A computer search of the U.S. Census Bureau's statistics proved he is in the top 3 percent of households across the United States. Paul, a member of the Mensa Society, the international organization of geniuses, says his IQ is in the 99th percentile. Smart? "There always are people wealthier and smarter than you are," the Jakubowskis echo.

You might conclude that the Jakubowskis are wealthy simply by looking at their income. Paul shows a $140,000-a-year salary on his 1998 W-2; Cheryl shows $6,700. The two live in an exclusive Cincinnati condominium in a three-story Civil War era building built by pork-packing barons. Paul is a technology manager at Procter & Gamble while Cheryl, 46, works about 40 weeks a year as a preschool substitute teacher.

"Back in the sixties, my dad made $6,000 to $7,000 a year," Paul said. "I was just like everybody else. I didn't have any perception of rich people or poor people. We didn't have a lot but didn't look for a lot. Life revolved around work."

Paul says his mother always worked. She owned a mom-and-pop 18-unit motel; his father had a series of jobs, including running a grain elevator next to the railroad tracks. Three brothers and two sisters completed the family.

Cheryl's mother started working when she was 12 or 13 as a government secretary and subsequently a welfare case worker; her father ran a filling station while she did all the books. . . . "If my sister and I wanted nice clothes, we made them; we learned how to sew. It was part of the small-town thing. If you couldn't do it one way, you went around the back door."

The couple met at the University of Nebraska and married in 1973. Paul majored in business administration and enrolled for extra hours so he could graduate early. That way he could enlist in the army rather than be ordered to Vietnam.

Cheryl never finished college. When the couple first married, they made a number of small moves. Paul went to Officer Candidates School while Cheryl moved in with Paul's parents. Paul still remembers his situation at their first apartment in Colorado Springs, when he was earning $341.67 a month and paying $135 a month in rent.

The couple's life changed dramatically, though, when Paul, after training in the army, got the military assignment of a lifetime. The couple found themselves living in a duplex at Fort Barry in San Francisco—a major change from their small-town roots. Cheryl found work as a teller.

Paul initially was assigned as an administrative officer. The army, though, had been in the process of winding down the war in Vietnam. "The personnel structure was all out of whack," he said. The changing environment resulted in his getting a job that would forever change the course of the couple's life. Paul became a protocol officer, carrying drinks and picking up tabs for worldwide dignitaries, a job that Paul considers a fluke. "It was a major's authorized job, but there weren't any majors around so they stuck me in it. It had nothing to do with qualification. I happened to be around."

The job was a dream come true. Paul's base was located in the middle of lush green parkland at the northern end of the Golden Gate Bridge. "We lived at the north end and I worked on the south end." His stomping ground was the 1,480 acres that are now part of the National Park Service's Golden Gate National Recreation Area. It not only was luck to be assigned to such pristine surroundings after an early threat of service in Vietnam, but he also was located near the area that served as a departure point for all service personnel going to the Pacific.

European VIPs at this time were touring the United States as guests of the government and often after stops around the country, their tours would wind up in San Francisco. Unlike other stops, which often lasted for a day during the week, the stays in San Francisco typically continued through a weekend, so the Jakubowskis had the opportunity to truly entertain.

The experience taught the couple what it was like to be high rollers. They began rubbing shoulders with the political elite. Among those Paul helped escort were Israel's Moshe Dayan and Golda Meir, and General Omar Bradley. They socialized with the late General George S. Brown, who had served as chairman of the Joint Chiefs of Staff. "I got to see how the really powerful people of the world carried themselves," he said. "I can remember wanting to leave the military because I wanted to be the person who got served the drinks rather than the one carrying them."

Besides noting the mannerisms of the elite who dropped into the area, Paul was also impressed by the salary of a four-star general. In 1977 it was $36,000. Paul's goal was to someday exceed that. That day finally arrived in 1983 while he worked at Procter & Gamble. "It was a right of passage," Paul says.

Back in San Francisco, much of the entertaining was at the lavish Fairmount Hotel. "It was a different life to be in the front row of the Venetian room." Paul's job was to pick up the tab and make sure the guests had a good time. On the other hand, he also had to avoid being mentioned in Jack Anderson's newspaper column on charges of throwing away government money. "I was being thrust into a completely different world with a completely different frame of reference."

While the events of those two years were the thrill of a lifetime, they also threatened to lead the couple to their demise. Credit cards had started becoming a way of life. They were an easy way to continue living the high life with their friends. "In San Francisco," Cheryl said, "that's what everybody did. You had a credit card for every major store in downtown San Francisco."

Paul finally left the army in 1977 and joined Procter & Gamble as a sales rep; the company offered a dividend reinvestment plan and a profit-sharing plan.

Meanwhile, Cheryl always managed to find work that would allow her to be with her children and Paul. "I was going to be a librarian," she reflected, but then worked as a bank teller. At one point, Procter & Gamble sent Paul to Lincoln, Nebraska, and Cheryl started working for a very small credit union. She learned accounting and went back to school to improve her accounting skills. She had a baby, and the family moved to Omaha and then Denver, where Cheryl worked in accounting for U.S. Home, the developer of the subdivision in which the couple then owned their home. The job let her work yet have time to run home to feed the baby.

The couple continued on to Dallas, where they desperately tried to buy a home in an area with a good school system. "Texas was booming with its oil patch. Interest rates were 12 to 13 percent. We bought a house that was in really sorry shape because it was the only thing we could afford," Paul said.

For the children's sake and the stability of the family, the couple vowed to put down roots in Dallas. It would be their 11th home in nine years. They bought a four-bedroom ranch house with a pool in the upper-middle-class North Dallas area. Their mortgage rate was 13 percent, but they were confident that Paul would get promoted. "We were house poor," Paul said, as he was earning about $3,300 a month.

It was hard for them to figure out where the money was going. They didn't leave home much because they had two small children, but they were footing the bill for their children's private schools. By 1985 the couple, in their mid-30s, had collected 20 credit cards (Visa, MasterCard, gas station cards, and department store cards). Added Paul: "I remember I gave her a Neiman Marcus credit card for Christmas." It was simply an impressive status symbol.

Although the couple knew how to work hard, there had been a gaping hole in both their childhoods because money was rarely discussed. How to manage it or invest it never came up in family conversations. As a result, Paul had nothing to fall back on—no voice in the back of his head that cautioned against the spending that was getting out of hand.

"My parents are children of the depression who squirreled away money," Paul said. While his parents disapproved of the younger couple's lifestyle, Paul was in the process of proving his independence. His brothers and sisters had remained close to home. He often avoided family gatherings because he knew his lifestyle would meet with the family's disapproval.

When the family did get together, money was never a topic of conversation. "It's a stretch to say it was a point of friction or anything like that," Paul said. "I knew exactly where they stood." Any time the couple needed something, they simply got another credit card. Because they were making more than the minimum payments, they were unconcerned.

It took a crisis to wake the couple up. The hard path to debt reduction led them to a more comfortable life than they could have imagined. It was buoyed by the bull years of the stock market and a dogged investment strategy.

The turning point came one night when Paul became concerned that they were getting fairly close to their credit limit on a MasterCard. "I was going to have to get another one," he said. "I asked Cheryl how much she spent. She missed it by half! Even

81

though no one had ever taken the time to teach me about money, I could tell that spending $1,400 when we would have estimated $750 was out of line. I could smell danger when I realized that our *perception* of what we spent was so at odds with the *reality* of what we spent."

Fortunately, Paul had begun using a computer at his job, and he had access to a portable one for use at work and at home. He decided to add a final item to his credit card—a budgeting program known as Managing Your Money. Although that program is no longer commercially available, Paul suggests that families trying to get their spending under control might purchase a similar program, such as Quicken or Microsoft Money.

At the time he keyed in the information the program requested, including all the family's assets and liabilities, the results were astonishing. Their net worth was a negative $20,000. That night, the couple had one of the biggest fights of their marriage—one that Paul says he now regrets. "Thank God our marriage was strong enough to survive it. I don't think we ever could have communicated if it hadn't been for the objective reality of what that printout said. When you put accurate data in front of mature people, they're going to react."

Had Paul and Cheryl relied on incomplete data or their own perhaps fading memories, Paul conceded, emotions could have taken control. That one fight might not have ended so quickly.

The spending had not been completely reckless, Cheryl stressed. "I had to have nice clothes for [the children's] private schools. We were buying a lot for the new home, which was bigger than the one we had come from." Paul drove a company car while Cheryl actually had been driving a two- to three-year-old diesel-powered Cadillac Seville.

Said Paul: "It would have been easy to say, 'Hey, you spent so much on that damn coffee table.' And she could have said, 'Yeah, but you put so much on that car.'" The printout, though, presented the stark reality. "To tell the truth, we didn't know what to do," Paul confessed.

Each time the Managing Your Money program pops up on the computer, it is accompanied by the following: "There is no dignity quite so impressive, and no independence quite so important, as living within your means," a quotation from the late President

Calvin Coolidge. The couple jointly vowed to incorporate that saying into their lifestyle.

Although Paul was at a loss initially for what to do, fortunately the program he purchased provided concrete instructions on how to prioritize spending and what to attack first. Paul also had read an *Esquire* magazine article that featured successful people, with descriptions of how they had become successful. In each case, the person went to a teacher and put into practice what the teacher advised.

Like the successful people spotlighted in that article, the Jakubowskis agreed to submit themselves to a teacher. In their case, the teacher was the computer budgeting program. Included in the program's advice was an admonition not to spend more than 15 percent of your income on shelter. "We were pushing 35 percent." It also suggested putting away 15 percent of your income into savings.

Initially, the couple started routing that 15 percent dedicated to savings to paying off the principal on their credit cards. "My idea of budgeting had been to make the minimum payments on credit cards," said Paul. "Instead, we turned a complete 180 degrees." They cut up all but two credit cards. "That was almost like putting a beloved pet to sleep," he said. "Our self-image was so tied up in the status they conveyed."

Fortunately, the family had some major help along the way. Paul's salary, which had been $450 a week in 1983 was steadily increasing. And interest rates were moving down, so their once whopping 13 percent adjustable-rate mortgage started costing them much less. They opted not to downsize their home at that time.

Meanwhile, Cheryl made a drastic change in her food spending. Instead of shopping at the local fancy supermarket, she drove to a discount supermarket and found she was able to save some $100 monthly on groceries.

The couple gave themselves allowances for money they didn't budget—$100 a week. "We gave ourselves little raises when we hit goals," Paul said. "To this day, we don't go to cash machines to get money to spend. I go once a week—after 3 PM on Friday afternoon —close to the weekend. That's all we spend. If we run out on Tuesday of the next week, we don't spend anything. It's so easy to go to a restaurant and spend $75 for a meal!"

The process continued. For about a four-year period, until 1988 or so, the family didn't take a vacation. Each year, Paul took one week of his vacation time and traded it in for cash that went toward wiping out the family's debt.

When you're dealing with two people, it's hard enough to turn the tide on credit card spending, but it becomes even more difficult when you add children. Constantly bombarded with television commercials and friends who have more than they do, children always make demands. Nevertheless, the Jakubowskis found ways around the demands made by their children.

Initially, it was difficult. "When the kids would want something, we would say the money is not there," Cheryl said. "They'd say, 'Go to the money machine and get it.' Children, it seems, simply don't understand the pressures of managing a household based on available cash. You have to explain that it's not that simple. The money's not in the bank. We made them understand that if we do this now, the end result is we can take you next summer to Disney World. That's the goal."

The couple was careful to explain to the children that there is a consequence for every action. They also got the children to buy into the household budget. Anytime one of their children wanted something, the child was encouraged to go to the computer to see exactly what the household budget was. Each child was given an allowance: 10¢ times their age each week and $1 when they were ten.

On top of that, the children were encouraged to qualify for bonuses, paid if they contributed to household chores above and beyond their duties. Extra cash was tacked onto the allowance if a child mowed the lawn or performed chores around the house.

On the other hand, if their rooms were dirty, the children earned less for the week. "I had them do the math and present me with a bill for their allowance," Paul said. The bills were due for payment on Saturday, which is when he often has the time to process them after a heavy travel schedule. "If they didn't give me a bill, I didn't pay them."

Paul said that the fact that he never learned about money when he was growing up taught him a major lesson with his own children. Involving the children in money matters is very important. By including them in the family budgeting process, it also impresses on them the tremendous power they had in their hands simply by watching what is spent.

Finally, the day came when the family got out of debt. "We bought a Plymouth Voyager van Christmas 1988. That van was a celebration that we could take on debt responsibly," Paul said, but the couple continued to budget. Instead of paying off debt, though, they were now routing money to investments, contributing regularly to Procter & Gamble's dividend reinvestment plan. The contributions continue. "We owned [the stock] at less than $10 a share," Paul said triumphantly. At this writing, it was $92 a share.

"Today, I keep two credit cards, a Discover Private Issue that we use for everything we can and a Visa for those places that won't take Discover. We charge everything possible—groceries, gas, pet care, college tuition."

But now the couple is careful to use credit cards to their own advantage. Paul hangs on to each receipt. The balance is paid off monthly and the 2 percent rebate the private issue card carries is also logged into their computerized budget to pay federal income tax from the year before. Each Saturday, the couple puts every transaction into their computer program, allocating each to a budget category.

The couple left Dallas in 1998 for Cincinnati to be near Procter & Gamble's headquarters. Thus, after a life of heavy traveling, Paul was able to travel a bit less, although he still has to check his schedule before making appointments to be certain he's going to be in town. The couple, with the move, gets to spend more time together, and Cheryl's work arrangement was specifically designed to be flexible enough to provide them more time together.

Their current condo cost about twice the amount they spent on their Dallas home; the most expensive condo in the seven-unit building is worth about $1 million. Paul believes that historically low interest rates made their new home in the Rawson Woods Nature Preserve near the University of Cincinnati an attractive deal. "I indulge myself in a dream media room," he adds.

The budget still runs, though, for the family in the computer. "He's got more money budgeted to spend at Christmas," Cheryl noted. Of course, the money is there because of planning during the rest of the year. When Cheryl wants to buy something, Paul tells her to check the budget categories in the computer. If something is on sale and she needs it in the current month, she'll discuss it with him. If they agree it's special, they'll cut back their spending accordingly the following month.

Their two children at this writing were both in college—a heavy cost that still causes financial concern. Their son was attending The

Citadel, where he had obtained a Navy scholarship. Their daughter was starting at the University of Oklahoma and had partially paid her way through music scholarships.

Despite the scholarships, the Jakubowskis still pay college housing expenses as well as travel for the children back and forth from school. Cheryl adds that since they have become empty nesters, they have made a conscious decision to give up the heavy maintenance costs that go with a pool and a large home. In celebration of their 25th anniversary, though, the family took a five-week trip, along with Paul's parents, to the South Pacific—a massive splurge that used up all their frequent flyer miles. "We saved for it and paid cash," Paul said.

The Jakubowskis drive a 1997 Toyota Celica, which the couple plans to give to their son if he brings up his grades. "I lost a company car when we moved, so we also bought a new Honda Accord," Paul added.

Their life has become financially easier, the two are the first to admit. But they recently had to learn another financial lesson: the importance of protecting your finances even after you succeed in accumulating them.

"Our daughter had a traffic accident last summer," Paul said. "We're in the midst of it right now." His daughter was uninjured, but there was a fatality. A nightmare? Yes, they chorus. Fortunately, the couple, as part of their financial vigilance, had purchased an umbrella insurance policy, which is easy to overlook if you have money. Umbrella insurance is designed to supplement homeowners, renters, and auto insurance coverage, kicking in after your homeowners and auto insurance coverage are exceeded.

Although the traffic accident had not been resolved at this writing, "the financial policy has given me peace of mind that would otherwise be driving me crazy right now. It's a very ugly situation," Paul said. "The way we looked at it when we got it," Cheryl said, "is he's the major earner. If he dropped dead tomorrow, what would I need to stay where I was, get the kids through college, and get myself a headstart in life?" Fortunately, the formula was available in their financial program.

CHAPTER 8

JOE L. DUDLEY SR.

From Farmhouse to Hair Care King

Joe L. Dudley Sr., 62, was left behind twice in grammar school. Slow and unable to concentrate, he also had a speech impediment. Born black, Dudley grew up in Aurora, North Carolina —the Deep South—and was raised with ten other children in a three-room farmhouse. His school had determined the reason for his problems: Dudley was mentally retarded, school personnel told his parents.

But Dudley always had food on the table and his parents—who encouraged him, nonetheless, to work at his education—filled him with expectations of success. Those expectations started at birth, when he was given the middle name Louis after boxer Joe Louis, at the time one of the nation's most successful black Americans.

Dudley's mother never stopped encouraging him, and Dudley took her words to heart. "Once a slow one gets it, he's got it," she told him. She was right. Dudley became a millionaire at 40.

Now his Kernersville, North Carolina, hair care products company, Dudley Products Inc., earns $30 million annually, according to *Black Enterprise* magazine. Ranked in the top 100 black-owned businesses, the company manufactures and distributes ethnic hair care products, provides cosmetology training, and has 425 employees.

The Dudley compound includes an 80,000-square-foot manufacturing and office building; the Dudley Cosmetology University, which claims to have graduated more than 14,000 persons; and a small hotel. The company also has eight beauty schools and a travel agency.

Joe and his wife, Eunice Mosly Dudley, 56, have two homes, one in Kernersville and another in Windermere, Florida, near Orlando.

"I really don't know what it was," Dudley says of his initial inability to make the grade in school. "Some say retardation. You could call it a learning disability." It was dogged determination and encouragement—by his mother, his wife, and one of the nation's most successful black businessmen—that helped set him on the right path. His wife, Eunice, is chief financial officer of Dudley Products.

The turning point, Dudley believes, was a relationship that went sour. In his junior year of high school, he was dumped by a girl he was crazy about. Hearing who her new boyfriend was, Dudley retorted that he was ugly. "Well maybe so, Joe," she replied, "but at least he's smart." (This is reported in Dudley's book *Walking by Faith* [Executive Press].)

Realizing that his lack of intelligence had turned off his love, Dudley gathered all the books he could find and began reading one every night. When he didn't understand a word, he checked the dictionary. He read each of his textbooks from first grade and worked his way up. In fact, after not being promoted twice, he made up part of one year.

It wasn't easy. Dudley milked cows and cleaned manure from the chicken coop—all while trying to get through school. He supported himself through the first year of college by working on the college farm caring for chickens. On Saturdays, he did housework for a professor. One of the worst jobs he ever held, he once told the *Greensboro News and Record,* was at Bethlehem Poultry. For $1 an hour, he would take chickens out of a vat and put them on a table so people could cut them up as they went down the line. He got a raise of 25¢ an hour when his job changed to scooping up chicken intestines after they were sent down a chute and putting them in a barrel. The money he saved from that job, though, helped him pay for college.

Dudley's big break came in 1957, when he moved into the basement of his aunt's home in Brooklyn, New York. He had worked out an arrangement with her that he would clean her house in lieu of rent. Searching for a high-paying job to help cover his college tuition, Dudley had been impressed with a well-dressed Fuller Products Company salesman he met and was hired by the black-owned Fuller Products.

Although both Fuller Brush Company and Fuller Products were door-to-door sales companies, Fuller Products was one of the nation's largest black-owned businesses at the time. For $10, Dudley purchased a box of perfume, hair dressings, cleansing creams, bath preparations, face powder, lipsticks, and colognes, and started pounding the pavement. Initially, his body ached from all the walking. So did his morale. Despite his hard work, sales tallied a discouraging $2.60, but he liked having the freedom to set his own hours.

A devout Christian, Dudley prayed at night, and his sales steadily increased each week so that by the end of the summer of his first year in 1957, he was making $100 in commissions.

Dudley brought the Fuller products back to college with him and continued selling them at North Carolina Agricultural and Technical State University, Greensboro, where he majored in business administration and graduated in 1962. He since has been awarded honorary doctorate degrees from his alma mater as well as from Edward Waters College, Jacksonville, Florida.

The key, Dudley wrote, was to greet his customers with a smile that warmed them up. He learned to be sensitive to their needs. He also refused to be discouraged when a door was slammed in his face. "Have a nice day," he'd say.

He tried to learn everything he possibly could from Fuller, which trained some 5,000 district sales reps. "No matter what the situation, go to work," was the Fuller mantra. The company, which peaked in the 1960s with $10 million in annual sales and offices in 38 states, grew steadily. It eventually controlled a department store, a theater, a newspaper group, and an appliance center. The company was also credited with helping to launch the careers of many eminent blacks, including not only Dudley but also John H. Johnson, publisher of *Ebony* magazine.

S.B. Fuller, who died in 1988, may well be an unsung national hero, Dudley believes. In fact, Dudley keeps Fuller's desk and chair in his own office and refuses to drive anything other than a Cadillac, the car of choice for Fuller. Dudley's company acquired the rights to what was left of Fuller Products in 1984, and Dudley continues to manufacture and distribute some original Fuller cosmetics.

"He had a mission of economic freedom and self-sufficiency," Dudley explains about his mentor. "Be job makers rather than job takers. His philosophy was for every disadvantage, there was an advantage. That's what I liked."

Dudley keeps the same positive attitude at his own company. When asked about the racism he and his wife were forced to endure on the way up the ladder, he skirts the subject, even though his book describes a zoning change he believed was provoked by racism.

"I didn't feel like I was deprived. There were so many poor people—white and black. There was no radio for us until we were older and no television and no real exposure. You always wanted to do better. You wanted to get an education."

His wife, Eunice, the daughter of a minister and a day care center–nursery school manager, has a similar attitude. She hadn't been quite as poor as Dudley but grew up in heavily segregated Selma, Alabama. "When you don't have anything to compare it to, you don't know specifically what's going on," she said. "I didn't realize how poor my whole state was until I moved away to New York." She firmly believes, though, that the racial prejudice and inequities of Selma actually fueled her determination to succeed. She is not alone, either, she says. "A lot who have come from Selma may not be rich, but a lot have done well in careers and professions because of the hardships and inequities."

As much as Fuller strove to make money, he also made it his mission to help some of the most poverty-stricken people of his own race. He recruited young blacks off the streets away from their involvement with drugs and alcohol and inspired them to succeed in direct sales. In fact, Dudley says S.B. Fuller helped him with what had started to become his own brush with alcoholism, a problem that had started in high school. After being designated retarded, it wasn't difficult to start hanging around with the wrong crowd. "My cousin must have been around 16 or 17 years old. He loved to make moonshine. He thought it was good money. I got involved with him." As an adult, reported the News & Observer Publishing Company in 1989, Dudley clearly made his point about alcoholism at a Chicago sales meeting by paying the Westin Hotel more than $700 to remove all liquor from each room's refrigerator.

Money clearly was not the overwhelming thought on Dudley's mind as a teenager. His good fortune actually occurred gradually and took him by surprise. "You continue doing the same thing and it gradually grows. Somebody else says, 'Hey, you know, this guy is wealthy.' You don't even think of it. You don't even feel like you're a millionaire—even today. I got so much joy out of what I was doing, the money just happened."

Dudley has tried to carry on the Fuller mission and clearly espouses his own: "It's very important—especially for African Americans—to see that you can be successful in America in the business world. I think that is important to give people hope for the future. I work the way I work because I enjoy it. I enjoy working with young kids who say, 'How do you do it?' I say, 'You can do what I'm doing, but you can do it better.'"

When Dudley started his own business, like Fuller he hired the downtrodden and inspired them to be good door-to-door salespeople. As the company has grown, however, door-to-door sales became a less critical segment of his business. Recently, he has been hiring experienced people with college degrees.

What turbocharged the sales of Fuller Products were emotionally charged motivational sales meetings and contests. Many similar strategies were adopted by Dudley when he started his own company by 1975. But at Fuller sales meetings, sometimes the salespeople, whose performances faltered, were laughed at in front of their colleagues. It was at one of those sales meetings, which happened to be a dark one for Dudley, that he met his wife. Eunice had just graduated high school and started work for Fuller Products to help pay for her college education at Talladega College in Alabama.

On her first day at the first sales meeting, Dudley was forced to sit underneath a conference table for about 15 minutes while the other salespeople in the room laughed at him—his punishment for missing a sales meeting. "There were team captains in each group," said Eunice. "One team competed against the other. A person from one team evidently ordered the punishment."

When queried about what might seem on the surface to be a belittling experience, Dudley laughs. He doesn't see it that way at all; rather, it was like a game. "I was put under the table because I didn't come to a sales meeting. I did a wrong and I was paying the price. I just figured when they go wrong, I'd be ready for them!" Dudley, though, didn't continue the practice in his own company because "times are different." Employees' skin may not be as tough as it was then. "It made us grow," but "today people are not able to take that type of challenge."

Dudley, along with other Fuller Products employees who were working there to put themselves through college, impressed and inspired Eunice. After seeing them succeed, "I felt if they could do it, I could do it too," she said. Following that sales meeting, a Fuller Products sales manager took Eunice out to sell; after approaching five homes, she felt ready to continue.

Eunice, a saver who has strongly believed in the power of money, always encouraged her husband to better himself. In fact, she initially refused to date him if he failed to meet his weekly sales quota, Dudley wrote in his book. The couple married in 1961. As other Fuller employees went on to open their own distributorships with the company, Eunice took a job in the office to learn the business end while Dudley focused on sales.

They saved almost every penny they made and in 1963 had their first child. Dudley was promoted to crew manager and then team captain—a position that, to his dismay, he was required to share with an arch rival. Although Dudley really wanted to be a branch manager, he never got the appointment he wanted so badly.

With his arch rival sharing his position as a team captain, Dudley redoubled his efforts to sell but was unable to meet his goals. He tried to motivate employees but was handicapped by his speech impediment. Dudley became depressed, and Eunice became frustrated with him as their needs were growing along with their family.

Although Dudley, dejected, finally was ready to throw in the towel and return to North Carolina and open a hog farm, S.B. Fuller, in front of his salespeople at a sales meeting, forced Dudley to think hard. What kind of money did Dudley think he could make as a hog farmer, he asked. Finally, Fuller offered Dudley a distributorship for a $2,000 investment. Dudley, taking a loan from his brother, opened a Fuller Products distributorship in Greensboro, North Carolina.

Eunice Dudley, then caring for two children, went to work for a law office and also handled the books of Dudley's distributorship. Although it sounds like an impossibly heavy workload, Eunice Dudley was undaunted. "Years ago, the options for outside activities were not as great." There were church activities, but life was simpler.

Dudley always encouraged his employees and motivated them. He managed to find money to help some of his salespeople get a car while his wife initially rode the bus to work. Sales at Dudley's Fuller Products distributorship were growing. Finally, when his wife became angry about the financial assistance he had given employees, he agreed to buy her a used car.

Fuller Products Company suffered as the civil rights movement got under way in the 1960s. Black Americans were just starting to finally obtain hard-earned rights, and Fuller, who had been very outspoken in his capitalistic beliefs, was perceived as a deterrent. It actually was the civil rights movement that many blame for nearly bankrupting the Dudleys' beloved employer.

Fuller had openly refused to participate in the civil rights protests. While most were rallying behind Martin Luther King, Fuller would tell them, "Stop that boycotting. Go there and buy the bus company; you can ride anywhere you want to ride."

What really angered black civil rights leaders, though, was Fuller's published comments that indicated the chief problem with blacks had nothing to do with racial barriers, but rather "a lack of understanding of the capitalist system. The minute that they can develop themselves so that they excel in whatever they do, then they are going to find that they don't have any real problems," Fuller told *U.S. News & World Report.*

Many African Americans, who perceived Fuller's remarks as indicating opposition to their all-important cause, began boycotting Fuller Products, causing his company to lose an estimated $8 million. Published reports indicate that Fuller Products already had been having problems from whites who didn't like the idea that a black man owned a company that manufactured white products.

Before long, Fuller Products was not paying its vendors. Dudley, while not directly affected by the boycotts, was unable to fill his customers' orders. He was forced to think about going on his own and finding another supplier. He located a company in Richmond that successfully manufactured hair products in a garage, and he bought the formula. He borrowed money from his sister to help finance the company's growth, and began focusing on his own product line. In 1969, the Dudleys began mixing their own hair care products in their kitchen. When they ran out of containers, they typed labels and put them on mayonnaise jars with help from their children. Dudley and his sales force first attempted to sell the products by knocking on doors in black neighborhoods.

There was racial unrest in Greensboro, and a North Carolina A&T student was killed, but, like Fuller, Dudley declined to get involved with the protests. The ethnic hair care business had just started taking off. Between 1968 and 1972, a loose-perm look, known as "the curl," became popular among black women, boosting sales of hair care products. Eunice Dudley says, though, that her company's success stemmed more from products that relaxed the hair and achieved a smoother look. "That [the curl] was capitalized on more by others."

While searching for empty containers for his products, Dudley had befriended several area cosmetologists, who told him of their need for an exclusive product line. Dudley's sales force immediately began filling that need only to learn that Dudley's suppliers were selling the same products in retail outlets. Dudley, who had marketed the products and enlisted cosmetologists to use them, felt deceived.

So he started manufacturing more of his own products, complete with an ironclad guarantee that cosmetologists who switched to his line would never find those products in the stores. He soon began getting orders from cosmetologists nationwide. Dudley was fortunate, as the ethnic hair care business in the 1960s and 1970s experienced double-digit growth. By 1975, Dudley Products evolved with more than $1.5 million in annual sales. Even today, Dudley Products has not sold any of its products through retail outlets. Only a few maintenance items, such as shampoo, hair dressing, and conditioner, are for sale to the general public—but through salons exclusively.

The early years had been lean, and Eunice was always careful to save all S&H Green Stamps and Gold Bond Stamps. She eagerly took advantage of all the dish and glass promotional giveaways at grocery stores and service stations. Today, she continues to clip coupons from newspapers and magazines, informing Dudley Products employees about true sales, "not jive sales." Every day she clips a local newspaper coupon that can be used for a free or discounted item or service as a way to cover the cost of the newspaper. "The coupons I don't use I bring to the office so anyone can get them."

She learned the hard way that when money is tight, every little bit goes a long way.

Eunice Dudley says she has carried over some of her household practices to the family business and points proudly to a ten-year-old Rolls Royce that she recently had had painted. Her Rolls Royce was a prize in a company contest that she used as a spur for suppliers to aid her in cutting the cost of supplies purchased by Dudley Products.

Suppliers typically offer lower prices if purchasers buy in bulk, but a small business may not need bulk amounts, and they lack the buying power to realize the benefits of buying in bulk. Eunice set about to do some tough negotiating, letting everybody she dealt with know that the prize for meeting her quota for reducing the cost of supplies was her beloved Rolls Royce.

The Rolls Royce cost $120,000, which took Eunice five years to earn. The Rolls represented but a fraction of the amount she saved the company during the five years. "I was able to negotiate lower costs for raw materials, containers, goods, and services," Eunice explained. "What I was able to do is start buying a lot of things by truckloads." By buying truckloads, she earned a price break on individual items. "I was mixing items to get truckloads. We were able to negotiate lower prices for bottles and jars."

She then would look at the low price she was able to negotiate compared with the price that the company otherwise would have paid over a specific period and earmarked those savings toward paying for the Rolls. Every time suppliers visited her, they asked how close they were to shaving costs enough to meet her goal. "They would try to help," Eunice said. "I appreciated it so much!"

The Dudleys, following Fuller's philosophy, believe in reading and have tried to instill in their employees an equal appreciation of books. Reading, though, largely occurs on employees' own time in reading groups. "Reading people are ruling people," S.B. Fuller often told his sales force. Sometimes those reading groups in which Dudley Products employees read silently last as long as six hours a week. "What we try to do is get people to condition their minds," Dudley says. Adds Eunice Dudley: "A lot of times you don't need the information [you find in books]. But there's something there that clicks. You're able to absorb it when you do need to use it."

At Dudley Products, sales meetings are convened two or three times every day, conducted either by Dudley or another executive. Dudley calls the meetings "mental gymnasiums for people to express themselves and do their job better."

"We had a young lady who had a difficult time with her personality," Dudley said. "I suggested that she go to a psychiatrist. She did. This morning she got up and told everybody about the experience. She was so excited because she had been wrestling with this."

After succeeding with his own product line, Dudley went on to purchase the Brooklyn branch of the still-troubled Fuller Products. S.B. Fuller had become ill and asked Dudley to run his company as president. Not wanting to disappoint his mentor, Dudley sold off some of his Dudley Products stores and moved his company to Fuller's headquarters in Chicago to monitor both Fuller Products and his own company at the same time. The Dudleys moved into an apartment on the 53rd floor—despite the fact that Dudley was afraid of heights. Perhaps that, he hints in his book, was an omen. Eunice worked as a purchasing agent at a manufacturing plant and also ran Dudley's manufacturing business.

After seven years, Fuller Products, while improved, still struggled. From 1976 to 1984, while Dudley was running both companies, the News & Observer Publishing Company reported sales of Dudley Products declined from $2 million to $1.3 million while sales of Fuller Products climbed from about $1.5 million to $2 million. Forced to deal with Chicago's cold weather, the couple couldn't afford to invest any more in Fuller Products without hurting their own company. The building in which Dudley operated needed insulation and began generating whopping $18,000 monthly heating bills. Finally, Dudley met a woman who advanced him $40,000 as a loan and ultimately came to work for him as a plant worker. "While the money she loaned me was very important, one of the greatest things was that she had trust in me and would put her money into the business," his book reported.

The couple bought the building in which they operated and paid the overdue utility bill but could no longer subsidize Fuller Products. Instead, they bought the rights to Fuller Products Company and decided to return to North Carolina. They attempted to sell the building, but the buyer failed to make payments. As a result of litigation, when the couple returned to North Carolina in 1984, they were forced to sign a month-to-month lease on a smaller building in Greensboro. Dudley said that after reading *Think and Grow Rich* by Napoleon Hill, he decided to drop the frustrating lawsuit and let go of his anger, forfeiting any money he might have received. He lost the building in Chicago and vowed to get another. "I'm not going to spend my life being bitter and complaining about what has happened," he wrote in his book. "Instead, I'm going to be grateful for the wonderful things I still have."

Dudley finally found a perfect site for his new office building. But when the bank refused to finance both the purchase of the land and the building construction, another companywide campaign was mounted. Dudley and his employees set out to raise the money in honor of Eunice Dudley's birthday. Sales managers were encouraged to meet quotas. The month of his wife's birthday, they succeeded in cutting a check to buy the land. A celebration marked its completion in 1986. At the new site, marketing, accounting, and customer satisfaction departments were added.

In December 1988, the company paid $2 million for 54 acres in Kernersville. Dudley Cosmetology University, a hotel and travel agency, and a 7,000-square-foot convention center followed. When the company's original location became too crowded, it built its current 80,000-square-foot headquarters, which opened in September 1994.

Dudley has been building economic ties with developing countries. He has met President Robert Gabriel Mugabe of Zimbabwe as well as South Africa's first post-apartheid president, Nelson Mandela. He has had similar exchanges with cosmetologists in Brazil.

In 1994 it was reported that Dudley wished to carry on Fuller's philosophy to be responsible for creating 220 millionaires. "That wasn't my program," he stressed to us. "That was Mr. Fuller's program. I'm just taking it on to make that happen. It looks like there's a possibility that we can do that. We have people in our 401(k) plan that we've had about six and a half years. A few people already have $100,000. They're very young. By 59 or 60, they will have that kind of wealth just in their 401(k) plans." Dudley says there was no one thing that he credits for his wealth. Rather, it was the culmination of all his hard work.

Dudley Products unveiled Dudley Cosmetics, a new makeup line directed by the couple's daughter Ursula. He has succeeded in keeping the business in the family. His son, Joe Jr., vice president, works in finance. Their other daughter, Genea, is in marketing. All graduated from Ivy League schools.

In the early days of Dudley Products, the couple plowed all their profits back into the company to fuel its growth. About 11 years ago, though, Eunice said they hired a financial planner with American Express to help them diversify their holdings. "We've tried to handle the money in a manner in which we've remained humble," she said. "A lot of times, people use it wrongly. We try to get people to understand it's not what you have, it's what you do with what you have and how you make people feel about being around you as you accumulate. Do you share it with family and employees?"

Today, Dudley speaks clearly. He says he overcame his stutter by reading out loud, practicing pronunciation in the mirror, and simply doing a lot of talking. "My job was to talk," he says. "I didn't do physical work. Because I did it for so many years, it was natural for me to grow out of it."

Dudley says the biggest misperception people have about money is that it is used interchangeably with success. Money, he claims, is not success. "You must be successful before you get money."

Nor, he says, is money happiness. "You've got to get involved in something and you've got to like it. If you're happy and enjoy what you're doing, God gives you the increase. You don't drink water to go to the bathroom. It automatically comes."

The Dudleys have been major donors, and Dudley estimates he has given close to $2 million to charities on an annual basis. In 1995 Dudley was inducted into the Horatio Alger Association. There are no written guidelines for where Dudley Products will give the money. But there is a company group that meets occasionally to review donations. Often, there is input from marketing. Plus, Eunice says, the couple makes personal donations.

Now, Eunice Dudley says, the company is conducting more specialized training programs. "There's an awful lot of product knowledge," she says.

The Dudleys continue to work—generally six days a week. Vacations, Eunice Dudley says, typically consist of an extra day on the way to a weekend conference. "I imagine at some point I will slow down and retire," she said. "Right now, I'm still too young."

Although published reports have indicated concern that Dudley's company could be bought out by a white manufacturer of hair care products, as has been the case with many other black-owned competitors, Dudley is not worried. Mergers, he notes, are happening all over. If he had it to do over again, he admits, he might have expanded his business a little differently. "I wouldn't have taken on the schools. I think I would help build direct sales more." He also might have thought twice about starting a hotel.

He doesn't believe his guarantee of exclusivity to salons is hurting growth opportunities either. "If you look at Avon, Amway, and Mary Kay, they're not selling to retail outlets. We've got 25,000 hairdressers selling my products and we're having them make money. After you make a certain amount of money anyway, what are you going to do with it?" He'd rather see other people reap some of the income.

Dudley exercises daily. While maintaining a grueling schedule, he doesn't feel strapped. "I do pretty much what I like doing. If I didn't, I would have to vacate from it."

While he works hard, he is careful to stop when it becomes too much. If he has a lot of speaking engagements, for example, he might tell his secretary not to give him anything more to do for two months. Plus, he said, having his own business gives him the freedom to leave at 2 PM if he wishes.

At this writing, Dudley was promoting a success seminar and offering a Rolls Royce as a prize. His objective is to teach some 400 to 500 cosmetologists and others how to run the business. The course is to cost $395. If they don't win the Rolls, Dudley says he hopes they'll learn how to earn enough money to buy one. While he frequently has held such seminars in the past, this marked the first where the prize was a Rolls.

CHAPTER 9

DAL LA MAGNA

Failing Entrepreneur
Succeeds with Tweezer Business

Do you sometimes think you can never get ahead? Few people have experienced as many business failures as Dal La Magna, the founder and chief executive of Tweezerman Corporation, Glen Cove, New York. It took years before the inspiration for the initial pair of stainless steel tweezers, on which his company was founded, hit in the most unlikely way. While La Magna was sunbathing nude on a California redwood deck, he discovered he had picked up a series of painful splinters in his derrier.

As he struggled with tweezers while bent over a mirror trying to remove them, La Magna became frustrated at their lack of precision and grip. Having better success with industrial tweezers, he developed the idea of his own brand and modified them with blunt edges for beauty shops.

By 1999, 19 years after the company's inception, Tweezerman Corporation boasted $15 million in annual sales. In June 1998, La Magna's company was appraised at $7.2 million; if he sells it, he estimates he would net $3 million minus taxes, definitely making him a millionaire.

La Magna, 53, flinches at the term *millionaire*, which has been used to describe him in the media. "It creates an expectation in America," he says. Although he has a good salary—$250,000 annually—he would have to sell Tweezerman to realize his wealth. "I'm not Ted Turner. I have potential wealth. I would say I lead a wealthy lifestyle. I have three houses. I can fly anywhere I want. I don't fly first-class because I'm still basically cheap."

There is good reason for La Magna's caution. His current success follows at least ten business ventures that flopped. "My life story is that I failed to get ahead," he says. "I failed so many times that by the process of elimination, I made every mistake I could make and finally eliminated all the possible problems I could have. Finally, I succeeded." La Magna's bout with painful splinters wound up being the key to repositioning his life as a 20-year success story.

To those who know La Magna, it is no surprise that he finally hit a business home run. He was a leader, not a follower, during his school days. As a child, he was an altar boy at St. Clares Roman Catholic Church, Rosedale, Queens, and he had dreams of becoming a priest. An honor student in high school, he always took stands on issues and talked about becoming an elected official.

His sister, Seri La Magna, once recalled the overwhelming attendance at a high school birthday party when he put up signs at a train station with directions to his house. "He expected 50 people. . . . Three hundred people showed up," she recently told *Newsday*. "Ever since he was a kid, he talked about running for office," notes his older sister, Teri Schiano, in the same article. "He's the only one of us with that aspiration." He also had an uncanny sense of how to attract attention.

La Magna was always a go-getter. He had guts like his father, a New York City fire fighter who doubled as a longshoreman so he could support five children in their four-bedroom middle-class home. The oldest son in the family, La Magna carefully took to heart one bit of wisdom imparted by his father: You have to have your own business. If you work for someone else, it will always be a struggle.

With his father's undying encouragement, La Magna had no shortage of money-making ideas. He ran a fistful of businesses, many of which drew admiration from classmates and friends, but none seemed to make it. Finally, one of his ideas panned out. It proved that sometimes creativity sprinkled with persistence and a pinch of focus can be what it takes. Fortunately, failure never stopped him; he learned from each mistake and moved forward.

The setbacks started early in life. While in high school, La Magna, who had been captain of his basketball team, sustained a head injury during a game and was diagnosed as an epileptic and had seizures throughout his high school years. He was a candidate for the Air Force Academy but couldn't go because he was classified as a 4F—physically unfit for military service.

Born in Brooklyn, La Magna hardly ever saw his father because he worked two jobs; his mother managed a bowling alley. With five children in the family, debt was a neverending part of family life. La Magna fondly recalls his father's attitude about the loan payment books that filled his pockets. "My father was very careful to keep his credit clean. His philosophy was to never pay his bills a day early but never pay them a day late. He always paid the minimum. I took that philosophy. I didn't feel poor. I lived definitely the middle-class life. I didn't feel rich."

His father always made it clear that he didn't want his son to lead the life he did. "He always lent me money and stuck with me from the beginning. He felt if I could create my own company and be successful, I wouldn't have to work all the time."

It also became very clear to La Magna at an early age that if there was anything he ever wanted, he'd have to get it himself. After all, it was virtually impossible for his parents to buy him anything expensive. If they did, they'd be obligated to do the same for four others. So when La Magna wanted a bicycle when he was nine years old, he decided to get one for himself. He won one. While attending Catholic school, La Magna won the bicycle—the prize for selling the most ticket books for a raffle of a Cadillac—and the respect of the nuns in his school.

"I sold 48 books," he said. The runner-up sold 16. La Magna won his bike by doing something decidedly different from his classmates: he sold to people he didn't know. He went to bus stops and solicited people getting on and off the bus. He took an old bicycle and rode further than his mother would like to have known he did, stopping at every store along the way. "I was playing on the fact that I was very young. I used to have a speech memorized. I said it really fast. I knew it amused everybody." Everyone agreed to buy from him.

La Magna's early success taught him a major lesson. "I realized that to be successful, you have to be successful with people you don't know. You don't break out unless you sell to strangers."

La Magna was an A student and the valedictorian of his grammar school class when his grade point average exceeded the runner-up by about one-tenth of one percentage point. Each year he had continued to win something for outselling raffle books.

In high school, he took up an important cause. Rosedale was on the approach path of what is now Kennedy airport, making it unbearable when the jets came in. "It drove most of the homeowners to set up kitchens in their basements, the noise was so loud."

In his senior year, La Magna determined that it was time the airlines did something for the communities they were oppressing. He rounded up students in the area to pressure the airlines to develop a youth center. Although he succeeded in organizing a movement and had begun to get petitions signed, the assassination of the late President John F. Kennedy stopped the project in its tracks —"We were all mourning for weeks"—the project died.

La Magna had realized when he was younger that he lacked the money to pursue one dream—becoming a politician. Although he began at Providence College in Rhode Island as a political science major, by his junior year he began taking courses from the best teachers he could find, no matter what they taught.

"I decided I wanted to follow in the steps of Voltaire," he said. Voltaire took four or five years off from his writing to make money in real estate and then was able to go back and spend time writing, he explained. "I felt I was going to spend time making some money so I could be independently well-off enough to go into politics."

His business ventures served as a challenging way to make spending money. He was always on the lookout for money-making ideas. And during his college years he learned—often the hard way—how to turn an idea into a reality.

At Providence College, where the quest to become a fast millionaire earned him a reputation around campus as an entrepreneur, he launched Christmas College Capers. The idea was for college kids who were going home for vacation to have a place to go for a night out and to dance, as well as to generate some cash. Among those he borrowed from was Christopher Dodd, a senior at Providence College ($400), who would later become a U.S. senator from Connecticut. The problem was that the dance had to be held in Taunton, Massachusetts (no hall in Providence allowed him to rent it), so La Magna was forced to move the dance further and further away. Nobody was able to get there. "We had 18 inches of snow and the only people who showed up were the band, who I had to pay; the police, who were required to keep the peace; and my lab partner." La Magna was out $1,000 and subsequently took a loan from his father to help pay creditors.

The tide turned when he and a friend entered a contest sponsored by a local TV station with a car as a grand prize. The objective was to guess the number of sixpence in an ale glass. The two, after carefully scrutinizing the rules, submitted so many entries that they couldn't help but be among the six who guessed the correct amount. Although they didn't get the first prize, they each won a Windjammer cruise. La Magna sold his for $600.

At Providence, La Magna had a landmark business success that helped to mitigate some of his other losses and keep him afloat financially. It was a computer dating service, dubbed "Cupid Computer," which he started in 1967 with a physics professor. "I was handling marketing. He was handling the computers." The charge was $5 a person. Students filled out applications by answering a series of questions about who they were and what they wanted. "We analyzed everybody in the pool. Say, somebody wanted somebody shorter than they were. The computer would eliminate all the people taller than they were. We took thousands in the pool and put them together. There were some perfect matches. Others barely matched. We had them all show up for a dance at the Sheraton Biltmore in Providence."

La Magna convinced a local radio station to promote the dance for free by allowing it to claim the dance as its own event. He hired the hit band the Cowsills, which at that point had not yet become well known but had been attracting a following in the Providence area. "Some $5,000 worth of applications came in the first week. We got over 1,000 applicants."

The concept held much promise and subsequently computer dating services did become popular. However, La Magna reflects, instead of carefully building his business, "I blew all the money on advertising and brochures. I had no discipline. I ended up losing all the money on what was a very creative concept."

There was one side effect to the computer dating service. La Magna included a couple of questions on the questionnaire about sex. Although it was intended for college students, the questionnaire got into the hands of some high school students whose mothers subsequently confiscated it. The archbishop of the diocese called the president of the college and La Magna and his physics professor partner were called before a disciplinary board, but no action was taken. But "three or four weeks later, my father called to say he got a letter from the college." La Magna says he froze, thinking he was in for more trouble from the computer dating service. Instead, "they selected me to go to Europe for my junior year. They didn't want to lose me but they didn't want me around."

La Magna was off on scholarship to the conservative Catholic community of Fribourg, Switzerland, where he tried out a computer dating service again. Launched with two others, a Frenchman and a German, who fronted the money, he advertised the service all over Europe with a unique result. "In America, we got over 1,000 applicants and no photos," he said. "In Europe, half the applicants sent photos. Ten percent had no clothes on—which both stunned and delighted my two partners." The service in Europe was not as successful as his American venture, but his partners recovered their expenses. "There were no profits left."

While tuition was covered and La Magna had a place to stay, pocket money was a necessity abroad. Although dancing was prohibited in the village, societies were permitted to conduct one dance a year for fundraising. So La Magna and a friend took advantage of the loophole to launch Club Shindig. They started creating different societies and headed to the police station weekly to file applications for a dance at different locations in the village. The secretary who took their applications was an attendee at the dances, which grew in popularity until the local newspaper made the public well aware of them. La Magna's venture met its grand finale when its miniskirt dance, *Le Grande Bal Mini-Jupe,* made the front page of the newspaper. The slogan, "As the Skirt Ggoes Up, the Price of Admission Goes Down," drew public outcries and a warning phone call from the U.S. ambassador. La Magna was sent home from Switzerland in May instead of July 1, after yet another antic aroused the ambassador's ire. When La Magna's friend totaled a Volkswagen, the two turned it upside down in the middle of the town and began charging townspeople the equivalent of 25¢ for a chance to strike it with a sledge hammer. The event, which angered townspeople, clinched La Magna's deportation while earning the two $100.

On returning to Providence, La Magna in 1968 ran a nightclub —Bambi's—owned by the Cowsills in Newport, Rhode Island. He also served as the singing group's personal manager. The Cowsills went on to make several hit records, including "Hair" and "The Rain, the Park and Other Things," and later became the group on which the hit television series *The Partridge Family* was based. However, La Magna says he didn't make any money to speak of from the affiliation. "The basic problem was the father controlled all the money and everybody around them, including the kids, didn't really see anything. It was a real tragedy. I don't think the father was a crook, but everybody around them was stealing money from them. When the kids reached 21, I heard they were in debt to the IRS for thousands of dollars.

"I managed the debt the group had accumulated on the way to the top. I dealt with all the creditors. Every week I would call and talk to them. To his [the father's] credit, he paid off every single one of them." La Magna said he was particularly thankful because it preserved his own reputation as a man of his word.

Apart from the singing group's personal problems, their nightclub was doomed to failure from the beginning. "The rent was too much—$2,000 a month," La Magna said. "You've got to have a lot of dances for that."

La Magna admits that his college career suffered slightly because of the overextension from all his business exploits, and he graduated from Providence 250th in his class of 350. Nevertheless, his business ventures impressed admissions officers at Harvard Business School, which, to his astonishment, accepted him. "It wasn't that I was a genius. But I had four pages of businesses that I had tried and failed. For me, someone who wanted to be a millionaire, I felt like I had gone to heaven."

La Magna was fortunate. The period marked a turning point in philosophy for the Harvard Business School. Ranking first in the class was not necessarily the priority. The women's liberation and black liberation movements were well under way, and the business school was committed to getting away from its image as a stodgy, numbers-oriented, white, Anglo-Saxon, Protestant institution. It aggressively sought a variety of students and paid particular attention to potential entrepreneurs.

In fact, when La Magna was at Harvard, his apartment in Harvard Square overlooked some of the student antiwar rioting. "We watched the students organize and have what started out as a peaceful demonstration." Some kids set fire to a newsstand, and he saw police in perfect formation line up much like the Germans were coming. La Magna made a conscious attempt to stay out of it. "I did not want to be involved in rioting and destruction and being a revolutionary. I wanted to change the system from the inside. That's when I made the promise that some day I'd be a congressman or senator."

La Magna was certain that his surprise admission to Harvard Business School would be his ticket to finally realizing his dream of becoming a millionaire. But those hopes were soon dashed when he lost his entire first-year tuition, loaned to him by the school, the first day. (To this day, La Magna wonders why the school handed him a check for the loan rather than deposit it directly to a special student account.) Arriving at his dorm room, he overheard the previous tenant talking on the phone to a stockbroker about the company Global Marine. "I thought it was the greatest stock tip in the world!" La Magna bought call options on 5,000 shares. The excitement mounted.

News that the company had discovered gold in Vancouver was breaking. The first day of school, activity on the company was so great that it failed to open. A new price had to be set. "Here I was holding options on 5,000 shares." Unfortunately, the stock wound up opening 50 points lower when the company found that the gold would be unprofitable to mine.

Minus his tuition money, La Magna went to the Harvard Business School financial director and complained. "Why did you send me the money. Didn't you read my résumé? I'm a compulsive capitalist." To La Magna's further shock, the school re-lent him the money.

"If I had had an intelligent stock broker," he lamented, "he would have advised me to buy a 'straddle,' which is a put and call on the same underlying security." That would have cost 20 or 30 percent more per contract, and he would have made a lot of money because the stock moved so much. "The point is I shouldn't have been gambling."

Adding at least $60,000 to his negative net worth was a failed effort to convert outdoor drive-in movie theaters into drive-in discotheques, using a psychedelic movie La Magna produced along with the head of Harvard University's animation department. The idea was creatively similar to MTV, a subsequent success story. Unfortunately, La Magna's venture failed. "It rained 21 out of 31 days in July that summer. I was rained out 11 shows in a row."

In retrospect, he says the rain was not necessarily the greatest flaw in his idea. "The lesson was don't fall in love with your ideas. If I had just looked around me, I would have seen that people then weren't interested in dancing. They were going to concerts and getting stoned." One of the people who helped produce the Cowsills, Artie Kornfeld, who wrote the Cowsills' hit "The Rain, The Park and Other Things," had suggested that La Magna get involved with him and some others to help produce the rock concert Woodstock. La Magna turned him down, explaining that he was too busy with his drive-in disco venture. "Five hundred thousand people showed up at his concert and 25 police showed up for mine," La Magna said.

With an accumulated $65,000 in debt, La Magna realized he was in trouble. He dropped out of Harvard Business School to make enough to pay back his creditors, but there was a glimmer of hope. Coca-Cola had been interested in his idea of the drive-in discos. "I got a verbal agreement that they would give me $100,000, which would have wiped out my debt." La Magna's hopes, though, were crushed again when the news came out that cyclamates, which at the time were in the company's diet drinks, might cause cancer. Coca-Cola eliminated experimental promotional budgets, and La Magna's proposed project was killed.

"There I was with no project, out of school, and in debt." So he opened up the Kinetic Light shop, selling psychedelic lighting in Harvard Square. He changed the name of the store to Aquarack when waterbeds became popular and began adding waterbeds to his wares. That business failed because his landlady evicted him out of concern that the weight of the waterbeds would collapse her building.

Dejected, he returned to Harvard Business School and graduated in 1971. His debt had soared to $100,000, including his cost of tuition as well as money he owed from his ventures. But the ventures didn't stop.

La Magna spent six or seven years trying to produce a movie—a Gothic thriller called *Keepers of the Night*. While staying with a friend on Park Avenue in New York, he tried raising money. "The movie got pretty far. I cast it—did everything. I just couldn't raise $1 million. Even though I had a Harvard business degree, I didn't know enough rich people." He told the *New York Post* that when he tried to pitch the flick to Jerry Lewis in a supermarket, Lewis responded, "Kid, you're crazy! Get out of here."

He finally succeeded in becoming coexecutive producer of the movie *Something Special* starring Patty Duke in 1984. Produced after the founding of Tweezerman Corporation, the film cost him $250,000.

La Magna admits that it's tough to find a more depressing experience than watching venture after venture flop or barely break even. Finally, he went home to live with his mother, who had, by that time, separated from his father.

Ten years out of Harvard, he had made $1,500 that year. He had been trying to be a movie producer along with painting houses and living in a film commune. He laments how a Harvard Business School classmate at a tenth year reunion told him he brought down the average earnings of his Harvard graduating class $80 a year.

La Magna was at a low point in his life. But he hadn't lost his keen instinct for spotting an opportunity. It was merely dampened by failure after failure.

Finally, he took a $200-a-week job as a contract administrator with Apoca Industries Inc., where he watched workers using industrial tweezers. Recalling the painful splinters he had suffered while living in Venice, California, the light bulb went off. He founded Tweezerman Corporation in 1980 with $500. "I created the concept of financing my business with credit cards," he admitted. "By the second year of Tweezerman, I had over 40 credit cards I was using to finance the company." Once you get a credit card and you pay on time, you get more. La Magna said he'd take a credit card, rush to the bank, and take a full cash advance. Often, he would use it to pay the minimum balance on another card.

Nevertheless, like his father he always paid his debts and within three years he had no problems getting loans from banks. By 1988 he had managed to pay back all his creditors. "One of the investors in the drive-in discotheque wrote me a note. I owed him $1,000. Twenty years after the fact, he never in his wildest imagination thought anyone would be so conscientious about paying the debt. I have a reputation that I'm not going to stick you. I'm not dishonest. I could have filed bankruptcy."

La Magna believes that honesty is a critical trait of any entrepreneur. "The first question is: Is that person honest? The second: Is he competent? The third: Do they get up every day to go to work? I always had those three ingredients."

Unlike others we've described in this book, La Magna didn't get ahead by minimizing his debt. "Right now, I'm in debt," he acknowledged. "I have personal debt of $500,000 plus $750,000 of mortgages on properties." At this writing, he owns two homes in Sea Cliff, New York, and a cottage in Port Washington, New York. Tweezerman has almost $4 million in debt.

When it comes to growing a business, La Magna believes you have to have debt. "You cannot do it without debt. Debt will always be part of my life. It's part of a dimension of a growing, successful business. You need equity and debt, although, right now I'd like to see less debt and more equity."

As far as his company is concerned, he's not worried about the debt. With offices in Glen Cove, New York, and Houston as well as 130 employees, La Magna says the key is debt service, or a company's cost of periodic payments to creditors. Tweezerman's debt service is only 10 percent of profits, "which is totally acceptable. If it were 50 percent of my profits, I would have a problem."

La Magna at this writing said he was retaining 50 percent of company profits to build up more equity in the company. He also was working on paying off his personal debt—partially at least by putting two of his three homes on the market.

He acknowledges problems can arise if you build too much personal debt by spending beyond your means. "Quite frankly, my personal lifestyle in the last ten years of my life has exceeded my earnings every year. I've awakened to the problem and since have cut back on my personal lifestyle."

While there is no problem meeting minimum payments, and creditors are lining up to give him and his company credit, personal debt can create problems in a recession. The value of your assets can drop. "The market value for your home could be $850,000, which supports a mortgage of $637,000. However, a recession could knock the market value down to $600,000. But the mortgage stays at $637,000. That's a problem."

After Tweezerman started turning a profit, business still wasn't a cakewalk. Entrepreneurs, by their very nature, are creative. When you're a creative person, it's difficult to concentrate on one thing—a problem La Magna struggled for years to overcome. "The most important lesson for me is to focus. Unless you focus on one thing and become an expert at it, you're never going to get up any steam. When I became Tweezerman, I only sold one tweezers for the first year and was only going to sell tweezers."

His first product was a splinter tweezers. La Magna then proceeded to a high-quality imported tweezers but managed to find 1,000 cosmetic stores he was able to do business with. The next product he added was a cuticle nipper. "Had I been successful with the splinter tweezers with hardware stores, my second product might have been a hammer. My being in the beauty tool business is really a function of focusing and my first success."

Once La Magna was able to focus on his single business, the next challenge was to manage his time and resources. "I worked out an equilateral triangle of approaching my business. An equilateral triangle has three equal sides. Those sides are producing a product, selling a product, and controlling the business end."

With your own business, he explained, nobody is telling you what to do every day. But he learned from his failed business ventures that one aspect of his business inevitably suffered, bringing down the other sides. To counter that, La Magna developed a plan to start the year working on the selling side—a natural because all the conventions and trade shows took place at the beginning of the year. Then he planned to start hiring his sales force and producing sales brochures. Starting in May, he intended to get into production and work on product, often traveling to Europe. The last four months of the year, when he was required to focus on taxes anyway, he'd concentrate on the control aspect of the business, including financial statements, computers, and taxes. "I would have to change my mental attitude from one phase to another. I would not work on any sales projects when I was in my financial mode."

La Magna believes that if you examine an equilateral triangle, you'll note that all sides are in touch with the others. While he might be focused on marketing, for example, he would keep in touch with the production and control areas. So anytime there was a control crisis, such as a need for more money, he would jump in and solve it. His budgeting also was based on that equilateral triangle. "I'd put one-third into product, one-third into brochures, and one-third into the computer system.

"Most entrepreneurs get themselves trapped by a lack of balance," he said. Often, someone will be out selling a product that can't be delivered. Or there might be a control freak who spends all his time doing accounting. "I have failed for every reason. I know the problems."

Often dressed casually at work, La Magna places great value on employees and once captured the Health Plan of New York Spirit Award. From day one, he believed his job was to take care of employees. The company conducts Quaker-style meetings in which employees are invited to stand up and say anything about the company they wish without fear of recrimination. In fact, his president at this writing, Lisa Bowen, came to the company when she was 18 and decided to stay rather than go to college. "She has a great sense of priorities. She understands the need to be a generalist rather than a specialist," La Magna said. "This is all from on-the-job training."

La Magna doesn't hesitate to make investments in his business even if it puts him in debt. "If we need computer systems, I buy them. If I need more space, I buy more space. It never stops me. That's a dramatic difference from the way it used to be in the eighties, when I had to be careful about everything." He always gets three estimates for everything he buys and, where possible, buys used instead of new equipment.

Creative marketing always has been a La Magna hallmark. At trade shows, he hired singers and gave them special lyrics about tweezers that they sang to popular tunes. In one publicity stunt, he appeared on Madison Avenue brandishing a giant tweezers. His quoted motto: We Aim to Tweeze. And in 1997, when La Magna ran for Oyster Bay, New York, supervisor, he quickly issued his own response to political leaders' cautions during the season that deer ticks threatened residents with Lyme disease. His company mailed media outlets a tick removal kit, including tweezers, small Ziploc-type storage bags for bringing the bugs to a doctor, and alcohol-soaked towelettes. "Tweezerman Helps Fight Lyme Disease with Tick Tweezers," headlined his news release.

At this writing, his Internet site offers a guarantee against manufacturing defects and a promise to repair or replace any defective implement at no charge. He also offers to sharpen implements that have become dull through normal use. Plus, there is an offer to repair a damaged implement for $5 or replace it with a new one at half of its current suggested price. Nipper springs may be repaired at no charge if they break.

The turning point in La Magna's life came when Tweezerman was able to turn a profit—"literally the first year of the company. In a movie, they would call this the plot point," La Magna quipped.

Boasting of its ability to remove hair with almost no pain, La Magna succeeded in selling his tweezers nationwide to high-end stores, including Bloomingdale's and Neiman Marcus, and finally squarely into the consumer market, particularly after being featured on *Oprah*. After making the list of *Time* magazine's best products of 1994, his company got added publicity when in 1996 he launched an unsuccessful but colorful bid for congressman from Nassau County.

La Magna says his company's second turning point came in 1997, when it went from providing a good living to being successful. "That happened when I reached $10 million in [annual] sales." His formula was to try to make a 10 percent return on sales. When that started happening in 1997, the company became extremely successful.

While much of La Magna's success is based on creativity and persistence, he says the Harvard Business School did help groom him for the big picture. "I could have easily found myself with a deli thinking I was doing well." Harvard introduced him to a network of like-minded and smart people prone to succeed. He also picked up the ability to think instead of memorize. "Every day we were presented with a business problem and had to make a recommendation to the president on how to solve it. I was taught how to think of a problem, devise a solution, and execute." At Harvard he also learned to read financial statements and develop marketing plans.

La Magna credits the national attention generated by his 1996 run as a congressional candidate with jettisoning business over his second hurdle. It was early on in his life that he told himself he would find a way to give to his fellow man through some kind of socially conscious community activity.

He has maintained that his chief motivation for running for Congress was the shutdown of the federal government in a

Republican stalemate. His candidacy appeared on both the Democratic and Independence party tickets.

La Magna spent $1 million—mostly his own money—to run in his Republican, largely working-class district. His ads carried the tagline, "La Magna. It rhymes with Lasagna." Complete with a British accent, they humorously referred to his opponent, two-term incumbent Peter King, as "King Peter."

King retaliated with ads claiming La Magna had been arrested in New York and once in the Midwest on drug-related charges. One of King's ads showed La Magna stroking his eyebrows with one of the beauty products La Magna sells to imply that La Magna was gay. King's campaign brought charges of unfairness by area Democrats.

La Magna responded that in the early 1970s, he was charged with trespassing for hopping a train in Kansas City. He contended that although he was carrying epilepsy medicine and initially was suspected of having an illegal substance, his sole conviction was for trespassing. He also admitted that in 1974 he made an illegal U-turn in upstate New York and spent three nights in jail because he refused to pay a fine as a matter of principle.

The portrayal of La Magna as a millionaire candidate by his opponent and the media made it difficult to raise money for the race. "I only was able to raise $77,000. I never planned to spend $1 million. I had to sell a piece of my company to come up with the money. Everyone around thinks I can afford whatever they want me to give them—whether it is a loan to my brother-in-law or something for family and relatives."

At this writing, La Magna, a father of two, was separated from his wife, but he says money had nothing to do with the separation. Yet money, he said, always has generated expectations. "It upsets me because I have the net worth, but I don't have liquid assets. It starts with everybody involved with me from my "ex-wife" to my son, friends, and relatives. They come to me and say, 'You should lend me money.' Now I say, 'No, I will have to borrow to lend it to you.'"

The perception that he has money tends to be a detriment to relationships. "It's my experience that women expect men to take care of them. The fact that I'm perceived to be wealthy puts a lot of pressure on me." Nevertheless, he enjoys the luxury of time he now has. His employees are trained to run the company. "So I can take all the time I want."

At this writing, he was renting a cabin and spending much of his time in Poulsco, Washington, just west of Seattle, helping out his brother. He keeps a 1994 Jeep in New York and drives a 1984 Toyota Celica in Washington. "I'm not a spender," he reiterates.

He also was on the advisory board of directors for the Social Venture Network in San Francisco, a national organization of CEOs and founders of companies promoting social responsibility. He is now taking his political energy and expending it on direct social change. "I'm working on a standards project of what a socially responsible company would be. My personal goal is promoting social responsibility to U.S. companies.

"Governments in the world are being replaced by big business. Some of the big businesses are more powerful than most countries. Money controls our election process. They have convinced Americans to downsize government. Government's traditional role is to represent and protect the interest of the people. That role has been dramatically reduced with the taxpayers cheering on the sidelines. They're told they're going to pay less taxes.

"Normally, government's role is to take care of society. Now, business needs to do that. Businesses should have the responsibility to customers and communities. Businesses should be concerned about the environment, employees, and communities. Tweezerman is very much involved in all of this. Were I a politician, I would be raising these issues through government instead of through other businesses."

La Magna says that despite an impending divorce and lost congressional election, he's happy. "I think if I lost all my money tomorrow, I'd be depressed for a while. But I would bounce back. My happiness has a lot to do with personal acceptance of who I am and my life. I'm healthy, have great kids, know a lot of great people."

No, he'll never retire. "If I'm not doing one thing I'm doing another. I'm spending a lot more time working on social ventures.

While La Magna still handles new products and new distribution, he can do that from anywhere. A steering committee runs his company. "I expect Tweezerman to be a $100 million company within five years."

In a *Business Week* article on the 20-year class reunion of the Harvard Business School class of 1970, it was revealed that a prank at the school that had generated media attention had been La Magna's doing. Each month, teams of Harvard Business School students were required to deliver to the library intensely detailed written analysis cases (WACs) at 6 PM and deposit them down a chute. They were exercises aimed at getting students to analyze complex hypothetical business situations and make recommendations to the president of the company. One unusually difficult case dealt with a cement company. It was La Magna who convinced the owner of a real-life cement company to send over a truck. The truck backed up to the chute so that it looked as though it was going to pour cement down it.

Although nobody at the time knew it had been a La Magna prank, the incident drew cheers by students who had gathered by the library. At his 25th Harvard Business School class reunion in 1995, La Magna was asked to stand up to take credit for the prank. That year, La Magna recounts proudly, he also helped raise the average class earnings.

CHAPTER 10

LISA G. RENSHAW

*Living in Parking
Garage Pays Off*

When she was 21, Lisa G. Renshaw chased a rat from a 10-by 12-foot room inside a nearly bankrupt parking garage just north of Amtrak's Penn Station in Baltimore so she could sleep. Unable to afford enough employees to run the garage, she made herself a bed out of a carpet remnant and moved in, living and working there for three and a half years.

Her father installed a shower and barricaded the door to her room with two locks; a kerosene heater kept her warm in the winter. Her mother called daily at 1 AM to make sure she was OK. Once, she was held up at gunpoint and the contents of her cash drawer stolen. Another time, she was threatened at knifepoint. Lisa's situation was bleak to say the least. She had no money but took a chance on starting a business. The five-foot-two-inch dynamo endured hardship that few could have tolerated.

Today at 38, she is realizing the fruits of her onetime nightmare. Her company, Penn Parking Inc., is based in Linthicum, Maryland, and generates $28 million in annual revenues. With 300 employees, it manages 68 garages and parking lots in Maryland, Washington, D.C., and Virginia. Renshaw's personal assets total more than $1 million. Penn Parking operates from a 2,500-square-foot office in an industrial park near Baltimore's airport. Even though Renshaw's stake in the three states' parking garage contract market is only about 5 percent—she is, however, the owner and

117

president and an area role model. She won the Small Business Administration's National Young Entrepreneur Award in 1987, which was presented by President George Bush; she was appointed to SBA's National Advisory Council in 1990; and given an honorable mention in *Inc.* magazine's Entrepreneur of the Year award.

Although Renshaw has a healthy respect for money, it was not the major force that drove her to success. "I liked independence" and wanted to "build something . . . to create."

Perhaps it was the influence of the town in which she grew up, Severn, Maryland. In that blue-collar town near Baltimore, everybody went to high school, worked hard, and made a living. Her father's family never went to college, and her mother was one of 15 children. Renshaw never thought about going to college, although she admits that her younger brothers and sisters did. Some of her desire for independence came from watching and helping her father, an independent contractor who worked on building single houses one at a time.

Renshaw learned to be patient as a result of seeing the time it took for her father's projects to come to fruition. That coupled with the frustration of dealing with the many people involved in a project taught her a valuable lesson: good things happen to people who wait.

Her dad had a couple of laborers who worked for him. Renshaw fondly recalls the time he bought a beat-up farmhouse without plumbing. "My mom refused to move in until my dad put in a bathroom." The house slowly grew into a large, nice house "because my father did all the work." To an extent, that's how Renshaw fashioned her business.

The oldest of five children, Renshaw, when growing up, would sell her services as a clown at birthday parties, though it was not a high-paying job. In fact, more of her stints ended as voluntary efforts. A tiny, withdrawn child, Renshaw faced unique challenges that forced her to build inner strength early on. She learned through her largely unhappy school days that she had better not live her life based on what other people think.

She was largely a C student, but once in a while would get an A, B, or D. "I was small and I was quiet and easy to hurt," she said. She was constantly pestered by bullies. "It just so happened these people followed me through elementary and junior high school. It made having friends difficult. The nice people in school didn't want to be my friends because they feared incurring the wrath of bullies."

The bullies would hit her in the back of her head with rotten apples during class. An eraser filled with chalk served as a weapon. "What happened is I became so introverted I was even a better target. In eighth grade, there was a point where it started to escalate. I had to make a decision whether I was going to fight back. I did." One of the girls who normally taunted her was waiting for her when she walked out of the gym one day. "I was tiny then. I jumped on that girl and was hanging on her. I ended up in the principal's office crying and upset." Three days later, that girl's cousin, a boy who was smaller than Renshaw, punched Renshaw in the face with his fist in social studies class.

"I had never been punched with fists before." He did it a second time and then a third time. "I turned around and tore into him. From that point, my life changed. I never ever would let somebody intimidate, pick on, or ridicule me. I believe that was all pivotal in laying the foundation for the way I am today."

Renshaw was faced with the decision of going through her life constantly being picked on or making a conscious effort to change. The decision: build her self-esteem.

Like the other entrepreneurs described here, Renshaw recast her unpopularity. Instead of caving into pressure, she used her negative experiences to build herself up. You can't always teach people everything it takes to run a successful business. Sometimes, the right mix of experiences must simply gel.

Renshaw's nightmare followed by opportunity came after she had been out of high school a few years. She was inspired by a pastor, who told the congregation that he wanted a job at a gas station so badly he would work for free.

Renshaw, who wanted her own business, had been working for her father as a laborer when she decided to try the tactic. She had overheard a garage operator talking. "I jumped in at the opportunity." Renshaw convinced the operator to hire her as executive assistant of the very troubled Chesapeake Garage. Her goal was to learn everything she could about the business in the hope he would take her on as a partner. "I didn't think the garage was being marketed correctly."

The garage, which had gone through a handful of operators in a five-year period, had been largely dependent on business from a nearby restaurant, which was being remodeled. During the remodeling, "less than 20 percent of the garage was utilized on any given day; revenues were down to $3,000 a month," reported *Warfield's*.

The restaurant never did reopen. But Renshaw saw the garage's potential, as it was near an Amtrak train station. "You don't understand business, baby doll," the operator said when she explained her idea to capture that valuable train business. Renshaw borrowed $3,000 from Household Finance at a 23 percent interest rate to let the garage operator keep the garage afloat and finance her marketing ideas. But the garage operator skipped town with the money.

"It was a fortune to me at the time," she reflected about the loss. It all happened very quickly—in less than one day." But she quickly manipulated control over the garage, even though she didn't even know how to use a stick shift. She was saddled with the garage's insurance costs and some five or six employees, who were being paid about $2 an hour under the table. The garage was in deplorable condition, but Renshaw was determined. She immediately changed the gas and electricity accounts into her name, changed the name of the company, and tried to renegotiate a lease with the owner, who was surprised to hear his tenant had skipped town.

Renshaw explained to the owner that she would like to run the garage herself. He responded, "But you're a little girl." "It wasn't malicious," she stressed, "but affectionate. I told him he didn't have anyone else who will run it." It was true. Nobody else wanted that garage because it was in such poor condition. "He didn't have anybody who would take it. If it had been a well-run, economically feasible operation, he would never have considered me."

She fired all but one employee. Because she had no money and the garage's hours were 5:30 AM to 1:30 AM, she had no choice but to move in. She immediately increased the rates from $4 a day to $5 and set her sights on the Amtrak train travelers who frequently had parked in another open lot near the train station. She developed a flyer, which she distributed in cold wet winter weather outside competitors' parking lots. "You parked in the wrong place," the flyer proclaimed, promising a free car wash for every five days a customer parked in her garage.

An employee taught her how to drive a stick shift using customers' cars. "I was very, very careful," she said. "I had to pay the insurance." In less than three years, *Warfield's* reported, the garage reached 70 percent capacity, which went to prove, Renshaw has said, that pity works.

Times were tough. Renshaw said she had strict rules that all garage windows were to be kept closed at night. Now that she was finally the boss, though, she had the right not to follow the rules and to change them. One night, when she slept with a window open, robbers got in and she was held up at gunpoint.

"People say your life flashes through your eyes," she said. Renshaw remembers wondering how large a hole a .22 semiautomatic would make going through her head. Her other thought, "Please, Jesus." Even though the robber left her with little cash, she still had to finish working her shift. Police arrived, interviewed her, and took fingerprints as she worked. When she finished her shift at 6 AM, she never will forget turning on the television set. The only thing on: *Helter Skelter,* a movie about the bloody mass murders by Charles Manson.

"One night, after living on that rug for three years, I wanted to give up," she admitted. It was her lowest point. It was cold in the garage. The leftover coffee in her cup was frozen. "It wasn't coming like I thought it would come," she told *Warfield's.* "Suddenly I hated parking." But she had put in too much sweat to give up.

Six months later, an open-air Amtrak lot came up for bidding. Renshaw, who was taking in $80,000 a year, won the contract. She installed a new fence and security system and raised rates to $8 in a market where daily rates averaged $5. Business skyrocketed.

Renshaw realized that to grow her business, she had to win contracts on more garages or lots. The key was to build customer loyalty. Besides offering car washes, she had her cashiers reward customers with little gifts to help solidify relationships in the hope that customers would remember to come to her garage when they got fed up with their current operator. At this writing, she was distributing these thank-you gifts: packs of flower seeds on the first day of spring; candy for summer; peanut M&Ms for fall; and packs of hot cocoa for winter. She also published a newsletter, "Penn Pal," for about seven years before discontinuing it because "we felt it ran its course."

One key to the growth of her business is the ability to pick up new garage or parking lot contracts. Generally, the landlords pay a flat fee or percentage of parking fees collected.

Renshaw says that she always tries to submit a fair bid and give better service. The problem with the large and publicly traded companies is they compete on a low bid, she believes. "What's ending up happening is it's coming back to bite them."

In 1994 she attracted local media attention by obtaining a $4.3 million contract to operate more than 35 properties owned by the Washington Metropolitan Area Transit Authority. She was among a dozen other bidders for the job. Although reports indicated that she had lost the contract at least twice, the original winners were unable to perform. The contract wasn't particularly profitable, but "it got her foot in the door so she could win more lucrative contracts running garages for private landlords in office buildings here," the *Washington Post* reported. She doubled her staff to handle the three-year contract.

Renshaw now can afford to feel more financially secure, although she says she really never has. "You're only one contract away from being out of business. I always stay on edge. It's not just for me. I'm responsible for 300 people. I never sit back and say I don't have to worry now. I could get out and be OK for the rest of my life. But it's the people in my company and their children they're sending to college."

At this writing, Renshaw was living in Severn in a small one-bedroom farmhouse. She had been married briefly at 19 but divorced six years later—a subject she doesn't like to talk about. The home has one tiny bath, and the ceilings are not quite six-and-one-half feet tall. Meanwhile, she is having a home built that has slightly more than 6,000 square feet, including the basement. It's all part of a 14-acre parcel she bought at an auction two years earlier. Her plan was to subdivide it into 11 lots and sell all but the one, so she won't ever have to worry about a mortgage.

The house is going to have large porches. "It's large but not oppressive. It's not like my house has to be better than everybody else's. I want a house that when people come into it, they feel comfortable. They're not overwhelmed and afraid to touch everything. I don't have to have 18,000 square feet."

The development project was the latest in a series of side businesses Renshaw had dabbled in, including an effort to set up gift-wrapping kiosks at malls—a venture that put her into debt. "I didn't know what I was doing."

Despite the occasional failure, though, life is much different from when she lived in a garage. She since has bought and sold two four-bedroom homes. "It's just that the things that would have bothered me ten years ago wouldn't be a blink on the radar screen now."

Renshaw faces new challenges. She has more responsibility and faces bigger financial pressures. She no longer runs just one location, where she can easily keep an eye on things. "You have 68. You have to set up systems. You're still responsible 24 hours a day 365 days a year. It never stops. It's not like a clothing store where you close at 7 PM. That never happens."

On the other hand, she has more flexibility with her time. "I don't have to put in a 5:30 AM to 1 AM day. I don't have to be in the office all the time. But I'm always thinking about the company. One time I took six working days off. I can put in four hours a day and accomplish what I have to accomplish. It's good I can leave. That's where I get my best ideas."

Also, she says, "I personally don't have to worry about money and I have money to do the things I like to do." Despite the financial security she has built for herself, Renshaw does not believe in debt and carries no debt on credit cards. "The only thing I would go into debt for is sometimes for the company in order to grow. I'm very, very conservative."

Renshaw doesn't have a car payment because she still buys used cars outright. At this writing, she was driving a 1994 Pontiac Grand Marquis. "I may have gotten Cs and Ds in school. But I have common sense that would run rings around hundreds of people." Cars, she notes, are depreciating assets that are not worth going into debt for.

When she operated her single garage, one of her biggest nightmares was having to file an auto damage claim on her insurance. Her worst business nightmares more recently have been taking over garages with active unions. When you take over a contract to run a parking lot, you often inherit the unions automatically. "Union leadership will make you out to be a bad guy before you even walk in."

One time she was taking over a garage in January. "The union had riled up all the employees by saying we were going to fire everybody." Rather, her announcement had been that employees would have to interview for the job. "It's not a guarantee for everybody, but there was no reason for us to get rid of anyone."

The union passed out flyers to employees and customers that made her appear to be the Grinch who stole people's Christmas, implying she was going to throw people out on the street just before Christmas. "I didn't back down. I had hundreds of phone calls from customers. I took every single phone call. If I was busy, I had somebody take the phone number and I returned every call."

In recounting the experience, her voice almost broke. "This is the hardest thing I've ever had to deal with. I was made out to be a bad guy even though knowing everything I've ever had in life I've worked very, very hard for, and I have such a protective instinct toward people who contributed to the company." Plus, she gives incentives to her key employees.

Renshaw rarely leaves her business; however, she does go to Disney World annually. "But I keep my trips to four nights. I call in every day two times."

Thinking ahead is important, she says. "I'm always thinking five years down the road." She tries to consider all the issues with contracts and health care and insurance and the staff. "Every decision you make could have ramifications."

There have been a number of fights—with competitors, unions, and taxes. So far, none have threatened the business. "There's little need to worry when you're a company and don't carry debts, and manage those you must carry very, very carefully.

"I'm not interested in going across the country and becoming a huge publicly traded company. I'm interested in doing a very good job where I am."

Too many people have the misconception that just because a person is wealthy, she has gobs and gobs of cash. "Just because you have assets doesn't mean you can go in live in Paris for the rest of your life. Lots of times, the money is going into the business. Everybody thinks you're rolling in the dough and you're an easy mark for borrowing money."

Renshaw admits she does get hit up lots of times for money. "If they ask, I cut the amount in half right away. Then I have to decide if I give this away, can I live with this if I don't get it back. I'm getting better at saying no than I used to be."

Renshaw is very active in her church and works with children there. "That's where I give and that's fine. It's nobody's business how much I give."

She admits that as business has improved, she has tended to become more generous. "It isn't really that I'm more generous." Rather, she tends to give more away proportionally because she has more proportionally. "A lot of people, when they get money, they get more tight with it. I haven't gotten more tight."

Although she didn't have a college education, Renshaw recommends it and encouraged her brothers and sisters to further their education. "But I don't think it should be used as an excuse not to go out there and enter into the real world. When you go to college, you should be decisive about what you want to go to college for."

On the personal finance side, Renshaw seeks professional help in managing her investments and retirement savings. Although she can run a business, she doesn't have the time to navigate the stock, bond, and mutual fund markets, particularly in today's volatile financial climate, where stock prices rise and fall 2 percent a day. Renshaw would rather have a financial advisor do the worrying.

She has hired a financial planner who has her personal assets in a combination of aggressive and conservative investments. Being an astute business person, Renshaw likes the idea of diversifying her investments to get the best returns with the least amount of risk. She might be an aggressive entrepreneur looking for parking garage contracts, but she won't bet the ranch on her retirement savings. She hates debt and hopes to grow her nest egg at a reasonable rate above inflation so she can meet her goals.

"I'm very good at parking cars. I investigated and tried to find a real good financial planner. I didn't just pick one out of the yellow pages. I got recommendations." She will use his recommendations until she sees something that makes her think it's not working. "My energies are into making the company grow—not learning all the ins and outs of the stock market. I pick very, very good people at what they do and monitor their performance."

Renshaw credits her success to perseverance. "I can't say that with any more firmness. You've got to be able not to get caught up in this bad thing that happened today. A good thing's going to happen tomorrow. It's a roller coaster ride. You've just got to roll with it."

Renshaw also believes that thinking five years down the road, not taking on a lot of debt, and not being overly greedy are the fundamentals to running a good business. "There are 1,000 decisions that are made all the time within the company. None of those make or break it."

At this writing, she was seeing someone special. But might she marry again? "If I can get him to say yes!"

Meanwhile, she feels that money is not a guarantee of happiness. Nevertheless, she would not trade what she has. "I can see there are definite benefits to having a 9-to-5 job and leaving it when you get home. But let's say you're not worried about the job. Then, people who don't worry about the job come home and are fighting over money.

"We all have good and bad in everything we do. I might gripe about things sometimes. If I could do it over again, I'd do the same things—even going back to elementary school and junior high. All these things factor into the person you end up being."

MARVIN B. ROFFMAN

Invests Bar Mitzvah Money in Stocks

Although Marvin B. Roffman, 60, grew up poor in Northeast Philadelphia, his family was used to saving. They had to be. His father made just $60 a month working in a delicatessen in the 1940s and early 1950s. Yet the Roffmans always got by.

Poverty didn't stop Roffman from reading and learning how to make money on Wall Street while in grammar school and high school. His fascination with tracking stocks in *The Wall Street Journal* paid off. Although his path to higher education was derailed because of a serious family illness, his early understanding of how important it is to be financially independent paid off handsomely. By the time he was fired by a prestigious Philadelphia brokerage firm in 1990, he was a millionaire.

In fact, he had noticed his investment portfolio swelling from six to seven figures—surpassing the million-dollar mark—when he was as young as 30. The financial cushion he continued building proved critical not only to surviving the loss of his job—which occurred right after the death of his mother—but also made it possible for him to challenge one of the nation's most flamboyant billionaires, Donald Trump, on an issue of critical importance to all investors.

Roffman was fired from his job as a securities analyst with Janney Montgomery Scott Inc. in 1990 after he was quoted in *The Wall Street Journal* predicting Trump's financial troubles. Roffman's prediction that Trump's Atlantic City, New Jersey, casino, Taj Mahal, would be hit with financial problems eventually came true. Roffman was dismissed after Trump wrote a letter to the brokerage firm complaining about Roffman's public remarks.

Even though Roffman was well off when he lost his brokerage firm job at Janney Montgomery Scott, he increased his net worth further when he took legal action against his employer and Donald Trump.

Roffman had been working as a casino analyst for Janney Montgomery Scott and coming under fire for his prediction of "cold winds" ahead for the Taj Mahal. The Taj Mahal's business, when the colder months came, failed to generate the estimated $1 million daily needed to cover its costs. Meanwhile, Roffman's mother had died on Christmas Day, 1989. "Right before her death, she said to me, 'You know, you better stop criticizing this Donald Trump or you're going to get fired.' She had this premonition. When she died, it really threw me into a tailspin." On March 23, 1990, her premonition came true. Roffman lost his job.

"Everybody grieves differently. . . . When my mother passed away, I was going to the cemetery two or three times a week. It caused me terrible grief. When I lost my job, that was the kiss of death. My work was everything to me."

Now, he philosophizes about that dark period of his life. Yes, tragedies can happen. His situation could have been worse, he reasons. After losing his job and being the subject of national media scrutiny, there was still double litigation to contend with. "I can tell you the more money involved, the nastier it gets. Litigation is the equivalent of war. Anytime you go into litigation, the outcome is going to be unpredictable. Law firms want to get paid for their out-of-pocket expenses." Roffman says he was thankful that the lawsuits were over within 13 months—a relatively short period.

Today, Roffman, who never married, co-owns a Philadelphia-based money management firm, Roffman Miller Associates Inc., and lives a financially comfortable life on his Haddonfield, New Jersey, estate. He holds no mortgage on the property and is able to spend more freely than ever before. His net worth is now, according to Roffman "more than $5 million." The investment management firm he co-owns manages $150 million of money. He charges a maximum 1 percent of assets per year for any account under $1 million.

Roffman quotes frequently from books about legendary investors Peter Lynch and Warren Buffett. His own style of investing is very similar and hasn't changed in more than 40 years. "It's quite simple. I'm a long-term investor—not a trader. I don't buy and sell stocks." He also believes in investing in companies you're familiar with and cites a decision by Peter Lynch, former manager of Fidelity's Magellan Fund, to invest based on his wife's fascination with L'eggs panty hose.

Like Lynch, Roffman also follows his instincts. Among his early investments that paid off handsomely: General Cigar. When the surgeon general's report came out in the 1960s on the dangers of smoking cigarettes, everyone started flocking to cigars, and General Cigar was subsequently taken over. Another star, New Jersey Zinc, was taken over by Gulf & Western Industries, which first became Paramount Pictures and then Viacom. "I still own Viacom. I made an awful lot of money on that over the past 40 years." Profits have been in the seven figures.

Roffman says that like Warren Buffet, chairman of Berkshire Hathaway, he likes to buy companies for less than their value per share if the company were to be sold, thus investing in stocks that are overlooked by many investors—that is, profitable companies with hidden values.

He likes to own just a handful because too many stocks drag down an investment portfolio, he believes. "I don't believe in over-diversification. Typically, at this firm [Roffman Miller], I would say the average portfolio has 20 to 30 stocks. We don't believe in owning hundreds of stocks. That almost guarantees a mediocre performance."

Roffman's good fortune stemmed from learning early on that the only way to make money is to save and invest wisely. Although he grew up poor, his family always talked about investing. Maybe it was wishful thinking. They didn't have much money, but they knew about the stock market.

Roffman, delivered by his physician uncle, grew up an only child in the predominantly Jewish section of Philadelphia. He remembers his father working about 70 hours a week for $15 a week. Meanwhile, rent for their three-bedroom home was $25 a month. Every week, his father would set aside money from his paycheck to make deposits into a savings account; CDs had not yet become available. "They always put food on the table and they always bought me toys," Roffman recalled. "In fact, in August 1948, we got a television set. It cost over $300. In 1948, that was like

$3,000 today. It was really a lot of money. We didn't have an automobile. My father didn't get an automobile until 1952."

Although Roffman always had hoped to attend college and received a scholarship for the first year, fate dealt a blow to those ambitions. His father, the sole breadwinner in the family, had developed lung cancer when Roffman was 17. At the time, lung cancer had a very low survival rate, and his father had to have a lung removed. The experience would seem to have thrown Roffman off track at an important milestone in his life. He had to abandon the scholarship and the path to higher education. Instead, he headed into the workforce to support his parents, who were 34 at the time. He never did graduate from college.

Roffman's innate interest in investing finally paid off. "My grandmother used to sit me on her lap and teach me how to read *The Wall Street Journal* when I was seven or eight years old," he recalled. Although it might seem an odd pastime for a woman in those days, his grandmother, while she didn't work, was very well read and talented. She played the piano, and investing had been commonplace in her family. Her brother had nearly lost all his money in the stock market during the crash that led to the Great Depression. So Roffman had grown up knowing all too well about the market's ups and downs.

"I've always been fascinated," Roffman said. In fact, he started picking investments with his Bar Mitzvah money, even though, because of his young age, he was forced to keep them in a custodial account. He read about company profits and losses and what market analysts touted in *The Wall Street Journal*. He tracked stock prices, earnings, and the economy and bought stocks when a company looked good.

Roffman proved to be an astute investor at an early age. Although he couldn't remember many of the stocks he bought as a young teenager, he recalls that several did well. It's no wonder. From 1950 through 1952, the stock market gained a whopping 40 percent. Those were tremendous gains for investors who were just beginning to recover from the losses of the 1930s and World War II.

By the time young Roffman, with a cash infusion from his Bar Mitzvah money, was ready to invest in his own account, the stock market had declined in value. So he bought some cheaply priced stocks with the little money he had, a year later turning a profit. In 1954 the stock market had gained a whopping 44 percent.

Early on Roffman knew his calling. He had already been molded in an odd way into the work ethic. His mother, like most other women during that period, stayed home to take care of her family. Roffman remembers his mother talking to his aunt on the telephone about his laziness. "He doesn't even want to have a job," Roffman recalls her saying. Roffman set out to prove her wrong. He got on his bicycle and got himself a job delivering newspapers on Saturdays. In high school he delivered prescription drugs. He had started working when he was nine years old and carefully saved his earnings.

After high school in 1958, Roffman got his first job for Elkins Morris Stokes & Company, a prominent Philadelphia brokerage that since has merged to become part of Prudential. That first brokerage job paid only $40 a week.

In those days, a college degree wasn't so important as it is today. "I took classes at the New York Institute of Finance," Roffman reflected. "I did study and got a diploma. I started working in the brokerage's research department, boosting the number of researchers the company employed to two. I used to go with the director of research, visit local companies, and do research."

Roffman recalls one of his first interviews on that job. It was with John Connelly, founder and chairman of Crown Cork & Seal Company. "He was very unusual for the chairman of the board for a large company," Roffman said. "He answered his own phone." Roffman was impressed by Connelly's hands-on style of management. In fact, he was so impressed that he not only produced a favorable report but he invested in the company himself. "It was extremely successful."

When Roffman started his first job, he already had figured that with an income of $200 weekly from his investments, he would be self-sufficient. "That was my goal at the time."

Roffman's father was very sick and had to miss work for a year while he recuperated from his surgery. When he recovered and returned to work, Roffman continued to live at home with his parents and was able to save almost everything he made, even though he always contributed to expenses. "If I earned $60, I would give $25 to my parents," he said.

Although Roffman invested at an early age, he didn't spend much. "I didn't buy my first automobile until 1965. Then it was $1,700—a brand new 1965 Volkswagen Beetle. Today that money doesn't even buy an accessory." It wasn't until 1981 that he moved out of his parents' home. He bought a house in the Society Hill area of Philadelphia. The area's revival started the city on a massive renaissance at a time when mortgage rates were 16.50 percent, "I bought the house for cash. It was an historical house built in the 1800s. I've always been successful in real estate and automobile purchases." He reported in his book *Take Charge of Your Financial Future* (Citadel Press) that in 1980 he paid $115,000 for the home and sold it in 1991 for $170,000—after the market had peaked.

Roffman abhors debt and cites a jolting experience he had in 1974 that helped bring him to that conclusion. "I was the Donald Trump of Northeast Philadelphia. I was buying convertible bonds at Gulf and Western" and borrowed money on margin. "At the time, I was getting 5.50 percent. I was paying something like a 5.25 percent interest rate on the money." It seemed like a great deal. "I thought, 'How can I go wrong?'" Unfortunately, margin has a variable rate, and, by the same token, prices of securities can fluctuate. "Within six months, it [loan interest] was up to 13 percent, and the average price of the Gulf and Western stock had gone down 70 percent. I got myself into a real bind."

His father loaned him the money to get out of his six-figure debt. "Never buy stock with borrowed money. What happens is you can lose control. No matter how right you can be long term, short-term circumstances can force you into selling at the worst possible time. It made me very debt-adverse."

Roffman recommends that people pay cash for as much as they can afford. Most people, he believes, are living beyond their means and mortgaging their future. It is not good to pay 17 percent interest on credit cards when the savings rate is 5 percent. It automatically puts you behind the eight ball.

"I don't like debt," Roffman reiterates. "Years ago when I was growing up, people used to burn their mortgages after they paid them off. Today, people take out second mortgages—home equity loans. When I was growing up, that was a disgrace. Unfortunately, what you have today is the vast majority of people don't have enough income to support them in a comfortable lifestyle. Most people today are spenders, not savers." Take a client who makes $700,000 a year, he said. That client spends $700,000. Roffman says he is working to get that client to start saving some money to avoid a drastic lifestyle change when the client stops working.

Roffman's net worth got a most rewarding boost when the New York Stock Exchange ordered Janney Montgomery Scott to pay Roffman $750,000 for wrongful termination. In addition, Roffman received an undisclosed amount from Trump in a settlement of the original $2 million federal court suit Roffman filed against him, charging interference with his employment contract and defamation of character. Trump's attorney in the case, John Barry, had called Roffman's suit "total nonsense" and contended Trump had no influence on brokerage firms' practices. And a published statement by Janney Montgomery Scott on July 19, 1990, had maintained that Roffman was not fired for his published remarks. Rather, the investment firm contended, he was fired for disobeying a superior's orders that he not send a second letter to Trump repudiating an earlier apology. Roffman considers himself privileged because he likes his work. "I know I'm in the minority. I was blessed with very wonderful parents. Knock on wood, so far I have my health and I feel good. A lot of people don't feel good about their work. They're very unhappy. Because you're working about half the time that you're awake, it's a major part of your life. Imagine having to struggle just to get into the office every day! I'm very privileged. I feel, in essence, I owe."

Since the Trump affair, Roffman has become something of a folk hero in the securities industry. "An analyst has got to be independent and objective," he told the *Philadelphia Business Journal* in 1990. "If he's not, he isn't worth two cents. And if an analyst isn't free to state an opinion, then the investment community suffers. I hope that this case might set some guidelines for analysts."

Analysts quickly rallied behind Roffman in what continues to be a critical industry cause. "The incident may have been the first in which an analyst lost a job over negative remarks," the *New York Times* reported shortly after Roffman was fired, "but Wall Street professionals say it has become almost commonplace for analysts to face lesser reprisals—from public ridicule and threats of being blackballed to loss of access to corporate information."

Fortunately, though, Roffman's financial cushion gave him the freedom to speak his mind, to put his job on the line, and to pursue legally what he had considered to be a terrible injustice. To this day, he believes his case against Trump illustrates one of the many conflicts of interest that continue to haunt brokerage firms.

"It's becoming increasingly difficult to put your trust in sell-side analysis [the reports that professional money managers get from the brokers they do business with]. Analysts are compensated not by how accurate their earnings estimates are, but on how much business they can generate. The mentality on Wall Street is to do transactions. They don't want you to buy America Online and keep it for ten years."

If you're an investor, he advises questioning the basis of the research on which your advisor is making a decision. Today, like Roffman, more investors are doing their own research and not relying on reports of brokerage firms.

Nevertheless, research reports often provide tallies on the number of brokers that recommend a stock to buy, the number that recommend a stock to sell, and the number that recommend holding what you own. "The smart people . . . when they look a buy, hold, or sell recommendation, don't consider the hold [recommendation] a buy. They consider it a sell. They don't even consider it like a hold. But the four-letter word *sell* is not used very much on Wall Street. For every sell recommendation, there are probably 100 buys."

Also, Roffman complains that "the mentality on Wall Street today is to build wealth by doing trading activity on accounts." By contrast, Roffman, along with many other financial experts, advocates not trading stocks but holding them for the long term.

"Traders usually wind up very unhappy. It's virtually impossible to trade and accumulate wealth." It's not only the cost of all the commissions you pay. "But if you're in a high income tax bracket, you can wind up giving Uncle Sam some 40¢ of all your capital gain if you hold it under a year. A year is an eternity for a trader."

Roffman believes his experience demonstrates how much financial independence means in life. He ranks it second, just behind good health. Had he not become a millionaire at an early age, he would not have been able to guarantee payment of the six-figure fees that his attorneys required before they would consider suing Trump and his brokerage firm employer. Plus, he might not have been in a position to start his business—something for which he had virtually no other option. After all, in the wake of his job loss and the flurry of media coverage that followed, at least ten brokerage firms in New York, Philadelphia, and Baltimore refused to hire him.

Now, he is finally getting his just reward. He is able to marvel at the luxuries he can afford—his six-bedroom Tudor estate, where he lives with his father, a caretaker, and two dogs. The home spans more than 5,000 square feet and is complete with a pool, fountain, greenhouse, and special temple, which is not necessarily for worship but to admire. Roffman graciously opens his home for tours by charitable groups, a major source of pleasure.

While at Janney Montgomery Scott, Roffman said there was a broker he respected very highly: Peter Miller. "I used to say to him, 'You know Peter, if I weren't in the business, you would be my broker.' I got fired on a Friday and all this got picked up in the media. Peter called me at home the next day. 'Does this mean I have your account?' he asked. That's how it all started. He and I were talking. He and I didn't like conflicts of interest on the brokerage side."

The two operated on the premise that the best way for an advisor to operate is on a fee basis rather than on the amount of business generated or on commissions from investments the advisor recommends. While many money managers require clients to have accounts of at least $1 million, Roffman Miller Associates opened managing investments for clients with as little as $100,000 to invest. However, the money management firm restricted clients to those willing to invest for at least three to five years.

In his book, Roffman credits the 70 clients in the company's first 20 months of operation to the fact that he opened the business to people who had $100,000 or $200,000 to invest. Now, he claims more than 300 clients, of which 40 percent are in the medical profession. The business grew largely through referrals.

Roffman continues to believe that handling smaller accounts is the way to go. This philosophy is contrary to many financial services providers who prefer to have larger amounts to invest because of the lower cost of the administrative work involved.

He cites an experience his company once had with a large pension fund to illustrate the problems that can stem from reliance on institutional business. "The pension fund was worth $5 million. We got the account because I was very friendly with the president.

We just lost that account after four years. It had tremendous performance and beat the S&P 500. The problem is the company was sold to a large company. They fired the guy we knew. They put their pension fund in with the larger pension fund. So it didn't matter how great we did or what the performance was. When you're dealing with institutions, you're dealing with people who can lose control with takeovers. There can be a lot of politics that comes into play." Besides, Roffman says, he actually enjoys the one-on-one contact he has with his retail clients.

Roffman admits that when he started his company, he didn't take a salary for about three years. Luckily, it was a sacrifice he was financially and psychologically equipped to make. Growing up, he had learned to go without a lot of things. As long as he was working toward his goal, he knew he would be successful.

"One of the reasons businesses fail is they don't have enough capital to get them through until they cross over the profitability line. In the beginning, there's a lot more money that goes out. We knew that. We had made plans that we would have enough capital to sustain the business for three years. Fortunately, it all worked out wonderfully."

Roffman had grown up watching every penny, but now, that has started to change. It was tough putting food on the table with his father bringing home so little. At this writing, he still owned a 1974 BMW and a Volvo station wagon. "I used to change the oil on [the BMW] and do the tune-ups." Now things are less restrained. With his accumulated wealth, he was able to buy his father an Acura Legend.

Roffman wants to take time to smell the roses and is just starting to enjoy the fruits of his struggles. The metamorphosis came in 1991, when he bought his Haddonfield estate. He began spending his money a little frivolously.

"Believe me, when I tell you, this is truly an outstanding property." His temple has eight columns with a domed roof and "serves no purpose whatsoever, except it's just wonderful to look at. It's very majestic. It has a dome that's 15 feet high and 12 feet in diameter and eight limestone columns. It's something that's so unusual."

He didn't buy the home as an investment for financial gain. "Is this money well spent?" he asked. "It is if it brings you pleasure." After all, he acknowledges, managing $150 million of other people's money can be a harrowing experience. "I take that very seriously. I take my clients' money more seriously than my own. Sometimes we have our stressful days."

The biggest challenge, he says, is getting clients to stay the course and not get panicky over media reports. Along that line, the most stressful time he remembers was July 17, 1998. That day the stock market began a six-week slide that settled just below the 20 percent drop that was officially termed a bear market. Although the market failed to meet the definition of a bear market, the average stock dropped as much as 30 percent. "A lot of people started to panic. Since we had opened our doors in 1991, we hadn't had any meaningful correction in the stock market."

Roffman says that it has not been unusual historically to have a correction every two years. He got through that period largely because his company specializes in face-to-face contact with clients and carefully explains its long-term philosophy up front. He also was careful to deal with the situation in his quarterly newsletter. "We like to minimize risk," he added.

He points with pride to an experience he claims may not only serve as a perfect illustration of successful investing but provides him with some of the most gratification he has received. Every year he goes into inner city schools in Philadelphia to lecture on the importance of saving. He gives each student a hypothetical $100,000 and has each pick 10 to 15 stocks. "We make them clients of the firm. We send them monthly statements."

At the end of the school year, four winners—those with the best performance—receive a scholarship toward a college education. First place gets $1,000 and the next three runners-up get $300 each. "If they don't go to college, it goes back into the pool for someone else to win."

In 1999 an investing class of 89 eighth graders in the Greenfield School in Philadelphia graduated from Roffman's program. "The combined total of every individual for that period beat the S&P 500! We gave them all a T-shirt that said 'Greenfield beats Wall Street.' The kids at the Greenfield School were investing a lot of money in Internet stocks. That's why they did so well." The children were picking based on what they knew.

The scholarship might be an odd prize to come from a man who never obtained a college degree. However, Roffman believes that education when he was growing up was not nearly so important as it is today. "It's almost a necessity if you're going to get a really good job." He acknowledges, however, that a lot of students may not be college material and may be better off learning a trade. "We have a guy here servicing the air conditioner today. I pay him as much as I pay a doctor."

The inner-school investing program is part of Roffman's effort to make children realize that you needn't get into sports or drug dealing to make enough money so that you don't have to work. There clearly is another way.

Just ask Roffman. "When I come home and drive down this gated driveway, I love it. It's so beautiful," he says of his current home. "I had a fence put around the house." The wrought iron is more than 100 years old for which he bought gold-leafed balls. "It's a crazy extra, but it looks so great.

"Since I bought this house, things have started to shift dramatically. I surround myself with really nice things. I like to go antiquing. I like to put a lot of money into landscaping and I like to keep the property very nice. I do it in an unselfish way. I make the house available for entertaining. I use the house for charitable things, so I'm sharing it with other people."

Roffman said one downside to having money is that he is constantly getting asked for political contributions. "I don't like to give money to politicians. The whole process really turns me off. Once you give money to one, you get on some kind of a list. I can't stand it!"

The keys to financial independence, he believes, are these: "First and foremost, be a saver. Don't do the kinds of things I do now until you've gotten to the point where you can afford it. And don't live beyond your means." Roffman's rules to live by, besides becoming financially independent, are to always tell the truth. "Don't be afraid to stand up for doing that."

As for picking stocks, he offers these tips:

- Be a long-term investor; don't try to guess where the stock market is going.

- Stay focused on the companies you're invested in—not what's happening around you in different countries. "You're a lot better off staying local in the United States and not trying to be all over the world. You're better off with large domestic companies that have a global presence."

- Be a patient investor. Don't look for quick fixes.

- Do your homework. If you can't do your homework, hire a professional to make decisions.

- Deal with people who don't have conflicts of interest.

Roffman acknowledges that he may be in the minority of people who are happy with what they do for a living. "There are many, many who are unhappy with their careers and jobs." Unfortunately, a lot are creatures of habit. It's difficult to get out there and make a change. Some people have financial obligations."

He mourns the fact that loyalty has left the American system and claims he tries to maintain it among his seven employees, including himself and his partner, by offering them shares in his company; providing good quality health insurance, including dental and prescriptions; and offering a membership in a local health club.

When he was growing up, his grandmother suggested that he work in a bank "because they would take care of you for the rest of your life." It's a good thing that he didn't listen. When Philadelphia's flagship bank, CoreStates Financial Corporation, merged with Charlotte's First Union Corporation in 1998, it announced the cutting of 5,800 jobs. On the brighter side, he says, there is hope today for those who wish to change their unhappy plights.

"We are in an age in which it is easy and inexpensive to start up a business. When I was growing up, they didn't have fax machines, photo copiers, or home offices. Today, you can do things and have your own Web site. If you're resourceful, you can do those things with very modest investments. Many already have done it and become successful."

CHAPTER 12

DAVID COPPERFIELD

Makes Millions from Magic Tricks

Talk about following passion.

Who would think that a magician could make more money than actor Harrison Ford, comedian Bill Cosby, and pop singer Michael Jackson? Illusionist David Copperfield did exactly that in 1997, according to *Forbes,* as the seventh highest-paid U.S. entertainer. With an annual income of $45 million that year alone, Copperfield, who religiously worked at his craft since the age of ten, ranked just behind Jerry Seinfeld and the Beatles. His pretax gross income in 1999 rose to $49.5 million, *Forbes* reported.

Copperfield, 43, was an only child, so poor he slept in the same room with his immigrant parents in a Metuchen, New Jersey, apartment. And later, when he was living in New York, his father, Hy Kotkin, who owned a clothing store, had to send him money to pay his heating and laundry bill.

The tide turned dramatically for Copperfield, a college dropout and fan of Broadway musicals since childhood, when he landed a lead role in a hit Chicago musical, *The Magic Man,* in 1974. The offer came after he had taken out an ad in *Variety* to promote his talents. The show's success led to a television special on ABC TV in 1977. From then on, business grew.

Published reports have indicated that Copperfield, reputed to be a hard worker and perfectionist who performs as many as 500 shows a year, is also a smart marketer and businessman. He made certain his annual television specials aired before his tours—thus drumming up interest in advance to boost attendance. And while most entertainers only perform one show daily while on tour, Copperfield typically performed at least two, permitting different levels of ticket prices so that more people could attend, a strategy that also doubles sales. He also made many foreign tours. Tickets typically sell at higher prices abroad than they do in the United States, often due to currency differences. Tickets in the Kremlin and St. Petersburg, for example, were reported to have sold for as much as $850 each.

Copperfield's financial success is not so surprising when you consider that he started developing his business and promotional prowess at the early age of ten. He had turned to magic then as a way to obtain acceptance as an awkward child. The landlord at the apartment complex in which he lived had stopped renting to families with children. His grandfather actually taught him his first magic trick at the age of eight.

Copperfield began performing informally as a ventriloquist, although he claims he wasn't very good. In fifth grade, he emceed a talent show. By age 12, he began conducting magic acts at birthday parties, dubbing himself "Davino, the Boy Magician." At $5 a performance, he was pleased with his audience's response, but he quickly discovered that he could command 20 percent more if he billed himself as an illusionist rather than a magician.

"What he wanted always with magic was to make an art form out of it, and he accomplished just that," Copperfield's father told the *New York Times*. "As a kid he could be a loner and be perfectly happy. He never had to come to his mother and say 'What should I do now, Mommy?' He always had an inventive mind." Kotkin told the *Los Angeles Times* that his son had been precocious, "looking for things and small magic tricks to do with his hands."

Copperfield, who sneaked into Broadway shows, was always fascinated by the talent of Fred Astaire and Gene Kelly. "At *Pippin,* the ushers let me sit on the floor," he told the *Times,* noting he gave the star, Ben Vereen, a little coaching on the show's famous magic number.

Copperfield began hanging out at the nation's largest magic shop—Tannen's in New York—and became the youngest person ever to get accepted to the Society of American Magicians. By 16, he was teaching magic at New York University in the evenings. He dropped out of Fordham University after just three weeks to star in *The Magic Man.*

Although Copperfield never did graduate from college, he did study acting at HB Studios. And he received an honorary doctorate degree from Fordham and delivered its commencement address in 1999. His parents, who he said always wanted him to be a doctor, attended.

Copperfield's early success gave him the self-esteem and confidence that has made him one of the entertaiment business's most astute promoters.

Phil Lobel, once his North American tour press agent on his 1997 tour to Latin America, was quoted as saying that before Copperfield left, his U.S. television specials were sent to each country and repackaged with locally popular television hosts. "The shows were aired months and, in some cases, weeks before his scheduled live appearances," Lobel told *Amusement Business.* Six months before Copperfield's arrival, Magicworks—Copperfield's worldwide producer and promoter, which is now a subsidiary of SFX Entertainment Inc.—flew in several South American reporters to see the show performed live in the United States and get a one-on-one interview with its star. Equipment was carried in three or four semitrucks, and set-up time was 72 hours before each foreign performance. In addition, an advance team visited an area one year earlier.

The tour involved a lot of work and money, but it all paid off. Running from May 8 through June 23 that year, it generated $13.4 million in ticket sales and broke box office records. "This show costs a fortune, but it makes a fortune," Lobel told the publication.

Henry Lo Conti Sr. of Agora Promotions in Cleveland, a company that has helped promote, publicize, and produce Copperfield's overseas shows, traveled to Budapest with Copperfield in January 1999. He told us Copperfield has a staff of 40 persons and typically contracts out additional crews.

With his two-year take of $35 million for 1991 and 1992, Copperfield's earnings caught the attention of *Forbes.* In a 1993 article, the magazine reported that Copperfield's dramatic success stemmed from a major change in his image. "He started like a stiff performer who looked like Donny Osmond in a rented tuxedo," *Forbes* stated. "Now he looks like an ersatz rock star, complete with motorcycle, studded leather jacket, and tight black jeans." He hit at a time, *Forbes* indicated, when baby boomers were looking for fun entertainment to share with their children, and he started incorporating rock music into his acts.

"I've worked with a lot of other acts," Lo Conti said. "They depend on business managers or attorneys or accountants. From what I can see from Copperfield, he runs his own show." He works with no agent, Lo Conti affirms.

Normally, Magicworks handles Copperfield's shows entirely, Lo Conti said. "It's not normal for someone like myself to be working with them. We almost became like the local promoter. They're not going to jump on a plane to go to Russia. We have to do the work."

Lo Conti became involved with Copperfield when, in his own travels, he noticed the market's receptiveness to the illusionist. In fact, that's how Copperfield wound up on his pioneer Russian tour. "I was in St. Petersberg in 1995," Lo Conti said. "I saw there was very little going on with Western world acts. I started talking to people there and named some acts. I don't know why I mentioned Copperfield." Lo Conti said that Copperfield, whose grandfather had come from the Ukraine, was one of the most highly recognized artists he had mentioned. "We sold out five shows in Russia [and] had to add another."

Lo Conti says that Copperfield, while on tour, takes on the Herculean task of making sure everything is running smoothly. For example, the first time Copperfield played in Russia was critical because it marked the 850th anniversary of the country. "We had a late load in at 10 PM until 8 PM the following evening," Lo Conti said. "He'd show up 1 AM on the stage to make sure everything was being handled properly—right to the point of where the audience is sitting and who's in the audience."

Long hours clearly don't seem to stop Copperfield. The *Los Angeles Times* once offered a dizzy sampling of a Copperfield schedule. He spent Wednesday filming commercials all day at a magic warehouse he owns for an upcoming TV special. Then he performed his show, *Beyond Imagination,* at Caesars Palace that night, after which he was driven immediately to Los Angeles so that he could spend Thursday editing his TV program. That night he returned to Las Vegas for another *Beyond Imagination* performance." After the show ended at 2 AM, he had another media interview, followed by interviews with *CBS This Morning* and other reporters just a few hours later. He had two more shows that night and two on Saturday.

Part of the appeal of these shows, added *Amusement Business* in a 1994 interview with Copperfield's producers, is that Copperfield's performance is not a magic act exclusively. Instead, he uses comedy, dance, and pop music.

Many have said that Copperfield actually is much more popular in foreign countries largely because he jokes with his interpreters, often playing on words. The ploy, particularly in Germany, where he is known as sex wizard "Coppi," has made him a superstar. Lo Conti told us Copperfield goes so far as to fly interpreters to the United States to rehearse with him before his foreign appearances so the timing is exactly right. "It's the comical way in which he tries to imitate the language," Lo Conti says.

Unlike other magicians who perform the same act daily, Copperfield is challenged to come up with new illusions almost constantly for his television specials. Published reports have said that he carefully guards his magic secrets and publicly lashes out—often with sharp barbs—at those who reveal them in public. He requires anybody who works for him to sign contracts promising not to divulge his secrets. Generally, nobody is permitted backstage.

Copperfield also carefully controls the media. Often, the only way reporters can interview him is by submitting a series of written questions in advance. When we submitted our written questions, he failed to respond.

He also is known to go out of his way to make an impression with movers and shakers when he performs. Take his 1996 show *Dreams and Nightmares* that was developed with renown director Francis Ford Coppola. The show was reported to have grossed more than $1.2 million in each of the five weeks it ran. Copperfield, according to the *Chicago Tribune,* was careful to invite the following people backstage: Tina Brown, then editor of *The New Yorker;* Graydon Carter, editor of *Vanity Fair;* designer Tommy Hilfiger; director Steven Spielberg; and Anna Wintour, editor of *Vogue.*

As for the invited reporters: "He didn't care whether they were writing about him or not," New York press agent Richard Kornberg told the *Tribune.* "It was a brilliant strategy to change the way in which he was perceived."

"Look, I've always wanted to be accepted and liked," Copperfield had responded to the newspaper. "Magic has taken a back seat [to legitimate theater] for far too long."

Meanwhile, Copperfield's six-year engagement to supermodel Claudia Schiffer certainly didn't hurt his popularity among both international and American fans. He met Schiffer while performing in Germany, spotting her in the audience at one of his shows. He brought her onstage while he attempted to predict the type of graffiti audience members would write on the wall. Within six months, they were engaged. Copperfield rented Little James Island for his proposal and gave her a $5 million ring. Some have said the relationship was contrived to boost both their careers, but Copperfield angrily refutes those charges. In fact, he and Schiffer won a judgment against *Paris Match* magazine, which a French court said erroneously reported that the relationship was contractual. Their engagement subsequently ended because of their heavy work schedules.

Copperfield has said it takes him anywhere from six months to two and a half years to develop an illusion. And he develops as many as five different technologies for each, so if fans guess how he does a trick, he can easily shift gears. He once reported that he consults a specialist when he needs help with the technical aspect of an illusion. "I usually farm out little parts of it so no one person knows how to do the entire thing," he told the *Chicago Tribune* in 1990. Performance rights for illusions cost anywhere for $10,000 to $100,000, Andrew Kole, an illusionist who is credited with creating many of Copperfield's illusions, told the *Arizona Republic* in 1998.

Magic tricks can be very risky. Copperfield told the *New York Daily News* that while doing a rope trick on stage in New Jersey, he cut off the tip of his finger. "Blood was everywhere and the tip of my finger was sitting on top of my scissors. I was in shock and didn't know what to do. I said to the audience, 'Ladies and gentlemen, I think I cut my finger off' and the audience started to applaud! I was rushed to the hospital and they sewed the tip of my finger back on."

Now, the once awkward and withdrawn teen leads a jet-setter's life and has a street named after him in Metuchen. A look at his tour schedule indicates he now takes more week-long breaks.

"We juggle careers by having three schedules," he told the *New York Daily News* while engaged to Schiffer. "I have my schedule, she's got her schedule, we've got our schedule. We have a two-week rule. We're never away from each other for more than two weeks."

Copperfield has a lavish penthouse apartment in Manhattan, although he has said that he travels so much that he really has no set home. Published reports also have said he doesn't drive, drink, or take drugs and is even reported to have a personal trainer. Homes, or at least, real estate investments of the entertainer over the years have been in Paris, Lake Tahoe, and around Las Vegas as well as in Hollywood Hills, California.

Copperfield is known to spare no expense on his illusions. He wants them exactly right. It was reported that he spent $700,000 to develop the apparatus that allowed him to fly on stage in the early 1990s.

USA Today said in 1993 that the reason he and his CBS producer, Joseph Cates, split up six years earlier is that Copperfield wanted to put more money into his television specials, which he considered loss leaders to sell concert tickets. "I paid a million bucks out of my own pocket for cost overruns during one CBS special in the Bermuda Triangle," Copperfield told the *Los Angeles Times* in 1988. CBS said policy prevented it from confirming or denying production costs.

More recently, Copperfield's "obsession with expensive, unprecedented illusions" was blamed for the 1999 collapse of David Copperfield's Magic Underground, which was to have been a theme restaurant in Times Square. The project, reported to have lost $34 million, was 45 percent owned by Copperfield. But Copperfield, according to his attorney, Albert Rettig, had put up none of his own money in the venture. Copperfield supporters, the *New York Times* reported, had argued that the magician merely was "intent on creating something worthy of his name rather than yet another theme restaurant that would be dismissed as schlock."

Copperfield has put his passion for magic into his investing and owns an International Museum and Library of Conjuring Arts. The library, in which Copperfield has said he has invested at least $10 million, includes a collection assembled by Carl M. Rheuban, a magic buff and former chairman of the defunct First Network Savings in Los Angeles. Since Copperfield turned heads by purchasing the collection for $2.2 million from the Resolution Trust Corporation in 1991, its value has swelled.

The museum now has on display the collection of Dr. Robert J. Albo, believed to be the most important collection of old magic props. In addition, it acquired the Cole Collection, believed to be the largest magic collection in the United Kingdom.

Among the artifacts reported to be lodged near a military test site in southern Nevada are pennies once held by Abraham Lincoln during a magic trick; a wand, handcuffs, and escape tools that once belonged to Houdini, and a book published in 1584 that is believed to be the first ever written about magic.

"I'm very unmotivated by the money aspect," Copperfield stressed to the *New York Times* in 1996. "I put my money into three things: my show, my museum, and my personal life." *Esquire* magazine noted in 1994 that he paid a whopping $2 million for the yacht *Honey Fitz*, on which John F. Kennedy once rode, as a gift for his former fiancée.

The magician had been born David Seth Kotkin before adopting the name David Copperfield when he was 18, recognizing at an early age that David Kotkin wouldn't necessarily have star power on a marquee.

Today, the magician has become a household name, often referenced in news articles that are seeking to describe a master illusionist. Copperfield's astonishing and awe-inspiring stunts, which included making the Statue of Liberty disappear in 1983, escaping from Alcatraz prison in 1987, and levitating across the Grand Canyon in 1984, helped earn him command presidential performances.

Copperfield in 1991 and 1992 received Emmy awards or Emmy nominations for his television specials and was named Entertainer of the Year in 1981 by the American Guild Variety Artists. In 1982 he founded Project Magic, a national rehabilitation project that helps disabled hospital patients learn magic tricks to strengthen their motor skills; and in 1996 he became the first American to produce an American television special in Communist China. Yet Copperfield has not been content to limit his magic to tours and television. He authored two books: *David Copperfield's Tales of the Impossible,* an anthology of original stories dealing with magic and illusion, and *Beyond Imagination* (both published by HarperPrism).

Copperfield admits that if he had one wish, it might be for less worry. "There's always going to be that lady in the front row," he told the *New York Times*. "That's the one you care about."

CHAPTER 13

HUMBERTO CRUZ

Frugal Columnist Saves
More Than $1 Million

Coming to this country unable to speak English might inhibit some people's effort to accumulate wealth. Not so with Humberto Cruz. Of course, when Cruz fled Cuba for the good life in America, having a high net worth was the last thing on his mind. All the 15-year-old was thinking about was learning English and getting a good meal. Confronted with the realities of life as an immigrant, he decided to take the bull by the horns.

Cruz, 54, not only speaks fluent English now but he is best known for his syndicated personal finance newspaper columns that run in 66 newspapers through the Tribune Media Services. A check on his Quicken program put the combined net worth of Cruz and his wife, Georgina, at $1.7 million. That, he says, includes their home and possessions.

Although his columns are well read, Cruz largely credits his high net worth to the basic instinct of having food on the table and to anger at a couple of well-chosen lenders.

He and his wife of Miramar, Florida, had been looking for a home with their daughter, Veronica, now a high school teacher. A $126,000 home was the lowest-priced home they could afford in the neighborhood where they wished to live. "We applied for a mortgage and got turned down."

Cruz was incensed that a lender evidently didn't consider him a good enough risk for that mortgage. "We went to another lender and got approved for a $100,000 mortgage. But to be approved, the lender forced us to liquidate an annuity and incur all the surrender charges," Cruz reported angrily. "Unless we upped the down payment, we would not qualify."

Not only did the Cruzes have to come up with $26,000 down to buy their home, but the prize for that $100,000 loan was a whopping 11.25 percent interest rate!

To this day, Cruz often recites to the penny, like a mantra, that ugly monthly payment that prompted the couple to kill the mortgage within a two-year period and never owe interest again: $1,152.34. The Cruzes kept right on paying that amount, but after that period, they paid it directly to themselves into a series of growth-oriented mutual funds. The strategy paid off handsomely.

Cruz never had had a goal to become a millionaire. He was driven by a sense of priorities. Cruz and his wife, both only children, were born to middle-class families in Cuba. Although they didn't know each other then, their families left Cuba in 1960, shortly after Castro had nationalized the companies for which their fathers worked. Cruz was 15, Georgina a year older.

Cruz's father, a sales supervisor with Texaco, had decided it would be better for his family to be raised in a country that had no communism. But Humberto's early years in Cuba represent a period of his life he has largely blocked out. He does remember friends or their parents who had been beaten or thrown in jail. "I didn't realize the magnitude of what they were doing," Cruz said of his parents. "I was concerned about going to school."

Georgina's memory of those days is a bit more vivid. Her late father worked as a credit manager at Nestle. He left his job on the basis of principle. Nestle had been a Swiss company with Swiss investors. Yet the Cuban government, on taking control of the company, made no effort to contact those investors.

He was outraged! "[Georgina's father] felt that if the government could take over his company and other companies, it could say the very next moment that your house is mine and your car is mine," Georgina remembers. "What was there to stop them?"

Like Humberto's family, Georgina's family brought to this country only what they had packed in their suitcases. Both families brought 300 American dollars because based on what the family evidently had heard from others, $300 was "the acceptable amount of money you could leave Cuba with and not get into any trouble." Both families independently arrived in this country safely, although there had been reports of random searches at the airport. "You had to strip down to complete nudity and these goons would come and search you," she says. "Women would search female passengers and men searched male passengers."

Dollars, at the time, had been circulated in Cuba as widely as Cuban pesos, which, many believed, soon would prove worthless. Nevertheless, Georgina said her family did bring an additional 100 pesos in their exodus just in case they returned to Cuba and needed cab fare. For Georgina, the experience was a terrifying one she will never forget. Her father had told his employer he was leaving on vacation; otherwise, he might not have been allowed to leave. Her family escaped the reported airport searches, but her plane, which was supposed to take off at 5 PM, failed to leave until almost midnight, adding to their fears. Her family first went to Miami to stay with relatives. From there, her father attempted to contact Nestle to find employment. They were told to go to New York to contact the Argentinian consulate and there he obtained a work permit. Fortunately, he was able to resume his former job as a credit manager. The family, which had moved to Argentina, subsequently left that country amid heavy inflation and followed a path to Los Angeles, Chicago, and then Miami.

Meanwhile, teenager Cruz had arrived in snow-covered New York. He was unable to speak English and was sharing a one-bedroom apartment with his parents and an aunt and uncle. "We slept in the dining room. My uncle and his wife slept in the living room. I remember my uncle getting a job in a factory and having to take the train for three hours to get to his job."

The Cruzes subsequently moved to Kansas City when Cruz's father finally did land a job with Texaco but no longer as a sales supervisor. Unable to speak English, he was forced instead to start all over again in the sales department in a new country. "It's like being an editor and starting all over as a reporter," Cruz said.

Cruz's mother, who had been a housewife primarily, also was forced to find work as a clerk, and Cruz concerned himself with learning English. Although he would have been a junior in high school, he had to repeat his sophomore year just to learn the new language. There was a valuable lesson, though, that his family's sudden poverty taught him: You can't spend what you don't have. "I recall the joy and accomplishment when we got a new mattress. We saved for three months!" he said.

Cruz was earning $1 an hour as a cashier in the school cafeteria and for cleaning up the high school gym. "I needed money, so I asked. You don't need to know English to clean the gymnasium."

Life was tough. Sometimes he missed lunch. Unable to speak English, he had to point to what he wanted in the school cafeteria. Other times, he simply wound up with the wrong thing. "It took me a while to make friends," he added.

He had arrived in Kansas City in December 1960. By the following February, he had started making himself understood. "When you're thrown into an environment where everyone else speaks another language, you learn it. You have no choice."

His success, though, stemmed from a unique form of self-discipline. He would try to go through one article of the *Readers Digest* each day for the express purpose of teaching himself the language. "I would sit in the room with the *Readers Digest* and a dictionary." Why *Readers Digest*? The stories are short and they're written in simple language. "It would take two to three hours to get through an article. In a month, I would get through 30 stories. It taught me the tremendous power of doing things a little at a time." The dictionary got worn out very quickly.

Cruz admits he was very depressed for about a year as he got acclimated to his new life in the United States. Although he was poor, money never had been an obsession. "I detected the fact that we needed to eat. I detected the fact that in high school, a lot of other kids had cars. A lot of schoolmates worried about dates and being the most popular kid in school. I was worried about learning English and putting food on the table. I didn't enjoy high school."

But a football game on television presented him with what he considers a defining moment that helped change his life. The Denver Broncos were way behind in the game but catching up. It was late in the fourth quarter. "The quarterback threw a Hail Mary pass." Cruz, in his clearest English yet, uttered the words, "He's got it!" That particular moment, he says, meant so much more than just a victory for the Broncos. It proved that Cruz finally had gotten the grasp of English he had been working so hard to learn. Perhaps even more important, it showed what you can achieve when you don't give up. It also proved that anyone has the power to come back from behind. And it was that football game that marked Cruz's transformation from Cuban to American culture.

Cruz's diligent studying of the *Readers Digest* had paid off in spades. Once he had the English language licked, he quickly progressed to becoming sports editor of his high school newspaper. His interest in writing was enhanced while he was studying English. He and a student from Finland stood in front of the other students conducting, as an exercise, a type of newspaper-style interview. The school newspaper's journalism advisor helped fan Cruz's talent, taking the time to fix his copy and providing the fatherly advice he so badly needed.

"Clearly the sacrifice my parents made is obvious to me now," Cruz says. While he had a tough time at 16, he realizes now that it had to be much easier for him at a young age than for his parents, who were in their 40s. Cruz's parents didn't speak English. Nor did they have much money. Nevertheless, even though they couldn't afford it, they told him not to worry about the money. Cruz, though, knew deep down that he *did* have to worry. "I realized I could not possibly count on them to pay for college."

He managed to complete his first two years of college at Kansas City Community College on a no-expense scholarship he obtained himself based on his high school academic record. His only cost, he says, was a $7 per semester activity fee.

But to maintain his scholarship, he had to keep up his grades, which included obtaining a B in physical education. Although physical education might be a breeze for some, for Cruz it was the class that threatened his future. Maintaining his scholarship depended on the results of a phys ed test that included a basketball free throw. Whether he made the grade in that phys ed class actually depended on whether he made the basket. "It was one shot—making it and qualifying for a scholarship or missing." Fortunately, he sank it.

Miami started beckoning Cruz. He had been attracted to Florida, the state where many Cubans, including his family, had gone for summer vacations. Although Americans tend to vacation in Florida in the winter, Miami's summer is a little cooler than Havana's, providing the ideal vacation spot for Cubans.

Cruz put himself through the University of Miami, where he graduated magna cum laude through a work-study scholarship. He worked 15 hours weekly on campus in exchange for tuition, choosing to put in his duty at the school library. He also worked as a sports editor for the school newspaper, the *Miami Hurricane*. When he walked into the office to see if he could work for the paper, the editor assigned him on the spot to cover a soccer game. He left the school newspaper, though, when offered a choice of staying there or interning for the *Miami Herald*.

Cruz's first full-time job on graduation was at the *Kansas City Star* as a reporter. He worked there for eight months. Sometimes, inspiration for change can be fueled not by a burning career objective but rather by outside forces. In Cruz's case, another defining moment struck when Mother Nature exerted her influence on his 3:30 PM to midnight shift on December 31, 1967. "It was one of the windiest, coldest days in the history of the city. I walked through the parking lot. It was so incredibly windy that it was painful to get my hands out of my pocket. I said, 'the hell with this!' I decided I was going to quit work without having a job."

Deeply moved by that cold, miserable night, Cruz moved to Florida permanently. "When you're single and 22, you can afford to do that. All I had to my name was $2,000, about half of which I used as a down payment on a car, a used Volkswagen Beetle." It was the only car that he ever bought on credit. He was driving around downtown Miami when he saw a Room for Rent sign. As it turned out, all the rooms in the home were rented, but he was able to sleep on a couch on an open porch for about $10. (Whether that was a weekly or monthly rate, he doesn't quite remember.) He kept his clothes in the car but was allowed to use the rest room. He took a job as a credit investigator for two months so he could eat.

Cruz began working at the *Sun-Sentinel* in Fort Lauderdale in May 1968. His initial salary left him with less than $100 a week after taxes. For his first apartment, he paid $52 a month in Lauderdale-by-the-Sea. One year later, he moved to an $80-a-month apartment and from there it was on to a one-bedroom.

He had been noticing a byline in the *Miami Hurricane*, which he read, of his future wife, although he had never met her until they were fixed up by a mutual friend. The friend had recognized how similar Humberto's and Georgina's lives had been and how alike they thought. "Humberto called me," she said. "But I said to him, nothing personal, but I really don't go out on blind dates. So nothing happened."

She was smitten, though, by his pleasant-sounding voice, and asked some of her University of Miami journalism professors if they knew anything about him. "My God, they had wonderful things to say." She followed up with a note to Humberto at the *Sun-Sentinel* explaining that if he still wanted to meet, they could meet for coffee at the student center. They subsequently met at a Cuban restaurant and went to see the movie *Ryan's Daughter.*

The couple married in 1972, and she moved into his apartment. He became assistant city editor. "Despite the fancy job titles, our combined salaries were enough for a one-bedroom apartment," Cruz said. When Georgina had their child, she decided she would freelance so that she could stay at home. At this writing, she is primarily freelancing travel stories.

The couple graduated from a one-bedroom to a two-bedroom apartment and by 1978 had saved enough to buy a $50,000 home in Lauderhill. "It took seven years to get enough for the down payment!" Cruz said.

As their daughter grew, they decided to buy a more expensive home, which required that fateful $100,000 mortgage. Although the rate had been 11.25 percent, the couple figured out a way to profit. They were able to sell their former home, which had appreciated from $50,000 to $80,000. To expedite the sale, they agreed to take back the mortgage at 12 percent—three-quarters of 1 percent more than their own mortgage. While that may have seemed like a sound business strategy, the Cruzes' homebuyers decided to pay off that mortgage early. Suddenly, the couple found themselves holding the $45,000 balance.

Immediately, they turned around and applied that money to the principal of their own larger mortgage. Applying money to the principal of a mortgage in its early years can have a dramatic effect because a very tiny proportion of initial monthly mortgage payments represent principal; the overwhelming majority is interest.

While the payment of the lump sum didn't actually lower their monthly mortgage payments, the couple was astounded at the amount of interest they were saving. "We got excited about the possibilities," Cruz said. He immediately used his year-end bonus to pay down even more of the mortgage. They aimed at wiping it out entirely. "For a period of two years, we started saving like crazy."

During that period, the couple began writing down every expense. They didn't go out to eat. Instead, they went for walks on the beach and in the park, pastimes that are free. "Going to the library was free. Our motivation was to lose that 11.25 percent mortgage." Buoyed by the additional $45,000 the couple received for their home, they were able to pay off the rest of that mortgage in just two years.

A couple's sacrifice for the good of a long-term goal can often create friction between spouses—particularly if one has other needs. Fortunately, in the Cruzes' case, both were in total agreement. They wanted avidly to wipe out their debt. For Humberto, it wasn't only the mortgage's high rate that prompted his commitment but a stronger motivation. "I wanted to show those people who gave me such a hard time to qualify for that mortgage that they were incorrect. We *were* a good risk!"

Georgina already had been brought up not to borrow. In fact, she had worked her way through Northwestern University and the University of Miami rather than take out a student loan. Fortunately, she had worked as a secretary in Chicago for Time Life, which offered to pay half her tuition as a company benefit. It hadn't been easy. It took her three years while working to finish what otherwise could have been one year at Northwestern University's downtown campus. When her parents wanted to move to Miami during her last year, she was forced to finish at the University of Miami, working part-time for the Institute of Molecular Evolution. "If I would have started borrowing money, it's true I would have graduated sooner," she explained, "but I would have been $20,000 in the hole, and I would have had to pay for that."

So she fully understood the value of retiring that pesky mortgage. "It really didn't kill me," she reflected. "You've probably started a diet. The first day or two, it's bothersome to you. After that, your stomach gets used to the new ration.

"What I tried to do is avoid temptation. I would avoid the malls. A lot of people go to the malls for a social thing and wind up spending on things they hadn't given a thought to. I avoided that. When I went to the grocery store, I tried to come with a list, go once a week only, and get out as quickly as I could. To this day, I clip coupons on Sunday and Thursday—only for things I would buy anyway."

The couple avoided buying on impulse. That wasn't as difficult as it might have been because their home happened to be in a newly developed area and wasn't very close to many stores. "We would go for picnics at the beach, walks in the park, festivals or fairs that were free or where admission was very low cost. We went to the library a lot and got books and records."

She says she also took their daughter to Storytime Fun and free movies at the library and made good use of Florida's free beaches and low-cost museums. And she and her daughter took an inexpensive ten-week mother-daughter craft course. "We went once a week. It taught us how to do collages and pottery. We would often come home and do it on our own for recreation." They also walked on nature trails and gathered leaves and petals.

When the couple succeeded in paying off the mortgage, they decided to route that famous $1,152.34 to investments. Cruz put the money in five no-load funds, including Fidelity Puritan, Babson Value, and a Strong stock fund. "Based on what I know now, five was too many. Three would have been enough." With five mutual funds, some held the same blue chip growth companies as others, canceling out their advantages.

Cruz acknowledges that both the Fort Lauderdale area real estate market and the stock market were on his side. Besides earning a profit on the sale of his first home, he happened to pay off his mortgage in November 1987—one month after the stock market crash of October 1987. So his investment plan was fueled by the added momentum of rock-bottom stock prices in Black Monday's aftermath. Cruz's net worth climbed and finally hit the $1 million mark in 1994.

Cruz shifted to writing personal finance columns after *Money* magazine discovered his ultraserious savings strategy. In a 1990 article, the magazine dubbed him a "Robosaver."

"I was assistant city editor," Cruz said. "I was sitting at my desk and had five minutes to go to the next meeting. So I literally took lunch and moved to another desk. By accident, I sat in the business department." While seated, Cruz overheard a conversation a freelance reporter for *Money* was having with the magazine. They were looking for live bodies to exemplify certain savings traits.

"This conversation was going on out loud next to me." Like a child back in school, Cruz dutifully raised his hand and said to the writer, "But I do all of that. You can use me for *all* the traits." The magazine did.

When the article was published, Cruz received phone calls from people all over the country asking for financial advice. "One was a nurse from Texas. She started crying on the telephone. She said she needed financial help and didn't know what to do." She suggested that he start writing a column. When he posed the idea of a financial column to his editor, the editor said, "Fine. But do it on your own time."

So Cruz came in one morning at 6 AM, wrote a column, and showed it to the business editor. "The business editor looked at it and said, 'This is what everybody else does. It's no good. Make it personal.' She threw it back at me."

Cruz redid it, injecting himself and his wife into it more frequently. This time the editor liked it, and Cruz began writing a column every other week. Shortly after that, the column was popular enough for the editors to suggest that it be syndicated. They began having conferences with the *Sun-Sentinel's* parent, Tribune Media Services, and the column was in 13 newspapers in its first year. In 1995 Cruz officially became a business columnist. Until the article in *Money* magazine, none of his coworkers had been aware of his savings habits.

Cruz continued to work. At 55, he would qualify for a much higher pension and continued medical benefits. Adding to Cruz's wealth is a company employee stock ownership plan (ESOP) that offers a percentage of an employee's base pay each year in shares of Tribune preferred and common stock. Generally, he once reported in his column, he expects to get 10 percent of his pay. However, in one year, earnings went up so high that he earned 17 percent.

In fact, "in one year," one of his columns detailed, "the value of my Tribune Company Employee Stock Ownership Plan, or ESOP, zoomed from a little less than $82,000 to more than $146,000, a 78 percent increase." His ESOP account grew more in that year than his salary for more than a dozen years at the newspaper.

Cruz now says, though, that although employee stock plans have made many employees wealthy, he doesn't necessarily consider his own a major factor in his wealth. First, he can't touch that money until his retirement—a fact he has been very thankful for in down years. "I'm sure if a lot of people could have touched it, they would have gotten out at the wrong time."

Cruz's parents have died; his wife's mother was living with them at this writing. After his wife's father died, they received his 1992 Toyota Tercel. Apart from that, they had just one car of their own, a 1997 Toyota Corolla. No Lexuses, Cadillacs, or Rolls Royces. In fact, published reports have indicated Cruz formerly drove a Volkswagen Rabbit with no radio. Some have gone so far as to consider him a tightwad and cheapskate. Cruz expounds on the report that the Rabbit had no radio. It also had no air-conditioning, the door didn't open, and the window was stuck halfway. "If it rained, we got wet."

Cruz denies that he's a tightwad or cheapskate. It's all, he says, about priorities. "For some people cars are extremely important. For me, they're meaningless. I get excited to get where I'm going. It doesn't matter what kind of a car I'm driving."

Driving is a bit more luxurious now, though. His current $16,000 Toyota Corolla does have a radio, a sun roof, air conditioner, and leather seats. In fact, his wife already has proclaimed firmly that their next car will be a Mercedes. But, she stresses, it's not necessarily because she aims for a lavish lifestyle: "I feel it's a very good quality car and probably will be our final car. We will keep it very nice."

Cruz subsequently did buy another home—the nicest he has ever owned—but one worth much less than he can afford. He paid for the home with cash. Although he could afford a half-million-dollar house, the Cruzes spent $167,000 for their three-bedroom, two-bath, 2,068-square-foot house. Cruz stayed true to his commitment never to owe anybody interest. The couple previously owned a home with a swimming pool but realized they lacked the time to use it much, so the new home has no pool. "When we want to go for a swim, we go to the ocean." Again, it was an issue, not necessarily of cheapness, but practicality: their home overlooks a beautiful lake.

"Most people buy more house than they can afford," Cruz believes. Once they do, they're not just supporting a home with a mortgage. They're spending on insurance, furniture, house decoration, and electricity. "It's hard to save money." In addition, "I don't think you can count on home prices to appreciate the way they did in the 1980s. How many square feet of house can you live in at one time? The family room can go away with half the living room, and you won't miss it."

Cruz maintains his really cheap years were just two—those two years the couple saved like crazy to pay down the 11.25 percent mortgage. Now, he and his wife's combined salaries leave them in the 28 percent tax bracket. "The only thing that pushes us above that is our syndication income [a share in his syndicated column profits] and dividend income." Nevertheless, they eat out in restaurants both days of the weekend and typically go somewhere—often to a movie.

Georgina adds that they have indulged in a big-screen television, and for their daughter's birthday spent $900 a night for three rooms at the concierge level of Disney World's Grand Floridian. They also often take annual trips to Europe or the Mediterranean.

Cruz takes on the myriad financial planners who advise that keeping money invested is wiser than paying off a mortgage. "All you hear about is asset allocation," Cruz says. The very type of asset allocation that planners recommend substantiates why it's an advantage to pay off your home, he believes. Chances are, you would earn 6.50 percent or 7 percent in bonds if you made that investment. "So what's the point of paying 6.50 percent to 7 percent interest to someone else? Imagine the return you're getting on the money you're not spending."

Think you should keep a mortgage because the interest is deductible on income taxes? Cruz believes that that tax advantage is one of the most misunderstood concepts there is. In 1999 a married couple who didn't itemize would have a $7,100 standard deduction on their income taxes. "A mortgage is only good when the interest you pay exceeds the standard deduction and only to the extent that it exceeds it."

Say you owe $10,000 in mortgage interest and you're in the 28 percent tax bracket. A married couple would only be able to deduct 28 percent of $2,900, which is the amount over the $7,100 standard deduction for a married couple in 1998, or $812 in interest. "It's true you can invest in stock instead," Cruz says. "But you're assuming stock market risk. There are no guarantees. Paying down your debt is the same as investing and getting a return equivalent to your interest rate."

Another overlooked reason not to owe mortgage interest, he believes, is cash flow. Once you stop making a monthly payment to a mortgage company, you can take all that money and invest it for yourself. It adds a feeling of security.

Cruz thinks that the most significant thing anyone hoping to achieve wealth can do is avoid getting into debt. "Avoiding interest and asking yourself if you really need something before you buy it are keys."

Another important factor to financial success is writing down expenditures. That's not denial. It's like a diary: Once you write it down, you have something to look back on and reminisce about. When you write down $20 for a present for your daughter's birthday or $3,000 for a trip for your anniversary, you can then look at your notes and realize that you really enjoyed those occasions.

In the meantime, you also notice what items you're spending on that don't give you pleasure. "It clearly helps identify areas where it may be possible to cut back. Do you think IBM doesn't know where the money is being spent?" By the same token, the exercise can also identify areas in which you should be spending more.

A computer program is not a necessity for tracking expenses, Cruz says. All you need is a pencil and paper, although he enters every expense on a Quicken program, which allows him to calculate net worth and figure percentage returns on investments. "My wife leaves yellow stick 'em notes on the kitchen counter—33¢ for postage, $12 for a haircut, and such and such." Even his daughter has tried tracking expenses—but for merely three months. "She said it was illuminating," he said, noting it served to make her realize all the sodas and junk food she was consuming.

Cruz says the greatest catalyst in his financial success was paying down that initial mortgage. "It proved it was possible to achieve something that looks impossible. We have not made a monthly payment for rent or a mortgage since November 1987. We still would be paying that. That mortgage today would not have expired."

Now, he and his wife maintain traditional IRAs. When the Roth IRA became available, the two immediately funded that type of IRA to the maximum. They also contribute the maximum to their 401(k) plans, and Georgina contributes the maximum through Keoghs. "We both have fully funded Keoghs," he says, explaining he gets a portion of income from his syndicated column. The couple maintains variable and fixed annuities. Although variable annuities have come under fire for high fees in the media, Cruz confesses that he has two very low-fee variable annuities: Vanguard's and T. Rowe Price.

Cruz considers himself a "small millionaire." Happily, he says, he is nowhere near the point where everyone is hitting him up for money. Neither he nor Georgina has brothers or sisters. Financial demands from needy friends or relatives, Georgina believes, are more apt to come to people who receive a windfall or are ostentatious.

"The downside of money," Cruz says, "and I'm happy we're nowhere near that point, is to delude ourselves into thinking that money is the most important thing. It is not." Among the things that have been much more important, is the birth of his daughter. "Even when we had five people in a one-bedroom apartment, that support for one another and family is a memory I treasure." Another important experience: "The first time I saw snow on the ground."

His millionaire status has not made an impact on either the couple's life or relationships. "We are friends with a couple who don't read the paper. They don't know about our net worth." Cruz is also the first to admit he's made some bad investment decisions —the time in 1990, for example, when he put some money in the Mutual Series Fund run by Michael Price. "I thought it was a very good fund, but it was a terrible year for value funds. It went down 10 percent and I pulled my money out at the bottom. The fund went on to gain 20 percent. . . . I look at it as a lesson.

"It's foolish to get discouraged. I made losing investments in things that have come down. Anybody who has not done that is not an investor or is a liar. With investing, if you get more right than wrong, you're going to be all right."

A key to making money, he says, is setting a goal. Initially, his goal was to keep food on the table. Then it was to get a mattress. Then it was to pay off the mortgage. "When you have that goal clearly in mind, it's a lot easier to resist distractions. It's an eye-opener." People need to ask themselves what's important and set priorities accordingly.

Cruz says that his money has bought him a secure future and the ability to do what he likes with his time. In the near future he hopes to cut his work hours, and the couple hopes to do more traveling and more reading, and return to school; Georgina hopes to study art appreciation. Cruz enjoys learning about computers, and the two also hope to volunteer in schools.

In the meantime, Cruz downloads Navigator Plus into his computer and figures out what will happen if he no longer works full-time and wants to spend a certain amount of money monthly. "We're already there," he says. "I have 150 CDs [compact disks]. There's nothing I want that I cannot get. All it took was two years of sacrifice. It was well worth it."

CHAPTER 14

SCOTT D. OKI

Microsoft Millionaire

It might have been fate that Scott D. Oki, 51, as a child had to walk down the hall to share a bathroom in a three-room tenement shared with five family members in central Seattle.

It actually was Oki's low-income Seattle roots that piqued his interest about an upstart Seattle-based company, Microsoft. The path led him to retire a multimillionaire in 1992. *Forbes* now pegs his net worth at $750 million.

Oki grew up in a largely black and Japanese American community. His parents, like many others in his neighborhood, had been placed in interment camps during World War II. The family finally scraped together $10,000 to buy a house with a backyard in the suburbs, so Oki was no longer playing in the city streets. Nevertheless, a modest childhood can sometimes create a keen eye for spotting an opportunity of a lifetime, taking advantage of it, and making it work.

"Being a Seattle native, I couldn't understand what a software company was doing in Seattle," Oki said. After all, software companies wanted to be in California's Silicon Valley. His curiosity prompted him to conduct more research and ask around what the company was doing in his hometown. "I saw a very aggressive product strategy."

Oki had been in California doing consulting work after leaving his own software company, which had split up. Microsoft was in its early days of assembly language products. "They were a language company. Yet they were starting to get involved in the operating system world with CPM 80—although that wasn't their product. They had developed a product called Softcard, and I had heard they were aggressively pursuing spreadsheet graphics in the applications market. I said that's an awful lot for one company to do."

In the early days, Microsoft's customers were primarily programmers. Oki particularly liked the idea that Microsoft was focusing on turnkey products for the consumer. He had no question that the company was aggressive and smart. What he did question, having already been through a start-up and breakup of a computer company, was whether Microsoft could pull it off. "Getting into product segments dilutes focus. There's a lot of risk in adopting a very aggressive strategy."

Nevertheless, Oki wrote a letter to Microsoft Chairman Bill Gates seeking employment. He then had a choice: (1) Take a job as marketing manager-special accounts at Microsoft at $40,000 a year with a 10,000-share options package with the ability to invest in 10,000 shares of Microsoft over a four-and-one-half-year period "at a price of maybe $1 a share"; or (2) go with Micropro in California's Silicon Valley at an annual starting salary of between $60,000 and $70,000.

Clearly, Oki says, he was never driven by money, or he never would have gone with Microsoft in 1982. As fate would have it, he arrived just one year after the first IBM personal computer, powered by MS-DOS, was unveiled. Oki hadn't known about that momentous deal at the time. "I had heard through the grapevine that he [Gates] had contemplated doing something with IBM." However, none of the details had yet been made public. It was only by asking questions at his initial meeting with Bill Gates that Oki developed an inkling of what was going on. It was that alliance between Microsoft's Bill Gates and IBM that prompted the software industry to focus on IBM-compatible machines rather than on Apple computers, revolutionizing the entire computer industry.

"Microsoft had a reputation for paying below market," Oki said, although he had made it clear in the beginning that he wanted the stock options. And Microsoft stock finally paid off. Oki seized every opportunity during his performance reviews—often with Bill Gates himself—to lobby for more stock options. While he wasn't sure what other employees did, "I would try to get as many options as I could, forgoing even salary increases. I would much rather have the increase in remuneration come with stock options."

How many stock options he received varied with performance. "As an example, when I was promoted to senior vice president, I got 100,000 options." Now, Microsoft has a more structured options program in place.

Very often, employees, when obtaining stock options, take the conservative route and cash them in immediately—typically for instant profit. Oki's strategy was to let them sit. He exercised the bulk of his options when he left the company in 1992. Announcing Oki's retirement, the *Seattle Times* reported that Oki held 202,000 shares in Microsoft stock worth $24 million, a figure that Oki now says sounds about right. "I never really thought much about making it in the financial sense. That didn't come until there was talk about Microsoft going public in 1986. When the company was in the midst of deciding if it wanted to hit the IPO market, I had a sense of OK, gee whiz, I'm going to be a millionaire." The only options he had cashed were a few while he was building a home.

Oki, as Microsoft's senior vice president of sales, marketing, and service, was making $140,000 a year when he left the company in 1992. He was not required to exercise his options, so it wasn't until he retired in 1992 that he was forced to cash in the options for stock. To this day, Oki says he holds onto the Microsoft stock. So far it has proven a smart move. Between 1993 and 1998 alone, according to Standard & Poor's, the stock grew at an annual rate of return of 65 percent. Based on those figures, the value of the stock doubled every 13 months! Oki at this writing had no plans to sell the stock anytime soon. "It's a fundamental belief in the vitality of the company. When I stop being bullish on Microsoft, believe me, I'll be an active seller of Microsoft stock. But it's still a very well-run leader in the industry. I see nothing to change that."

Oki is chairman of Oki Development Inc. in Seattle, a for-profit company that invests in whatever he wants. He admits he likes high-tech companies. At this writing, he was in the process of building a new golf course—The Golf Course at New Castle—whose designers are professional golfers Bob Cupp and Fred Couples. He also owns homes and commercial office space in Washington and Scottsdale, Arizona, "where hopefully the market appreciates at fairly significant rates." He owns four golf courses, including Echo Falls Country Club and Indian Summer Country Club in Olympia.

He also owns a professional soccer team, the Seattle Sounders; a company, Nanny & Webster, that manufactures baby blankets for companies to buy as gifts for employees who have babies; a cigar store; and restaurants. Much of his profits are plowed back into his nonprofit Oki Foundation, which Laurie, his wife since October 1988, presides over. In fact, Nanny & Webster gives 100 percent of the profits to charities, while the Seattle Sounders donate the greater of 100 percent of the profits or 2 percent of ticket sales. Oki was expecting his for-profit companies to have between 400 and 500 employees by the time his new golf course opened. That compares with some 3,000 employees he oversaw when he finally left Microsoft's U.S. division.

A father of three young children, Oki has a home overlooking Lake Washington in Bellevue on more than an acre as well as a home in Vail, Colorado, but says the family doesn't wear wealth on their sleeves. He admits, though, that his wife drives a van and a Lexus, while he drives a Mercedes.

He now spends 80 to 90 percent of his time at the Oki Foundation, which is based in a converted church. The decision on how he allots his time is his own. He generally leaves home between 7 AM and 7:15 AM and frequently continues until the evening, either going alone or with his wife to a variety of functions in conjunction with close to 20 organizations he is involved with.

Unlike when he was at Microsoft, weekends are off-limits— time dedicated completely to his family. Oki also has the freedom to take as much as two months off for vacation. "If I were still working at Microsoft, I'd be working weekends. If we wanted to take an extended vacation—it was never an option at Microsoft. The longest vacation I ever took was two weeks and that was for my honeymoon."

It's all a far cry from the way his life started. Oki's father had worked as a post office worker and his mother as a secretary. Oki's parents, Oki, and a younger brother and sister shared their home with their grandmother. At one point, the family, like other Japanese-American families in the neighborhood, earned extra income by packaging tackle. They had been subcontracted out by a local fishing tackle store to put three pieces of tackle per package in a plastic wrapper. Commandeered by his grandmother and sitting around the kitchen table, the family took in about a nickel for each package. "My grandmother would do it all day long. We would do it at night."

Although he grew up in a low-income neighborhood, Oki never wanted for anything. "We never felt we were poor. We lived a very comfortable life. The Japanese community at that time was very closely knit. The church played a significant role in holding the community together. No one really had that much. Your peers look, feel, and smell and do the things you're doing."

Oki had been active in the Boy Scouts, an organization he actively supports to this day. He had played and participated in the drum and bugle corps his father had founded. Education was always emphasized in the Japanese community and particularly in Oki's family. "I remember my father telling me that education was unbelievably important. Once you get an education, you can't lose it. You can't misplace it. It's not something that can be given to you and you sell. . . . Once you have an education, that sets the stage." Oki's father had high expectations for his son, although he never had completed college himself. Yet "he had studied chemical engineering prior to being interned in World War II," Oki said. His father wanted his son to have a better fate. "He wanted me to be an electrical engineer and work for Boeing."

At first, Oki tried to meet his father's expectations. "His dream was my dream." Oki always did well in school, particularly in the sciences and music. He started at the University of Washington in Seattle but lost momentum so that by 1969, when the war in Vietnam and antiwar protests were in full swing, Oki was dropping his classes. The war, though, had nothing to do with his performance; he simply was taking advantage of his newfound freedom away from what had been a very closed community. Oki preferred to spend his time shooting pool and playing cards. "I didn't go to school and didn't go to class. It didn't take long before my grades had been uncharacteristically low. I fell off the bandwagon. I didn't flunk. There were courses I dropped because I knew I *would* flunk."

Ironically, in 1993 Oki received a prestigious gubernatorial appointment to serve on the Board of Regents for the very school he had dropped out of. He took that appointment in conjunction with the University of Washington very seriously and was also active with the University of Washington Foundation. "It was partly because of my success at Microsoft and partly because of my ethnicity," Oki speculated about that appointment. "I think they were looking for diversity. I was very honored."

At the time, though, his poor performance had serious repercussions. He lost his student deferment. While he was at the University of Washington, Oki drew a very low number in the draft lottery. He received a draft notice and was ordered to report for a physical. "I said I really didn't want to go in the army. So I decided to enlist for four years in the air force."

Oki began to travel and see the country. The air force thrust him out of the sheltered life of Seattle's tight Japanese-American community. Fortunately, Oki was able to stay out of combat; he played the drums and traveled. "I was the only Japanese American in my unit."

He flew almost every weekend around the country to some function—"whether it was a general retiring at an air force base or someplace else. I saw quite a bit of the United States. It was an eye-opener for me to see how other people lived."

Prior to the stint in the air force, the only traveling Oki had done was an occasional vacation to Portland, Oregon, or Vancouver, British Columbia. "Growing up we never had much money to travel." He also married for a brief time while in the air force but subsequently divorced.

His time in the air force had created within him a new kind of spirit. He realized that he disliked environments in which logic, at least in his own mind, didn't necessarily prevail. "In the military, the modus operandi is you take orders from superiors—whether you think they make sense or not. You're not paid to debate the issue. I hated that environment." On leaving the military, he vowed in the future that he would try to steer himself into situations in which his opinions counted for something.

The major advantage of his stint in the air force from 1969 to 1973 was its providing him an almost ideal opportunity to reapply himself and get an education. His duty was so light that he was able to take courses, courtesy of the United States Air Force, at the University of Colorado. This time, he recommitted himself to his education and graduated magna cum laude with an undergraduate bachelor of science degree in accounting and information systems.

Oki had been excelling in science and calculus. Recognizing that his father's wish that he become an electrical engineer wasn't going to happen, he decided to switch to business. "It seemed by default to be an area that was a marketable degree. I didn't want to be a teacher. I didn't think I wanted anything in the liberal arts area."

As IRS rules got more and more cumbersome, the demand for accountants was definitely on the rise. Oki went on to get his master's degree in business administration at the University of Colorado, with some prodding from a counselor. The counselor advised him that he could take some classes in the last quarter of his undergraduate semester that would count toward his MBA. That way, he figured, he could get an even better job.

Getting that MBA, though, wasn't easy. Oki was working full-time as a programmer for Looart Press, a local company in Colorado Springs, that subsequently became the popular catalog company Current. He went to school at night under the GI bill while earning $9,000 a year in his job. "If I left and went to work in the private sector, I would never go back for an MBA," he reflected. But he was single at the time and able to make education the focus of his life.

In 1975 he left Looart Press and joined Hewlett-Packard in Colorado Springs. As a senior cost accountant, his starting salary rose to $16,000 annually. "I hated it. But Hewlett-Packard was a very large company, and they were more than accommodating by transferring me to a brand new division they were starting in Fort Collins. That was my first taste of a start-up environment. I was hired as product marketing manager in this new division, taking care of my technical background and accounting. I loved it and did fairly well."

The new division was transferred to California in 1978 and 1979 and became part of the general systems division within Hewlett-Packard. "I stayed with the company for another year and started getting thoughts of doing something on my own."

Oki was getting tired of the slow decision-making process at Hewlett-Packard. Feeling stifled, he talked with a few guys he had met at a party about going off on their own. They wrote a business plan and quit their jobs. One of the four founders had a connection with some investors and was able to round up $3.5 million to start a software company, Sequoia Group Inc., in Larkspur Landing, California.

The company wrote software and packaged it with hardware in an attempt to provide a turnkey solution for doctors to handle their back-office functions. While it's hard to imagine doctors being without computers today, pushing this system at that particular time was not an easy job. The new company's business plan called for a steep increase in hiring along with deploying a national sales force. Oki handled the product marketing, documentation, testing, and customer service.

The market simply wasn't ready for the product. "Doctors just weren't embracing the need to have these things called computers helping their back-office function. This was back in 1980–1982. It preceded the whole world of PCs. This was software written for the minicomputer."

The company had reached a major hurdle in its growth plans. Two of the company's founders, including Oki, had wanted to cut prices for the systems and increase the volume sold. "We had an underutilized factory. We weren't selling enough units." On the other hand, his partners were seeking a second round of financing. To entice investors, they wanted to hold prices so they could show the business's potential for a high profit margin.

Oki and another founder finally left the company, and in 1982 Oki began consulting in San Francisco. It was while he was consulting that he became aware of Microsoft.

He had viewed the split-up of his own company as one of the turning points of his career. "It was a painful process. That affected me. There was scar tissue in terms of making a lot of mistakes. It was working until your fingers were raw—there isn't more time in the day to work. That environment is a very intense environment." Slaving for an unknown outcome was difficult.

Oki learned from that experience. "I think the first thing I would tell anyone is passion rules. Almost everything else takes care of itself. Most people end up doing things they fundamentally don't want to do. If you contrast that with doing something you really love to do—thinking about that business or whatever you're trying to accomplish, maybe even dreaming—that's the kind of environment people will find stimulating and rewarding."

Oki considers himself a high-level, goal-oriented invidual. "Even though I might have had a setback, you set new goals. . . .

One of the things I have learned in being at a very early stage of my career with computers is that I love computers. There wasn't a single time in my career where I wasn't involved with computers. When the computer industry went from mainframe to minis to PCs, I was fortunate to follow."

On taking his job with Microsoft, he founded the company's international division, which in four years grew to account for 42 percent of Microsoft's revenues and more than 50 percent of the company's profits. To launch the division, he told *Washington CEO* that he worked three years without a day off. "Upon boarding an airplane in Sydney, Australia," the magazine reported, "a flight attendant told him he was Pan Am's number one most frequent flier," having logged 400,000 miles that year. That was just Pan Am.

He also turned around the U.S. division by aggressively lobbying for the company to develop a Windows-based strategy despite the fact that Microsoft's Windows software, which allowed people to use an IBM-compatible computer by clicking on the computer screen with a mouse, initially was panned. It wasn't until Microsoft's 1991 Windows 3.0 version that the famous software actually took off.

Oki says he was undaunted by Microsoft's early failures. "It actually wasn't as big a deal as some might imagine. Virtually every Microsoft product had experienced the same thing—whether it was a word processor or spreadsheet. In the first incarnations, the products weren't very successful. It wasn't until Microsoft came out with the second, third, fourth, or fifth version that they actually got it right." Even its national hit, MS-DOS, met with resistance initially.

Microsoft's U.S. business grew from $69 million in 1986, when Oki took over that division, to $571 million at the end of fiscal year 1991. Under his leadership, the company developed strong partnerships with resellers—companies like Egghead Software. Those partnerships have since been considered a model for the industry.

Computer & Software News in 1989 reported on one Microsoft promotion Oki was involved in. Microsoft had dedicated $5 million to a four-part winter reseller promotion that 1,700 dealers were expected to participate in, it said. The two-month campaign spanned in-store demonstration stations; a retail merchandising promotion; seminars; and a direct mail campaign. Retail demonstrations featured Microsoft Mouse, Windows, Flight Simulator, Works, and several language packages, while the seminar program focused on getting Excel into a greater number of corporate accounts.

By offering four separate components, Oki had said at the time, Microsoft hoped to "tailor the program to individual dealers." "The catchword is flexibility," Oki was quoted as saying. "We hope to meet as many needs as possible." It was all part of Microsoft's plans to run "three large promotions per year that tie together its entire product line, as opposed to smaller campaigns," the publication reported.

Oki explains that Microsoft had a rough time at first. It didn't have dominant market share. None of its products in the United States were market leaders. "It was hard trying to convince resellers that they should be paying attention to our marketing programs versus others'." There were long discussions with reseller leaders explaining why doing things the way competitors were doing failed to generate demand and build market share.

Microsoft aligned itself with that distribution channel largely, he says, by fighting a herd mentality. Many competitors concentrated on what he terms "stuffing the channel." In other words, they would try to get the reseller to buy as much of their software as possible. They figured if they could get these resellers to dedicate their scarce cash resources to buying their product, the resellers wouldn't have resources left to buy products of competitors. It was a faulty strategy, Oki declares. Once the channel was "stuffed" and the other software vendors did little from a marketing standpoint to move the product off the shelf, much of the software simply got returned. That's why the resellers appreciated Microsoft, he says. Microsoft invested in software that tracked product sales: "We made sure they didn't have more than one month's supply of any of our products." And Microsoft's relationship with this important distribution channel mushroomed.

A number of other software companies were highly successful, Oki muses. "Maybe they haven't created the kind of wealth Microsoft has, but back in the early days, we had no clue—not an idea. Not even Bill Gates had any idea it was going to turn out the way we have. We had faith in a successful business—sheer will and perseverance—a competitiveness that allowed us to succeed."

Published reports in early 1990 had cited Oki as a candidate to succeed Jon Shirley, then president of Microsoft, when Shirley announced his retirement in 1990. But Oki became the third executive to announce his departure over a two-week period in 1992. Following Oki's departure, Michael R. Hallman, Microsoft's president selected by Bill Gates two years earlier, was dismissed. The departures came as Gates announced a new three-member office structure of the Microsoft presidency.

Oki publicly stated that the management changes had nothing to do with his departure. "It's pretty simple," he told the *Seattle Times*. "This has everything to do with spending more time with my family. . . . I want to be part of their growing up, and it's hard to do that in an environment like Microsoft, where the commitment level is so incredibly high." He maintains that his family was the primary reason he left Microsoft. "It was purely a decision to get more balance in my life."

Now, Oki spends the bulk of his time in the nonprofit world, often, published reports have said, attending board meetings in jeans. In 1997 he was one of several executives that helped to raise a whopping $60 million for United Way in the Seattle area. Other recent gifts at this writing included a $1 million contribution to Seattle Children's Theaters; a $1 million challenge grant to Children's Hospital; and an endowed professorship at the University of Colorado. He also founded the Japanese-American Chamber of Commerce.

Oki told Tom Brokaw on an NBC TV report a few years ago that he wants to give something back to the world as a result of his success. "Our family was always connected to the community. We weren't very well off. And now that I have the time and the financial means to do something positive, a lot of that is pointed in the direction of the community."

He admits that when he and his wife set up the Oki Foundation in 1986, they put a few thousand shares of Microsoft's stock options in the foundation largely as a hedge against taxes. The proceeds, which are worth millions today, are used to help children.

The Okis have since chosen to make the foundation their passion; and Microsoft is frequently cited as a major contributor to Oki's philanthropic efforts. When the couple first started their philanthropy, they weren't sure what they wanted to do with the foundation. They decided to focus on children largely because they have three of their own. "Maybe because they're the most helpless and underrepresented," Oki adds.

"We wound up writing a lot of small checks to a lot of different requests, not wanting to say no." Now they know they went about their business of philanthropy the wrong way. Although they get hundreds of requests annually for money, they have devised rules for making grants—for example, only grants to local organizations and only for children's health and welfare.

The couple also learned that they can be more effective by leveraging the money. Instead of just giving a $1 million gift to Children's Hospital and drawing matching gifts that might have totaled $2 million, for example, Oki set up a challenge. For each gift, the Okis matched the first $10,000. The effort motivated others in the community to join in and raised $11.7 million instead of the mere $2 million initially anticipated.

Oki has learned that it's more work giving money away than it was earning the money in the first place. Now, whenever the foundation makes a gift, the couple replenishes it by diverting some of their Microsoft stock to the foundation. Based on tax law at this writing, putting the appreciated stock into the foundation rather than cash avoids capital gains tax on the donation. However, he warns, IRS rules keep changing.

So far, Oki's wealth hasn't caused any trouble, but he regrets that more young people in his area are not more involved in philanthropy. "All this wealth has been accumulated in such a short period of time. For most people, it represents a dream come true. What I would like to see is people thinking harder about philanthropy and giving back to the community at a much earlier age than is typical."

CHAPTER 15

DENNIS L. LARDON

Ramp Agent Grows with Southwest Airlines

For Dennis L. Lardon, 56, success was a no-brainer. It was the early 1970s; he had just been divorced and desperately needed a job, when few were available. So when a friend, who had worked for American Airlines, suggested that he talk to an interesting new start-up, Southwest Airlines in Dallas, he decided to apply.

Southwest hired Lardon in 1971 as a ramp agent, loading baggage onto airplanes. He had no airline experience nor did he ever finish college.

Lardon still works for the airline. But he earns approximately $100,000 annually as director of flight attendants. Once among a total of just 198 Southwest Airlines employees, Lardon now oversees close to 6,000 in his department alone. He doesn't, however, consider his impressive salary the major source of his wealth. The source has been the company's profit-sharing program, which, unbeknownst to Lardon when he first started, was initiated two years after he began loading baggage. At this writing, Lardon's profit-sharing stash alone was worth $3 million, diminished some by two divorce settlements.

Fortunately for Lardon, who really never had thought much about investing, the whole deal was automatic. The company simply started paying benefits to its employees—quarterly cash bonuses to Lardon were initially about $185 after taxes. "Most of it stayed in stock."

Then there was profit sharing based on company profits and employees' level of responsibility. Published reports said the company strived to pay at least 15 percent of its pretax profits to employees. Again, employees received shares of Southwest stock, depending on what an employee and the company earned.

In the mid-1980s, a 401(k) retirement plan, in which the company matched up to 100 percent of an employee's contribution, was added. More recently, key employees are also awarded stock options; Lardon's stock options started in 1991.

A combination of greatly enhanced company benefits and a major increase in salary has allowed Lardon to graduate from his original 1960 Comet to a new $65,000 Lexus sports utility vehicle for which he paid cash. He also paid cash for a lot on Horseshoe Bay, a golf-lakefront community some 45 miles west of Austin. He expected to start construction on his retirement home by year-end 1999. Whatever he feels like buying, he does—not that he necessarily believes he needs a lot of extravagances or expensive jewelry.

That wasn't the case while he was growing up in the 1950s. He remembers wanting to buy a pair of white "bucks," the latest style in shoes at the time, but his parents had refused to give him the money. Lardon's father, a construction manager who invested some money in his company's stock, had been a product of the depression. There always had been food on the table, and Lardon's father paid for his schooling in addition to frequently giving him $5 or $10 in spending money.

Lardon picked up some valuable advice from his father. "His overall attitude is you gotta try. You may screw up and fail, but you gotta try. It's OK to screw up."

Lardon was born in St. Cloud, Minnesota, and grew up with his two younger brothers in a three-bedroom, two-bath, brick home in the San Antonio, Texas, area. While money wasn't plentiful, the children had nice clothes to wear to school, and the family had two cars.

Lardon graduated in 1962 from Alamo Heights High School, located in one of the better school districts; he had been active in sports—football, basketball, and track—but his grades were unimpressive. "I was there to have fun. I did. I did not like school. I never learned to study properly. Therefore, I was memorizing everything. It just didn't work for any type of retention."

His best subjects were math and science; the worst, history and English. He attended San Antonio Junior College but left before graduating. Nonetheless, Lardon recommends college. "I once worked for a guy who once told his employees, 'The hell with college.' I would never do that. I was awfully fortunate to work for a company such as Southwest Airlines. They allowed me to do what I needed to do without four years of college. A lot of companies, though, think you have to have that piece of paper. I think education probably allows you to develop your abilities a little more."

Although his father helped him pay for college, he earned spending money by working as a lifeguard during the summer and at a gas station the rest of the year. After deserting college, he went to work full-time in management for a now defunct 70-store grocery chain between 1964 and 1969. Subsequent jobs included sales and food broker in addition to a brief stint as an investigator for a retail credit company. "I hated the job," he said of the credit company position. "It was insurance investigation—reporting on people's habits. I thought that was just way too nosy for me." He was particularly turned off because he was forced to tell insurance companies that people were doing some of the same things he was doing.

Lardon was married and divorced three times. "I don't believe there'll be a fourth," he chuckles. At least one of his ex-wives now works at Southwest Airlines, yet the two are on amicable terms.

He is not bitter. In fact, he's happy, largely because he always keeps a positive mental attitude. He blames money as a negative influence only in his first marriage. And that was because there was a shortage of it!

When Lardon was hired at the San Antonio station of Southwest Airlines, he lacked not only a college degree but also airline experience. "But it doesn't take a brain surgeon to load luggage on an aircraft." The benefits at Southwest Airlines at the time weren't much. Lardon earned a piddling $425 a month, paying $190 a month for rent and initially skimping even on necessities, such as car insurance. There *were* medical benefits and also pass privileges that come with the job; he could fly for free between Dallas and Houston. Occasionally, he could get an offline pass to go somewhere on another airline, but most other airlines, at the time, didn't recognize Southwest.

For the first five years at Southwest, Lardon lived largely month to month. But he loved the job. The initial group of employees had been unusually close-knit, meeting often for get-togethers at people's houses and for celebrations. "Rather than a place of employment, it was almost like a family atmosphere. A lot of times the husbands of customer service agents would come out on Fridays and Sundays and help us load bags when security wasn't as tight as it is now. They liked to hang out there because it was fun. We all got along very well."

Now, he boasts that his love for the company probably is the reason he missed only ten days because of illness in the 28 years he has been with Southwest. "I was able to learn all I could about the job on the station level. There were no boundaries. You could do anything you wanted to do."

Lardon, though not yet in the most prestigious job, originally enjoyed some major benefits. San Antonio was the smallest of the three initial stations operated by Southwest Airlines; and there wasn't much baggage to handle there. Originally, he was one of only about 20 employees stationed in San Antonio. "We had only seven flights a day to Dallas," he said, so he had a great deal of extra time to do other things. And there were no closed doors. Once, Lardon noticed a stack of checks on the station manager's desk. Having previously worked as a manager, he recognized them as "hot checks" from passengers who bought tickets. "I recognized the attachments and markings on the checks from the banks and I said, 'Why don't you let me do these things?'" The station manager was happy to have the assistance. After all, in the early days, Southwest had not hired a collection agency, so each of its three stations had to handle its own unpaid bills. In some cases, the accounts merely missed funds and checks had to be run back through the bank; in other cases, the accounts had been closed. "They had to be worked," Lardon said. "You do your best to find them. Some you had to write off."

Lardon said that in San Antonio he also learned how to sell tickets and work the operations end, taking boarding passes from passengers. He worked on the manager's report at the end of the month and learned how to do deposits.

It wasn't long before Southwest Airlines began revolutionizing the airline industry. Created June 18, 1971, with a mere three

Boeing 737 planes that served three cities—Dallas, Houston, and San Antonio—the airline, by year-end 1998, operated 280 planes and provided service to 53 airports in 52 cities in 26 states. Southwest has grown largely by shunning the computer reservation systems used by travel agents. Instead, it has offered low-fare, no-frills service while keeping a fierce grip on costs. Fortunately for Lardon, who had been in on the ground floor, the airline always has viewed its employees as a key ingredient to its success. But rather than paying the highest wages, it offered a generous profit-sharing program.

The company has always been a firm believer in promotion from within. That attitude, along with aggressive upbeat advertising, published reports have indicated, has prompted employees to go the extra mile for the company. In fact, the attitude has been cited as an integral force in the airline, once the nation's underdog but now posting profits for 26 consecutive years, including an industrywide downturn in the early 1990s. In 1999 the company reported $4.2 billion in operating revenues and $433.4 million in profits.

Lardon was specifically cited in the book *Nuts! Southwest Airlines' Crazy Recipe for Business and Personal Success* by Kevin and Jackie Freiberg (Broadway) for exemplifying the company's spirit in its early days. Forced to sell a 737 to keep the airline afloat in those early days, Southwest faced the prospect of being unable to meet its flight schedule. A shutdown of its San Antonio station was forecast for a week later. The key to the station's survival was restricting to ten minutes the time for a plane to pull into the gate, unload passengers, load up, and leave. "Most of us, not having an airline background, had no idea that we couldn't do this," Lardon is quoted as saying. "So we just did it."

There were two things never said by employees in the early days: "One, we can't do it; two, it's not my job." Even today, the company is known for its culture committees that organize employee get-togethers. Job interviews, published reports have indicated, often require an applicant to tell a joke. It's all part of the company's effort to promote good service and a healthy attitude to entice customers.

"What we are looking for, first and foremost, is a sense of humor," Chairman Kelleher told *Fortune* magazine in 1994. "We don't care that much about education and expertise because we can train people to do whatever they have to do. We hire attitudes." The philosophy has paid off.

Lardon says it wasn't long before he got a call from his department manager from Dallas asking if he'd like a job as assistant manager in Houston. "I think it was, overall, the good rapport we had when he came to San Antonio."

Lardon had taken the job at Southwest initially because it was all he could find. Deep down, though, he truly wanted to be in management, particularly because he already had had jobs in management before. In his new position, Lardon took over when the manager wasn't there. "I was in charge of the operations of the station," which involved working nights and weekends.

Then, in 1973 he was offered an opportunity to return to San Antonio—his hometown—as station manager. "I wanted to move up. The next progression was station manager—somewhere. At that point, there were just three cities open."

Lardon was aware of a potential opportunity because he knew that Southwest had petitioned for permission to serve the Rio Grande Valley at Harlingen Airport, near Brownsville. So he wrote a letter to his vice president asking to be considered as manager at that station if permission were granted. Lardon never heard back about that position, but a station manager position in San Antonio, where he never had expected an opening, soon became available. Lardon got that instead. "I'm pretty outgoing, I guess," Lardon admitted. "I think sometimes personality can take you further than your abilities. I've always liked people."

Lardon's indoctrination into the stock market came only when the airline underwent many stock splits. When he started accumulating stock in his profit-sharing plan, it didn't mean much to him. For about five years after Lardon began working at Southwest, he was busy making monthly payments to pay off the balances on his credit cards. So how could he possibly think about investing?

In fact, he says, a boss he had early on at Southwest once gave him what, he now reflects, would have been the greatest advice ever: sell everything you can and buy Southwest stock. Unfortunately, "I didn't have any money and didn't have anything to sell," Lardon says. "That would have been unbelievable advice!" Over the years, he did manage to buy a little extra stock in the airline.

Lardon moved to his current job in 1981, when he was offered more money. While it seems like a large department to manage, Lardon notes that his employees—flight attendants—are largely absentee employees. "They're in California doing their job," he said. It is largely on the basis of peer reports or reports from customers that he evaluates them. The key: "We try to hire the best person for the job." He says he looks for someone who is a self-starter and has a positive attitude.

Occasionally, he has to terminate people, generally the result of bad attitudes. "If you've got to terminate somebody, I don't care how much they deserve to be terminated, you're changing somebody's life. It certainly is a very difficult thing to do. I do what needs to be done and move on." Furthermore, "I'm just lucky to be able to recognize when I'm getting negative and tell myself that it's wrong."

As Lardon moved up the ladder and Southwest's stock began splitting, he began paying more attention to his investments. "It was about 1977 or 1978 that I started getting up there to where there was a little money," he reflected. The biggest nut was the profit-sharing stash.

Lardon always used the money in his account to buy company stock, which was, for many years, the only thing the company permitted him to do with it. More recently, the company began to allow investing in a series of mutual funds. Largely from inertia, though, Lardon just kept his money in the company stock. "I'm not sure it was a wise choice. It was more ignorance about the stock market. Rather than take a chance, I left it where it was." It turned out to be a good choice, although not necessarily the one that financial planners would have recommended. Generally, their advice is to not keep all your eggs in one investment basket—just in case.

For Lardon, though, the company stock provided the greatest growth of any of the other options. It was only in the beginning of 1999 that he decided to accept the wisdom of general financial planning sentiment and move all his profit-sharing money out of the company stock and into mutual funds.

"It's not based on anything I know," he stressed. Rather, he was getting older and wanted to assume a little less risk. "I didn't want to risk losing what I had. It's great if the stock is $20 to $30 a share. But if it's $2 when I retire, I've got problems. I've got enough. I think this way it's better protected." His 401(k) plan, which is a much smaller sum, remained invested in Southwest stock.

With the profit sharing, Lardon says, you can take control at 59½. If you leave the company earlier, you can take it with you provided you are 100 percent vested. Anyone who worked at Southwest Airlines since at least around 1975 has at least $1 million or $2 million in the company's profit-sharing plan, Lardon believes.

Not everyone, though, stayed the course. "In the middle years, I've seen people who got $50,000, $60,000, or $70,000 in profit sharing. They figure it's a lot of money and say, 'I'm leaving.' They'll go out and buy a huge sailboat, have no job, and sit around for a while. Then, that runs out." That's one mistake, Lardon says, he avoided despite an incomplete higher education. "Certainly they were looking for short-lived gain rather than long-term gain."

Lardon says his 31-year-old son Gary, also divorced, has come to work for Southwest Airlines, long known as one of the nation's most generous companies in its dealing with employees. (At this writing, Gary was a dispatcher.) But even if his son stays with the company for 28 years like his father, Lardon says he doesn't expect him to make out quite as well through profit sharing because there is now a bigger pie. Profits are being divided among close to 28,000 employees rather than the initial few. Also, the company has halted quarterly cash bonuses entirely, although cash from previous bonuses is permitted to be used to buy more Southwest stock. Lardon says he's not worried much, however, about the security of his son's future at Southwest.

As for himself, he takes a few three-day vacations and enjoys golf and sailing. "I don't know how much I spend a year on charities. Somebody'll have a drive going on for something almost every day here. I give a lot of money from that standpoint. I generally say, 'Don't even tell me what it is. Here's your money.'" Work remains one of his loves. In the last several years, he typically has worked 8 AM to 5 PM. There are days, though, when he'll work until 9 or 10 at night even though he probably doesn't need to.

Despite the fact that money is not a major worry, Lardon uses only an American Express credit card and pays cash for major purchases. Those debt-ridden days still haunt him, so he now avoids carrying balances altogether.

Lardon is not necessarily aiming for further advancement but rather looking toward his retirement. "I'm extremely happy at what I'm doing. I work for a wonderful lady. I can't imagine things being any better. I enjoy my job. I love the people I work with."

Even now, though, he doesn't consider himself a major investor. "I don't have the confidence I need in myself, or a stockbroker as far as that goes, to make a lot of money. I do have accounts at Merrill Lynch. They're doing a good job, but it's not all of my money either."

CHAPTER 16

MAYA ANGELOU
Poetry and Novels Earn Millions

Maya Angelou may be best known as a poet, a profession known to produce many a starving idealist. But the 71-year-old black artist, while no stranger to rough times, has been reported by *Forbes* as earning an unusually comfortable living—at least $4.3 million annually in 1996. More than $2 million comes in annually from royalties generated by her published books, *Forbes* reported. She gets another $100,000 or so from a lifetime appointment as a professor of American studies at Wake Forest University, a position she has held since 1981, in addition to some $40,000 for each public appearance. In 1995, when her speaking fees were just $30,000, *Forbes* noted, she earned $2 million a year from speeches. At this writing, her published books number more than 20.

Angelou makes her home in a 17-room Winston-Salem, North Carolina, mansion. She has been reported to have a staff of three full-time assistants and an art collection that includes works by well-known African American artists John Biggers, Romare, Bearden, Elizabeth Catlett, and quiltmaker Faith Ringgold.

And Angelou has said she thought success meant having an attache case and a pair of shoes and bags that matched! It is ironic that wealth has befallen this woman, whose best-selling autobiography, *I Know Why the Caged Bird Sings* (Bantam), showed disdain for the wealthy. "I find it interesting that the meanest life, the poorest existence, is attributed to God's will," she wrote in the book that in 1970 won a National Book Award. "But as human beings become more affluent, as their living standard and style begin to ascend the material scale, God descends the scale of responsibility at a commensurate speed." Her poem "Alone," *Forbes* notes, refers to millionaires needing doctors "to cure their hearts of stone."

How did Angelou get to be in the very financial position of those she had once seemed to despise? She won't talk about money, according to her assistant at Wake Forest University. Her literary agent, Helen Brann, of Bridgewater, Connecticut, through an assistant of her own, echoed the sentiment. An interview about money, the assistant said, affirming that she spoke both for Brann and Angelou, is not "tasteful."

But based on published reports, her financial success began after her work as a journalist and activity in the civil rights movement. A conversation with writer James Baldwin, she claims, helped inspire her to publish her autobiographical *I Know Why the Caged Bird Sings*. The book, says *Forbes,* spent six weeks on the *New York Times* best-seller list as early as 1970 and led to demand for her as a lecturer and speaker. That same book, as well as others she had written, dominated the *New York Times* best-seller list again after she read her poem, "On the Pulse of the Morning," at the presidential inauguration of Bill Clinton in 1993. In 1995, *Forbes* reported, *Caged Bird* alone brought in at least $300,000 in royalties, "not counting some 100,000 sold as required reading in schools."

Perhaps there's good reason for money to be a particularly difficult subject for Angelou. Early on, it had been a source of intense struggle. It had served as the quest that propelled her on a journey through scores of different career paths that are the subjects of her best-selling autobiographies. She was the first "Negro" to be hired as a conductor on the San Francisco streetcars. More recently, she indicated that her enormous achievement in obtaining the financial security she so diligently sought for herself and her son did not necessarily offer the most satisfaction. "Success is not always fame or fortune," she stressed to the *Chicago Tribune* in 1994. "Success is picking up that burden and keep on walking and not letting the pain trip you up."

It has been a long and tedious journey for Maya Angelou—even with the success and wealth she has attained. She may well have paid a stiff emotional price to earn the dollars that stemmed from her ability to move so many people so deeply. Divorced from at least two husbands who have formally been acknowledged, she was born Marguerite Annie Johnson. At the age of three, she and her four-year-old brother Bailey were shipped by train to live with their grandmother in heavily segregated rural Stamps, Arkansas. Her parents had divorced.

For most of her younger years, Angelou was brought up by her beloved but strict and religious grandmother, whom she affectionately called "Momma." Angelou hung out in her grandmother's general store with her brother and a crippled uncle, where the poverty-stricken black population, much of which tediously picked cotton for a living, had stopped on its way to and from work. No matter how hard the blacks worked, Angelou had observed painfully, they never quite earned enough to get themselves out of debt.

Angelou's grandmother actually was one of the few black people in town who owned property and was not on welfare during the Depression. Instead, she kept her business going by very astutely offering her customers, who saw their already piddling wages drop, the ability to barter with her for store items. Meanwhile, the black townspeople lived in constant fear that crime in the white community would be blamed—often unfairly and randomly—on one of them. As a child, Angelou was suffering pain at one time and endured the added abuse of being refused desperately needed treatment by a bigoted white dentist.

Although Angelou had initially speculated that her parents were dead—she and her brother often commiserated about their abandonment—she finally got to meet her father. A one-time doorman at the plush Breakers Hotel in Santa Monica, California, he paid a surprise visit to bring her and her brother to St. Louis, her birthplace, to live with their mother. There, her life took a dramatic turn.

At the age of seven or eight, Angelou was raped by her mother's boyfriend. Although he was convicted and sentenced to jail, he never served because he was found murdered shortly afterward. Thinking she was to blame, Angelou voluntarily stopped talking for almost six years until she was about 13. Instead, she silently observed everything around her, went to libraries, read everything she could, and excelled in school. Angelou has subsequently cited her period of muteness as the possible source of an unusually sensitive photographic memory that has helped make her one of the nation's most respected writers. "There isn't one day since I was raped that I haven't thought about it," she told the *Washington Post* in 1981.

Angelou has credited a Stamps resident, Bertha Flowers, with encouraging her, through poetry, to finally begin expressing herself with actual words. The encouragement was fruitful. In 1972 Angelou, who never went to college, received a Pulitzer Prize nomination in poetry for "Just Give Me a Cool Drink of Water 'fore I Die."

A *Washington Post* article, written in 1981 after the release of the fourth book in her autobiographical series, *Heart of a Woman*, portrayed Angelou then as financially comfortable. She had traveled widely and had lived in Egypt and Ghana. Published reports say she has received as many as 50 honorary doctorate degrees and is fluent in as many as eight different languages.

Her icon status, however, emerged largely after she was summoned by former Arkansas Governor Bill Clinton to write his presidential inaugural poem in 1993. The Clintons, she had reported, used to come to see her lecture or read poetry when he was governor of Arkansas. Her poem was written in six weeks specially for the Clinton event, which was of particular significance to the civil rights cause. Both Angelou, granddaughter of an Arkansas slave, and Clinton had grown up in Arkansas. Meanwhile, when Angelou was growing up in that state, its former governor, Orval E. Faubus, had refused federal orders to integrate the schools.

Angelou's poem for the inaugural also sparked a renewed interest in poetry, which *USA Today* reported had been given only about 17 percent of English class time in the eleventh and twelfth grades in 1989–1990. By 1996, April had been designated National Poetry Month, although in 1995, the year before the tradition began, poetry, art, and literature still reflected just 3.8 percent of all book purchases, the Book Industry Study Group reported in the *San Diego Union-Tribune*.

Angelou had received the presidential call that changed her life from Harry Thomason, cochairman of Clinton's inaugural committee, at the end of 1992. "I was bowled over," she told the *Washington Post*. "I did sit down." The goal of the poem was to convey a theme that has permeated many of her works: people are more alike than unalike. The six-foot woman wore an AIDS ribbon as she recited her poem on national television. Prior to that address, said the *Dallas Morning News,* she had received 400 letters a week. Afterward, she got 1,500 and was reported—at least in 1993—to have answered them all.

A week after she read her poem on TV, sales of her already successful book, *I Know Why a Caged Bird Sings,* shot up 500 percent. "We have gone to press with nearly 400,000 copies of all her books," said Stuart Applebaum, a spokesman for her publisher, Bantam Books. Random House, publisher of her hardcover books, had said at month's end after the inauguration that it sold more of her books in January than in all of 1992—an increase of 1,200 percent. Just after the inauguration, Bantam announced the printing of her inaugural poem in a commemorative paperback edition. The first printing was 50,000 copies compared with a 3,000 to 10,000 initial print run for a typical book. By the end of 1994, it was announced that 500,000 copies for the second volume of her autobiography, *Wouldn't Take Nothing for My Journey Now,* would be printed.

The success of Angelou's books and the inaugural poem helped fuel her steady advancement as a speaker. It was reported in 1998 that she earned $35,000 a speech, compared with $60,000 to $70,000 paid financial guru Peter Lynch. By 1999 a *Forbes* report had pegged her fee at $40,000. While the Border Voices Poetry Fair paid dozens of major poets $1,000 to $7,000 to appear at San Diego State University, Maya Angelou's fee was $25,000 for her reading scheduled for April 7, 2000, according to the *San Diego Union Tribune.*

Angelou's success built steadily on a unique mix of experiences on top of a core of heavy reading as a child, an insatiable appreciation for the arts, and a good education. She moved to San Francisco to be with her mother and graduated high school in 1945 at the age of 15. The following year she gave birth to a son. She had studied dance with Martha Graham, Pearl Primus, and Ann Halprin, and drama with Frank Silvera and Gene Frankel. In one of her early dance acts, "Al and Rita," she partnered with Alvin Ailey, who subsequently formed his own renown dance group, Alvin Ailey American Dance Theater. She sang in San Francisco at the Purple Onion, performing along with other popular acts that included comedienne Phyllis Diller. Through her California entertainment contacts, Angelou met jazz great Billie Holiday. She was exhilarated as she got to see the world on a 22-country tour sponsored by the U.S. Department of State in a production of *Porgy and Bess.*

Angelou's efforts to support herself and her son threw her into show business, the civil rights movement, and heavy travel. In New York, where she went to perform, she joined the Harlem Writers' Guild and served as coordinator of Martin Luther King's Southern Christian Leadership Conference when a vacancy arose. She was there during the days that the quest for civil rights helped revolutionize black culture. She befriended people like comedian Godfrey Cambridge, who was performing while driving a cab for a living, and her inspirational source, writer James Baldwin. She even performed at the famed Apollo Theater in Harlem.

It was during her performing days that she took the name Maya Angelou. She had already been nicknamed Maya by her brother, who frequently referred to her as "maya sister." "Angelou" reflected a French twist of her married name—"Angelos"—while she was in San Francisco.

For all the achievements in her life, though, there were major lows. An unwed mother at 16, Angelou was forced to support herself through a host of menial jobs, including stints as a Creole cook, cocktail waitress, and madam of a house of prostitution. Stonewalled by the white establishment when she was looking for a job, she subsequently got divorced from her first husband, who was white. She attributes that breakup largely to the fact that she forfeited her own independence in the relationship. Then, another relationship—not clear from her books that it was a legal marriage—also ended. In that case, the culprit may well have been naivety—about both money and faithfulness.

While working for the Southern Christian Leadership Conference, Angelou had been dazzled by Vusumzi Make, a representative of the Pan African Congress from South Africa. She and this freedom fighter discussed marriage, but although in one book she indicated that they never quite formalized it, subsequent references referred to her as "Mrs. Make."

Financial planners typically recommend that couples, prior to or, at the very least, during marriage or a similar live-in relationship, meet regularly to discuss finances. Angelou, though, admitted she was completely in the dark about Make's. The two lived in a luxurious New York apartment. But Angelou wrote that she never had any idea how much money they had or whether bills were paid. Her answer came when she arrived home one day to find sheriff's deputies nailing an eviction notice on the door of the apartment. The couple were ordered to be out of their apartment within 24 hours. Although she, her son, and Make subsequently moved to Egypt, money also seemed to disappear there, and she began to notice evidence of unfaithfulness. The two finally broke up, and Angelou found work as a journalist to support herself and her son.

Another marriage, this time to feminist Germaine Greer's ex-husband, Paul du Feau, a builder and writer who once posed as a nude centerfold for the *British Cosmopolitan,* also ended. The *San Francisco Chronicle* reported that Angelou subsequently left San Francisco because too much in that city reminded her of du Feau. "I would go into one of 'our' restaurants, and he would be sitting there with some other dame," she told the newspaper. "I couldn't handle it." She left the city in 1980, according to the *Chronicle,* after the ten-year marriage was over.

Angelou's beloved son, Guy Johnson, also an author and poet, had suffered a broken neck in a car accident when he was a teenager. Johnson recently published his first novel, *Standing at the Scratch Line,* which drew mixed reviews. Her brother had suffered a series of strokes, and she suffered further trauma when her son's ex-wife kidnapped her grandson, Colin, in 1981 from the home of her son, who had legal custody. Angelou, once again devastated by loss, hired private detective after private detective to track down her grandchild. In January 1985, the *Los Angeles Times* reported, she went so far as to remodel her home, adding a room for her grandson that sported a picture of Big Bird. Months later, the two were reunited after she issued an anonymous plea on Austin, Texas, television. The child's mother, Sharon Johnson, ultimately pleaded guilty to child stealing and was sentenced to five years' probation, the *Los Angeles Times* stated.

These incidents and the death of her mother and grandmother devastated Angelou. She took refuge in writing, but she never wrote at home, she reported. Her home was too "fixed up," and she worried she'd spend too much time straightening up and not getting her work done. Instead, she went to homes of friends, an apartment, and, more recently, a rented hotel room. She has said she starts work at 5:30 or 6 AM after taking everything off the walls, and typically works until midday. She brings with her a yellow legal pad, a Bible, a dictionary, *Roget's Thesaurus,* and a bottle of sherry.

Angelou has said she is a workaholic, but she refutes comments that she's a natural-born writer. "That's like saying you're a natural open-heart surgeon," she says. One page, she reports, might take her as long as a week or two to eke out. Her trademark yellow pad, she maintains, was an important outgrowth of a conversation with her voice teacher in San Francisco when she was younger. On telling him that she felt like she was going mad, the instructor advised her to write everything down. So she did. The yellow legal pad has been an important tool ever since.

It is clear from published reports that Angelou, wherever she speaks, commands a unique inspirational presence, merging her talents in poetry with her learned skills of drama and song. She constantly draws sold-out crowds and triggers standing ovations. Her autobiographies have been said to be significant and straightforward chronicles of the black woman in 20th-century society.

Sometimes, an artist's success can be fueled by controversy. People often buy a work to see what all the fuss is about. In the case of Maya Angelou, controversy might have been a middle name. It started with her political activism during the civil rights movement. Later on, the American Library Association, frequently cited her works as causes célèbres during its banned book weeks. Between 1990 and 1999, the association reports, her books had received close to 60 challenges—that is, complaints or requests asking that it reconsider offering the book. The most frequently challenged of Angelou's books, the organization says, is *I Know Why the Caged Bird Sings.*

Other complaints over the years have been filed against school systems that sought to put her books on reading lists or make them required reading. As recently as 1999, the Unity, New Hampshire, School Board voted to ban *Caged Bird* from the reading list for seventh and eighth graders. But it declined to ban the book from the library. Some parents, the Associated Press said, objected to passages in the book that discussed homosexuality and hermaphrodites as well as a description of Angelou's getting pregnant while an unmarried teenager. Often, though, school boards have stood firm in making the books required reading. Angelou now says that at least one of her books is required reading in virtually every school system.

Angelou, who has spoken before gay and lesbian rights groups, has also been a target of hate. In 1994 she canceled an appearance in Emporia, Kansas, after The Reverend Fred Phelps, a disbarred lawyer and antigay activist, led a protest against her appearance in Topeka with chants and obscenities. She indicated the cancellation came out of fear there could be violence at her next engagement as fans attempted to protect her. It was reported that Phelps and his backers had targeted Angelou because of her affiliation with President Clinton and the "left-wing liberal fringe."

Angelou also experienced criticism on her own turf—Wake Forest University. She stated publicly that if she is ever someone's teacher, she is that person's teacher for life. Nevertheless, one student, based on his report in *The American Spectator,* didn't exactly see it that way. He criticized the university's whopping expenditures on her annual appointment as an American Studies professor.

John Meroney, at the time a senior at Wake Forest and editor of the *Wake Forest Critic,* complained of her frequent absences. "Angelou's name and photograph appear year after year . . . in Wake Forest's admissions applications, its annual reports to trustees and alumni, and the alumni magazine—but she has no meaningful responsibilities at the university," he complained. "She collects an annual salary well into the six figures, yet presently teaches no classes and has no on-campus office. When I asked her about her salary in proportion to the time she spends in the classroom, she replied that those who raise such questions 'don't understand the politics of a university.' Angelou does: Wake Forest could hire four real professors with the money they're paying her!"

Angelou's schedule has been grueling, one report citing as many as 60 appearances in three months. News of an appearance by Angelou is often revered and her talks forever discussed and quoted. A commitment by her to attend a YWCA fundraiser in Spokane, Washington, motivated a comment in that city's *Spokesman-Review.* It is a "dream coming true," the newspaper said, "a reminder that many good things are happening here."

Published reports, though, indicate that Angelou has been known to cancel engagements. Sometimes, illnesses have been cited as the reason, but other cancellations have been made with no explanations whatsoever. Yet others have been called off simply as the result of a better opportunity. One group, the African Overseas

Union, in 1999 went so far as to file a suit against Angelou for failing to show up for a scheduled appearance at which it was supposed to honor her with an Order of Kilimanjaro in 1998. James C. "Clay" Crawford, Houston-based attorney for the nonprofit organization, contended that she refused to return its phone calls and letters. The canceled appearance, it reported, cost the nonprofit group $50,000 to $75,000. Again, Angelou declined to be interviewed. As this book went to press, the lawsuit was still not settled.

In 1992 the *New York Times* reported that not long after Angelou agreed to give a commencement speech at Sarah Lawrence College for what the school might have regarded as a slightly high fee of $10,000, Angelou called back to decline, stating she had discovered a prior speaking commitment "for considerably more than $10,000" to IBM. Two years later, she canceled a program in Buffalo for the second time in one year. Reason: She was to be working on a Steven Spielberg project. "The first time was understandable," Campus West Principal Michael O'Brien had told the *Buffalo News*. "This one is not quite so palatable." And a reporter for New York's *Village Voice*, Michael Musto, reported in 1998 that he was once instructed to call Maya Angelou "Doctor" before she stood him up for a scheduled phone interview.

One definite enhancement to Angelou's career has been a special relationship with talk-show czar Oprah Winfrey. The two met when Winfrey, as a broadcaster in Baltimore, requested a five-minute interview. Winfrey, also abused as a child, read *I Know Why the Caged Bird Sings*, she told the *Los Angeles Times* in 1996. It marked the "first time I encountered a book about a person who looked like, sounded like, and felt like myself. It was transforming to know that the life I was leading and could relate to so well was considered important enough to be written about," Winfrey wrote.

Winfrey is considered one of the best people any author could possibly know. The daytime talk show hostess, on her nationally broadcast television show, has started Oprah's Book Club. Each month, Winfrey recommends a book to her worldwide audience; the mere mention of a book title is known to send it onto bestseller lists.

Besides being a guest on the popular television show, Angelou's autobiography *The Heart of a Woman* was the book club's seventh pick and the first nonfiction book named to Oprah's coveted list.

Angelou's publisher, Bantam Books, eagerly took advantage of the honor. "Anticipating high book-buyer interest, Bantam Books is printing 1 million copies of the paperback edition," reported *Daily Variety* in 1997. Bantam planned to donate 10,000 copies to schools and libraries nationwide. And lucky Oprah viewers and Angelou readers were selected to go to Angelou's home for a pajama party. Participants were treated to free pajamas and a home-cooked meal prepared by Angelou, who is famous for her cooking. It was Winfrey who threw her good friend Angelou a star-studded 70th birthday party bash for some 150 friends, who cruised the Caribbean for a week and visited the Mayan ruins in Mexico.

Angelou has not been content to limit her accomplishments to writing poetry and books, and public appearances. She has directed numerous plays, was nominated for a Tony award in 1973 for her performance in *Look Away,* and was nominated for an Emmy award as best supporting actress for her performance in *Roots* in 1977. In 1971 she was the first black woman to have a screenplay produced as a film—*Georgia, Georgia.* Most recently, she directed the film *Down on the Delta,* which came in under budget before debuting in 1998 to mixed reviews. Angelou has also written children's books, produced and starred in a number of television shows, and has been inducted into the Horatio Alger Association. In 1998 she was inducted into the National Women's Hall of Fame.

Angelou hints that the rough roads that have made her such an inspirational poet and writer are not necessarily over. "What was the most difficult time in your life?" a *New York Times* reporter asked in 1998. "I'd have to say now," Angelou responded. "It's hard for me because I'm in New York and Betty Shabazz [the widow of Malcolm X] isn't here. We'd always be together when I was in New York." She also lost another best friend, writer Jessica Mitford. The hard part of life is "the absence of the beloveds," Angelou told the *Times.* "Some people who start with you go on before you to their other destinations."

CHAPTER 17

TIMOTHY B. AND KAREN SCHMIDT FABER

Couple Creates and Sells Personnel Business

Becoming independent and then losing that independence can sometimes be tougher than starting from scratch. The characters of Karen Schmidt Faber, 37, and Timothy B. Faber, 42, were tested to the maximum when they gave up their apartment to launch their own business. But they pulled through and now they're millionaires.

After graduating from the University of South Carolina, Karen spent two years working on her own before starting a temporary personnel agency with her husband-to-be. In the first year of that business, 1987, the couple, who had been earning combined salaries of over $100,000, took a massive pay cut to $18,000. "We had no lifestyle," said Karen, who had put her furniture in storage. She took her work clothes and dog and moved into the three-bedroom ranch house belonging to Tim's mother. Tim, who gave up a benefit-filled job at IBM, rented out his furnished condo because the start-up company left him with no money to pay the mortgage. He also moved into his mother's house.

The couple—not yet married—were living down the hall from one another and working out of their new 700-square-foot office. While both pounded the pavement and dropped off business cards at local companies, they managed to entice one woman to work for a modest $12,000 annually to field the phone calls.

The business venture paid off with sales growing to $35 million. In March 1996, the couple sold the company, U.S. Personnel, based in Columbia, South Carolina, to Staffing Resources Inc. in Dallas for $21 million, taking 21 percent of the sales price in stock.

Now the couple continue to live in their first home in Columbia with their two young children; and they also own a beach house valued at $1.5 million. While Karen stays home with the children working largely with nonprofit agencies, Tim is chairman of Paradyme Corporation, a human resources outsourcing company in Columbia. He also serves as CEO of Orthopaedic Solutions, a small orthopedics distribution company that he intends to "make very big." In early 1999, the couple had sold a small subsidiary of Paradyme Corporation, HR Technologies, to Ciber Inc. of Denver. Besides having $6.6 million in invested assets, they have an annual income of $120,000 generated by tax-free municipal bonds.

Once the Fabers met, they made a great team. Their family backgrounds coupled with careful planning and finance education helped prepare them for the challenges they faced. The couple's union came about by chance. Each had different but complementary skills—a factor Tim believes is important for any marriage to survive a husband-wife business venture.

Tim was born in Ann Arbor, Michigan, the son of a dentist, who subsequently divorced his mother, a registered nurse, and moved to Orlando. "I got to see him pay bills, write payroll checks, and collect checks from his patients and deposit them," Tim said of his childhood, noting he was fascinated by the process. "I remember, as a kid, playing at a desk in his office and watching him fill out deposit tickets. I thought people giving him money for his work was a pretty neat thing." Nobody in his father's family had been college educated, and his father had put himself through dental school. Tim found himself attracted to the business end of his father's practice and participated in business programs when he was in high school. "To me, it's just like playing a game," he said of business. "It is fun to win."

His parents had been doing well financially and lived comfortably, but his father never had been flamboyant with money. "Every couple of years we vacationed—usually inside the United States." When his parents divorced and he went to live with his mother, it was another story. Life became more difficult financially.

After high school, Tim joined the Air Force for four years and was stationed in South Carolina, attending the University of South Carolina at night. After the Air Force, he continued his education with some assistance from the GI bill. He had made a deal with his father, whereby his father would pay for all his graduate but not his undergraduate schooling. Tim decided not to pursue a graduate degree and instead worked his way toward an undergraduate degree. "I worked all the time—literally at nights and on weekends full-time. One semester, I carried 21 credit hours. In other words, I was going to school more than full-time. I didn't have too many dates, that's for certain." Finally, he graduated with honors in 1983 with a bachelor of science degree in computer science and a minor in finance. Tim had been on a mission. Most of his friends were getting out of college by the time he had left the Air Force, "so I couldn't get through school fast enough."

While in school, he processed checks on weekends for a savings and loan in Columbia and also worked in the computer room, monitoring the ATM network. During the last nine months of school, he interned for IBM. When he finally graduated, IBM offered him a job as a systems engineer; after two years, he became a senior marketing rep, and two years later, he met Karen.

Meanwhile, Houston-born Karen, an army brat, spent most of her life moving around. Each move provided her not only a brand new experience but new challenges. Following her father, she had moved to Louisiana, Georgia, Kansas, Arkansas, Germany, and Virginia before winding up at the University of South Carolina. About every three years she suddenly was uprooted and forced to cultivate new friends. The moving around, besides broadening her horizons, presented her with the task of introducing herself to groups of new and different people. Later in life, these conversations she was forced to initiate in each new location provided the perfect training ground for sales. It made cold calling on people she had never met before at local businesses easy and fun. She graduated the same year as Tim from the University of South Carolina with a bachelor of science degree in finance and marketing. The couple at the time had been merely acquaintances.

Karen had never thought much about money until her family moved to Charlottesville, Virginia. "You're always surrounded by people in the same boat as you," she said of army life. But

Charlottesville, with its high per capita income and sprawling plantations, was different. "For the first time I thought about all the kids driving cars. I never had a car until I graduated college and bought a car." A group of girls that lived in Charlottesville had grown up in the late 1970s and wore expensive preppy clothes that were always well coordinated. "I didn't have anything against them. It was just a different crowd from the group I hung out with. I never felt treated badly. It's just they were the rich kids and my group was the middle-of-the-road kids. Then there were kids on the other side that came from low-income homes, and I was just fine right in the middle."

When you have few material things, childhood experiences sometimes remain etched in your mind. Later on, when opportunities arise, those memories help you spot a window of opportunity.

While living in Charlottesville, a boyfriend of Karen's had gotten a new car. "That was a big deal. I thought I had a boyfriend who had some money. I can remember going to Hilton Head with his family and thinking, 'Omigosh. This is what people with money do.'" That wasn't necessarily the catalyst, though, that prompted her to make money. After college, Karen worked as a banker for four months in Houston; having trouble paying the bills, she took a night job with Norrell, a nationwide staffing company. She subsequently worked in marketing with Temps & Company in Washington, D.C., and moved to South Carolina to set up an office in Columbia.

When she renewed her acquaintance with Tim, she was a regional vice president visiting IBM, where Tim was working. Hoping to get IBM to hire temporary employees, she stepped off the elevator onto the wrong floor. It was a fateful step. As she paused to ask the receptionist for directions, Tim, who had remembered sharing some finance classes with Karen, recognized her. "We waved and said, 'Hi,'" Tim said. Although the couple had graduated the same year, they hadn't seen each other in four years.

A series of meetings started both their business and personal relationship. First, they ran into each other at a bar the night they met at IBM. "It was a total coincidence!" Tim said. "We actually stopped and spoke at this bar. Then she went on her way and I went on my way. I was with a buddy, and we went into another bar a couple of doors down and ran into her again. That was the third time the same day. I got her phone number that time!"

Tim called her the following week, and they met downtown near where they both worked. "We literally talked about business the entire time. During the conversation, I asked her if somebody came to her with the money, would she be interested in starting her own business."

It was a strange question—particularly for a first date. However, it was one the two both wound up taking very seriously. Karen was taken aback. But the idea attracted her. "I said yeah, but I'll never have that kind of money," Karen recalled.

The self-reliance the couple learned as children paid off. So did the finance classes. The couple decided to take the risk. They used their life savings, convinced investors to help, and survived with flying colors.

Tim believes there are two ways to become wealthy. You can earn a large salary or make money for yourself. "The probability of making a lot of salary for someone else is pretty low unless you're a senior executive or successful surgeon. The highest probability is by doing something on your own."

Tim was a heavy researcher and had always been motivated to start his own company. He had been reading about the staffing industry, which Karen said, "I knew was very fast-growing." Karen, who Tim says wanted to go off on her own, had already done much of the financial work as a prerequisite for opening offices for the company she had worked for. Within seven months, they opened U.S. Personnel.

And the money? The whole time Tim had been at IBM, he had been a fanatical saver. He always had contributed the maximum to his 401(k) plan and the maximum to his stock purchase plan. "At IBM, they average the price of stock for over the quarter and give you a 15 percent discount off that price. So if the price of the stock were $50 a share, they'd give you a 15 percent discount off of that price. You could buy up to a certain percentage of your salary."

The company also had an automatic deduction type of savings plan in which Tim always participated. "I didn't need a lot to live on. When I graduated, I still lived in the apartment I had in college. The rent was $220 a month, and I had a roommate, so I paid $110 per month plus utilities. I didn't have a car payment. I was still driving the car I had through college."

Once Karen agreed to the business idea, the couple met again. "We had to identify what the cost was going to be. We started putting together business plans and ran the financials over and over again," Tim said. The couple determined the business would cost $55,000 to start up, and they contributed between $30,000 and $35,000 themselves. "We got $20,000 from my brother and dad, her grandparents, and friends, who put up $1,000, $2,000, or $3,000," he said.

Karen says one special investor, who put up $5,000, was an English professor who had been a retired navy captain. Because her father had a similar background, she had run into him often at the officer's club, and they had become good friends. "He's like a grandfather to me. When we started U.S. Personnel, I talked to him about it."

The retired captain's return on his initial investment, according to Karen, was at least $500,000. Now he travels a great deal and is careful to send her postcards from wherever he is. The post-cards always carry the following closing message, "Thanks for making this trip possible." "He was a guiding factor in college and one of the people I never wanted to let down," Karen said. "If I had lost that money, I would have felt terrible!"

Karen credits the heavy planning the couple did with paving their way to success. But even the best-laid plans don't always go the way people hope. "If we had it to do again," she said, "we would probably plan even more."

Dividing the duties, Tim says, was a no-brainer. "I didn't know anything about the staffing business," so that was Karen's bailiwick. On the other hand, Tim handled the accounting, financial, and legal end of the business. Because the company initially had no money coming in, he retained his job at IBM between the fall of 1987, when the company started, through mid-December, when he began working full-time at U.S. Personnel and both started marketing and selling. Through the startup of the business, the two became romantically involved and married in June 1989.

Fortunately for Karen, sales came easily—critical to a start-up company that had no business whatsoever.

Tim says his unique experience with both his father's small, one-person entrepreneurial shop and IBM was invaluable. Even though U.S. Personnel was a medium-sized regional company, its training program, for example, was competitive with its largest competitors internationally, thanks to the IBM influence. "There were speakers, video tapes, and slides. There also were class photos, bowling trips, awards, T-shirt giveaways, and trips out for pizza and beer. People walked away from the training programs knowing what they were supposed to do. I saw competitors grow up in small businesses, but it would take them years and years to think of this stuff," Tim said.

Despite all the planning, the first year was a close call.

U.S. Personnel had been off to a good start until three weeks after the doors opened. The stock market crashed, stunning potential clients. Many businesses were fearful of laying out money because they didn't know what the repercussions would be. "We didn't have any business to lose, so we just kept on marketing," Karen said. "We were marketing maniacs."

She'd take a stack of business cards, a map of the city, and start looking for office buildings. "We would go out and drop off business cards with receptionists and find out who the decision makers were," Karen said. Then, she would call the decision makers to ask if they had received the card and if they had five minutes to talk about her company. "You'd build a relationship, send them a note, and invite them to lunch."

But the stock market crash wasn't the only thing that hindered efforts to get business. In January 1987, Greenville, where the company started, was hit with a 14-inch snowstorm. "I woke up in the morning and it was snowing," Karen said. "My car had bald tires. I can remember trying to get to the office. Nobody went to work for a week." Schools were closed for almost two weeks.

Without people working, a temporary personnel office couldn't function. "I was motivated by fear after that," Karen said. She began spending entire days going on sales calls with little breaks in between appointments. As a result, business started picking up, but their troubles weren't over. In the temporary personnel business, employees are paid on an hourly basis. On the other hand, clients who hire them often don't pay the agency for 30 to 60 days. It's a common problem that can prove devastating if a business is unprepared. In a sense, the couple found that they had overmarketed. "We got so many orders, the hours we were billing to clients was skyrocketing." But even though the business had started soaring, the couple was unable to find a bank that would grant them a loan to tide them over until their clients paid up. "We were a new start-up business and had no assets," Karen explained. Banks, it turned out, only wanted to lend to people who already had money.

Finally, a small Greenville bank agreed to give them a $15,000 term loan, which is just what they needed. The couple immediately put the money in the bank. They began running out of cash and thought they'd be forced to tap it. The day before they might otherwise have had to take that dreaded move, however, they were surprised by a $17,000 check from Michelin, the tire manufacturer. Michelin just happened to have its North American headquarters in Greenville and had been a loyal client. "By the end of the first year, we made a $95,000 profit, which we used to open our second office in Columbia," Karen said.

The company hit its first-year projections exactly. From there, the growth was uphill, and the company diversified its staffing services. By the time the company was sold, it had 19 locations in 7 states.

For a business to be successful, hard work goes without saying; skill and education often help too. But the couple credit much of their success to careful planning and their pumping profits back into the company. Critical elements for the business start-up were a cash flow analysis for a year and a business plan. The couple also drew up brochures in advance. "A lot of people start a business and don't do enough planning," Karen said. "Most businesses run out of money." Also, she said, too many people are afraid to take risks and sacrifice. They are simply unwilling to live a year the way the Fabers initially did—having no lifestyle and earning $18,000 annually. For seven months, Karen had a mere $13,000 to live on.

Tim agrees that the growth of the company was spearheaded by the fact that the couple took very little in salary and chose to reinvest the bulk of the money back into the business. "One day we woke up and said we can actually pay ourselves some money now. We don't have to put it into the company." The company became an Inc. 500 company in 1992 and 1993 and won the U.S. Chamber of Commerce Blue Chip Initiative Award in 1994.

Did the Fabers' hard-earned new wealth change them? Did they go wild and spend it all as people who come into a fortune often do? If you met the Fabers, you would think they're your average middle-class neighbors. Although the couple's net worth had grown, Tim says he didn't start feeling wealthy until 1995 or 1996. "That's when we realized that if we wanted to, we could pay ourselves $1 million or $2 million a year and the company still could make money," he said. "That's when it hit. We didn't do that though. We kept putting money back into the company—primarily because we wanted it to get bigger and bigger and bigger."

For Karen, the realization that the couple had plenty of money didn't dawn on her until they actually sold U.S. Personnel. "I still don't feel wealthy," she said. "We're very lucky."

She acknowledged that she never thought she would own a beach house, which she still considers a luxury. "For all those years, we had a great net worth and no cash. We just didn't pay ourselves that much money until we agreed to sell."

Karen says her parents taught her some valuable lessons through their own sacrifices. Her mother, although graduating fifth in her high school class, didn't go to college. Instead, she helped put her husband through college. "They bought me everything I absolutely needed but very little of what I just wanted. I didn't go without food or shoes. I'm trying to do that with my kids."

At this writing, Karen is president of Children's Unlimited, a nonprofit adoption agency for special needs children that the state can't place. She is also on the board of Paradyme Corporation, does volunteer work for the University of South Carolina, and had served on the board of directors of First Bank, Beauford, South Carolina, which had just been sold. Tim is president-elect and on the board of the South Carolina Philharmonic.

Karen drives a Ford Expedition; Tim, a BMW sedan. They're in their original home, on which they've built an addition, which Tim estimates is worth about $450,000. They also have a sailboat.

Tim says he doesn't believe he's living very extravagantly, and Karen, he adds, needs very little. They don't live as well, for example, as a very good friend who has an 8,000-square-foot home with "a weight room, media room, a couple of dens, and a 600-square-foot playroom for the kids," Tim says. One of their homes is attractively located on the beach. The couple maintain their same friends, and life has changed very little, although they have chartered a jet once in a while for the family, and they might travel more than the average family.

Karen says she has more flexibility in her life. Although she originally had stayed on as a vice president for Staffing Resources, the company that acquired U.S. Personnel, she stopped working daily in May 1997 and took up tennis. "Once my little boy is in kindergarten and this Orthopaedics Solutions is doing well, I'd like to do something with that. I don't see myself having a lot of free time."

Tim says that his money has allowed him to concentrate less on the money and more on the sport of winning on his deals. "In October 1998, I really got to the point where I was completely retired. By the end of November, I had bought a minority interest in Orthopaedics Solutions. That's how it is with me. Once I get out of one thing, I can't wait to get into something else."

He says that he has learned some valuable business lessons along the way. For one thing, when you become wealthy enough, it can be more profitable to invest in your own selection of small companies that might either be acquired or go public than it is to go through a stockbroker.

"When you get to the point where you're making significant investments in the stock market, be your own venture capitalist. The advantage for me is I can make investments in companies at early stages. Granted, some are going to fall on their faces, but the ones that make it big are going to make it so big!

"To take $10,000 and get a couple hundred thousand out in a couple of years, you've got to have some serious luck in the stock market."

It's important, though, to do a lot of homework to invest this way. To find good potential investments, Tim suggests notifying all the accounting firms you've ever dealt with to let them know you're interested, contacting local venture capital groups, and notifying your attorneys.

Tim learned another major lesson when he sold one company because the couple felt there was an opportunity to increase its value faster. "It's been a couple of years, and we're still working on increasing that value," he said. "We have a substantial amount tied up in that investment and it's not liquid, which is a problem. We can't use it for other opportunities." The sale was to a private company that intends to become a public company. "Knowing what we know now, I would have chosen to sell it to a company that was already public." To have an interest in a publicly traded company, he said, at least provides liquidity. "The value might drop, which is a financial risk. But you know you could trade those shares."

Now, he says, the couple has 70 percent of their assets in illiquid investments. "I would prefer to have no more than 30 percent in illiquid assets and keep it that way. My investment horizon is now very short as a result of going through this transaction."

Tim's February 1999 sale of Paradyme HR Technologies was to a company traded on the New York Stock Exchange. Paradyme grew from a small professional employer organization that had been part of U.S. Personnel and that the couple kept and recapitalized. "We grew that company and made several acquisitions," Tim said. In 1998, its sales were $190 million. Tim says he would advise any investors who have made a lot of money and are seeking to grow their wealth to take 50 to 75 percent of their money and put it in something "very, very safe. Take the rest of it and do it again." Keep doing that, he advised.

Even though investments have enormous potential, he said, it doesn't pay to be illiquid when you could be creating immediate income simply by investing in municipal bonds.

Although wealth hasn't changed the Fabers as people, they admit that the way certain other people see them has changed. Dealing with that hasn't been easy.

Tim attributes the change in others' treatment largely to a newspaper article that noted they gave $1 million to the University of South Carolina's business school. "I had breakfast before I chatted with you," Tim said. "Somebody wanted me to buy into part of a bank. Then there was someone who wanted me to give to the Boy Scouts, and someone wanted me to sponsor a golf tournament."

He admits it's very tough to say no to people. "At some point in time, it becomes ridiculous. You have to identify functions you're going to support with a lot of zeal. I can't tell you how many times I've heard it's *only* $1,000."

After the couple sold U.S. Personnel, some people who didn't know them well acted as if they had hit the lottery. Close friends quickly corrected the insinuation, pointing out how hard the couple had worked. "It was a little irritating," Tim said.

Karen said that when the article about their University of South Carolina donation appeared in the paper, people started treating her differently. "It's sad," she said. "All of a sudden, I got calls from people I hadn't talked to in years—kind of touching base—not asking for anything. Everybody is trying to guess how much you have, not that anybody ever asks."

Karen says she has some concerns about how the money will affect her children. "I don't want my children growing up thinking they don't have to work for what they're going to get. I want to get them everything they need and just a little of what they want. I don't want them thinking of our family as wealthy. But because I worry about it, I think I'll be OK with it."

EPILOGUE

Now that we've told you how a number of ordinary people—and not so ordinary people—have become wealthy, let's figure out what we can learn. After all, once you have the money you need, most of your problems will be solved, right? Well, not exactly.

Forbes has reported that people who pursue money as their central goal are not necessarily in the greatest shape in other ways. They are more prone to behavioral problems and physical ailments, according to a six-year study by Richard Ryan and Timothy Kasser across 13 countries.

Psychologist Olivia Mellan, in her book *Money Harmony*, (Walker and Company, New York) also stresses that "money does not equal happiness, love, power, freedom, self-worth, or security. Money equals dollars and cents."

In a survey of 49 of the richest people listed by *Forbes*, 37 percent reported their happiness levels were less than average, according to an ABC TV special report on "The Mystery of Happiness."

What's wrong in the lives of these people—if not the lack of money? Try these bugaboos that experts report tend to ruin the lives of persons who are well-off financially: isolation; the inability to listen; pressures of being in the public eye; and neglect of family because of busy schedules. Could any of these factors be keeping you from enjoying the true pleasures of the money you already have?

One thing is for sure: Relationships are important. Much research indicates, for example, that married people are less likely than single people to die from strokes, accidents, flu, tuberculosis, and various forms of cancer. Perhaps it's the closeness of a relationship rather than the written contract that's responsible.

Other factors that researchers have pegged as more important to your emotional well-being than the amount of money you have include independence, having an important purpose in life, and a good sense of humor.

So what can you do to make certain that you are counted among both the financially well-off and the happy?

Examine whether your perspective on money is a balanced one. If not, make a list of ways you might change.

If all your money is creating a lack of time in your life, list what functions or affairs you might stop attending this year. If you desire relationships, determine what activities you can participate in—possibly in the community—to start cultivating quality friends.

Could it be important to spend more time with friends or family members? Maybe it's time to pick up the phone.

If you're among the monied people who are feeling worthless, perhaps doing much-needed volunteer work is an option. Also, determine whether you're sharing enough jokes and good humor with enough people.

Meanwhile, if you're scoring well in the emotional part of your life but ignoring your money a little too much, perhaps you need to consider taking a more active role in your financial affairs.

More people today are achieving financial success. In 1998, 4.6 million households had a net worth of at least $1 million—up from 2.9 million in 1995, according to the Federal Reserve Board's Surveys of Consumer Finances. How do these people do it? Their motivation comes from within. In some cases, it was the desire merely to make ends meet. In others, it was an effort to be independent. What they did do is take advantage of opportunities because they wanted to better their life.

Authors Thomas J. Stanley and William D. Danko, authors of *The Millionaire Next Door* (Longstreet Press), found that 86 percent of millionaires are first generation. In other words, they did it on their own. The authors also found that the average millionaire is a 57-year-old married male with three children.

While, unfortunately, there is no precise formula for making $1 million, there are some common themes in this book that seemed to run throughout the stories we heard.

- The millionaires we interviewed had strong encouragement from at least one family member. In the case of Chi Chi Rodriguez, it was his father who made him realize from a very young age that he would be successful. Judy Walker credits her mother and grandmother for supplying encouragement; for Del Hedgepath, it was his mother; and for Fran Kelly, it was both parents.

- Many of the millionaires we found were especially challenged in some way as a child. The experiences, instead of sending our millionaires cowering into a corner, made them stronger and helped mold their abilities to overcome adversities. David Geffen and Lisa Renshaw were bullied as children. And Dal La Magna, one of five children, learned when he was young that he'd have to get anything he wanted himself.

- Those who became millionaires set some type of goal. That goal, as we said earlier, was not always to make money. Sometimes, as in the case of Humberto Cruz, there were a series of goals. The first for him was to put food on the table and then remove a high-rate mortgage on his house. In the cases of Dennis Lardon and Scott Oki, the initial goal was as basic as finding a job—a simple goal many of us already may have had. They just happened to choose the right employers at the right time.

- Many had the inner strength to make considerable sacrifices—although not always for dramatically long periods, maybe merely a year or two. For Humberto Cruz it was the two years it took to pay down his mortgage. Timothy and Karen Faber toughed it out for a year before their company started turning a profit. Lisa Renshaw lived in a parking garage for three years before her business took off.

- Many were unafraid to take risks—whether leaving money in the volatile stock market like Dennis Lardon and Scott

Oki or starting a business in what might have seemed an impossible situation such as Lisa Renshaw, Jay Thiessens, or Marvin Roffman. Dal La Magna's risk was accruing mounds of credit card debt.

- Often, these millionaires had a unique ability to sell people on new ideas or to manage well. In some cases, such as the Jakubowskis and Humberto Cruz, management of the business involved family members. In others, a unique brand of business management fostered the growth of a company— for example, the cases of Jay Thiessens, David Geffen, Dal La Magna, Joe Dudley, and Lisa Renshaw.

- All of them read a lot or took aggressive steps to learn from others. Joe Dudley went so far as to encourage reading groups at his company. Del Hedgepath—although he never finished college—admits he read many books several times. And Jay Thiessens, even though unable to read, learned from audio or video books and seminars.

- Our millionaires followed their passions regardless of what other people said or thought. Although David Copperfield's parents would have liked him to become a doctor, he focused on becoming a magician from an early age. Maya Angelou was determined to perform and write; ultimately, all her loves and skills came together to create a unique breed of talent. Scott Oki loved computers and accounting and accepted a job with Microsoft even though the salary was not the greatest. Marvin Roffman, by firmly standing his ground over a negative analysis of Donald Trump's casino business, wound up in his own successful business.

- None of these millionaires like personal debt. Even Dal La Magna, who grew up in a household where personal debt was commonplace, acknowledges debt has drawbacks. Humberto Cruz's road to wealth actually began by paying off a mortgage. Dennis Lardon, even though a multimillionaire, reports he sticks with one charge card that he pays off monthly. And Lisa Renshaw was working to develop homes so that she could live in her own new home mortgage free. A key to Judy Walker's business success in buying homes and fixing them up: being able to offer troubled homeowners hard cash.

- All had the ability to bounce back from failures and keep on going. Despite the difficult times, they didn't give up.

We hope these profiles inspire you to learn even more from the significant people in your life and to become more financially successful at whatever it may be that you choose to do.

REFERENCES

Chapter 1: Del Hedgepath

Fussell, James A. "The Look of Loot Is Changing as More Folks Cash in with Savings and Investing." *Kansas City Star*, 13 April 1997, G1.

Meyer, Gene. "Landlord Should Start Diversifying Assets; Hitting $1 Million Milestone Will Mean Taking Different Risks." *Kansas City Star*, 12 Feb. 1995, F8.

Chapter 2: Juan "Chi Chi" Rodriguez

Berkow, Ira. "Golf: At the Head of the Senior Class." *New York Times*, 5 July 1987, sec. 5, p. 1.

"Chi Chi Rodriguez Tees Up America's New Year Celebration." *PR Newswire*, 12 Oct. 1994.

Chi Chi Rodriguez Youth Foundation Web page at <*www.chichi.org*>.

Cortez, John P. "Julius Keeps the Score for Sports Promotions; Leading Marketers Rely on Consultancy's Numbers." *Advertising Age*, 1 June 1992.

Diaz, James. "Chi Chi has a last laugh—Chi Chi Rodriguez was once best known for his one-liners, but now his unparalleled success on the Senior tour is no joke." *Sports Illustrated*, 23 Nov. 1987, 38.

Friedman, Jack. "At 51, Chi Chi's Still Laughing; Now It's on the Way to the Bank." *People,* 21 Sept. 1987, Jocks section, p. 51.

The Golf Talk Live, "Chi Chi Rodriguez." Cable News Network Inc., 1999.

McConnell, Doug, and John Davis. "Flu Bug Bites Rodriguez, but He'll Play." *Phoenix Gazette,* 1 April 1993.

McCoy, Doris Lee. "Golf's Good Samaritan; Chi Chi Rodriguez." *Saturday Evening Post,* March 1989, 62.

Murray, Jim. "Jim Murray: He Always Has a Crowd Rooting for Him to Win." *Los Angeles Times,* 4 March 1993, Sports section, part C, p. 1.

Pate, Russ. "Some Golf Ads Click; Others Clink." *Adweek,* 22 April 1991.

Phalon, Richard. "Big Bertha's Sweet Spot." *Forbes,* 11 May 1992, Companies/Industries section, Up & Comers, p. 130.

Radosta, John. "At 45, Rodriguez Remains the Blithe Spirit of Golf." *New York Times,* section A, p. 12.

Rude, Jeff. "Take a Look at Many Sides of a Golfer Named Chi Chi." *Dallas Morning News,* as published in the *Houston Chronicle,* 7 June 1992, Sports section, p. 4.

Serafin, Raymond, and Cleveland Horton. "Golf Boom Fits Carmakers to a Tee." *Advertising Age,* 15 July 1991, News, p. 17.

"Some Pro Golfers Show the Touch—Midas Touch," compiled by Robert Fachet, *Washington Post,* 9 Nov. 1994, Sports section, p. F2, Fanfare.

Stancavage, John. "Staking Out Your Strategy Quick, Short-Term Gains Key to Stock Contest." *Tulsa World,* 11 Jan. 1998.

Straud, Ruth. "Special Report; Marketing to Hispanics." *Advertising Age,* 13 Feb. 1989, S-9.

Symonds, William C., with Brenton Welling. "The Boom in Golf as Baby Boomers Hit the Links." *Business Week,* 27 March 1989, 76.

Symonds, William C. "Golf's Old Greats Are Really Swinging Again." *Business Week,* 26 June 1989, 122.

Chapter 3: Jay Thiessens

"Reader's block. Jay Thiessens made millions, but one thing he couldn't make; any sense of the words he saw on a page." *People,* 9 Aug. 1999, 81.

Chapter 4: Francis "Fran" J. Kelly III

Farrell, Greg. "As Clients and Consulting Firms Hire MBAs, the Advertising Industry Evaluates Its Recruiting Policies." *Adweek*, 2 June 1997.

"Meet the New Millionaires." *Adweek*, 20 July 1998, New England edition.

Chapter 5: Judy Walker

Edwards, Audrey. "How I Made a Million: Savvy Sisters Tell You What You Need to Know to Make Your Financial Dreams a Reality." *Essence*, October 1998, 102.

Gargaro, Paul. "County Is Hot for Homes." *Crain's Detroit Business*, 7 July 1997, News section, p. M-22.

Hymer, Dian. "Agents Don't Get Rich Quick." *Miami Herald*, 17 Jan. 1999, H2.

"Integration." *The Columbia Encyclopedia*. 5th ed. Columbia University Press, 1993.

Mirick, Adam. "Metro Area House Prices Climb 11.4%; Increase, 3rd Largest in Midwest, Beats Mutual Fund Return." *Detroit News*, 13 Aug. 1998, Business section, p. B1.

Chapter 6: David Geffen

Albo, Amy. "The Benefactor 100." *Worth Online*, April 1999.

Dutka, Elaine. "Business: Little Shop of Winners at David Geffen's Entertainment Mill, the Hits Keep Coming." *Time*, 12 Dec. 1988, 60.

Goodman, Fred. *The Mansion on the Hill*. New York: Vintage Books, 1998.

Gubernick, Lisa, and Peter Newcomb. "The Richest Man in Hollywood." *Forbes*, 24 Dec. 1990, 94.

"Obituary of Laura Nyro, American Singer-Songwriter Who Found Success in the 1960s with Compositions That Were as Unconventional as Her Appearance." *Daily Telegraph*, 15 April 1997, 25.

Orwall, Bruce. "Observers Second-Guess Disney Handling of Feud." *Wall Street Journal*, 9 July 1999, sec. B, p. 3.

Seabrook, John. "Profile: The Many Lives of David Geffen." *New Yorker,* 23 Feb. and 2 March 1998, 108.

Sheff, David. "Playboy Interview: David Geffen." *Playboy,* Sept. 1994, p. 51.

Singular, Stephen. *The Rise and Rise of David Geffen.* Birch Lane Press, 1997.

Weinraub, Bernard. "David Geffen, Still Hungry." *New York Times,* Section 6, p. 28.

Chapter 7: Paul and Cheryl Jakubowski

Tobias, Andrew. "Do You Know Your Net Worth?" *Parade Magazine,* 14 Feb. 1999, 13.

Chapter 8: Joe L. Dudley Sr.

Dudley, Joe L. Sr. *Walking by Faith.* Executive Press, 1998.

Glascock, Ned. "'Slow' Student to Millionaire, Joe Dudley Willed His Success." *The News and Observer* (Raleigh, NC), 13 Dec. 1998, B1.

Hennessee, Melody. "Millionaire Finds Success in More Than Money." *The Herald* (Rock Hill, SC), 27 Sept. 1998, State section, p. 11B.

"Joe Dudley: Head of a Growing Empire." *Los Angeles Sentinel,* 9 July 1992, C-4.

McCauley, Byron. "Expanding Horizons." *Greensboro News & Record,* 3 April 1989, sec. C, p. 10.

Narvaez, Alfonso A. "S.B. Fuller, Door-to-Door Entrepreneur, Dies at 83." *New York Times,* 28 Oct. 1988, sec. B, p. 7.

Sellmeyer, Sheri. "Dudley Does Right." *Business-North Carolina,* June 1989, sec. 1, p. 74.

Times Wire Services. "S.B. Fuller; Door-to-Door Cosmetics Firm's Founder." *Los Angeles Times,* part 1, p. 30.

Chapter 9: Dal La Magna

Bard, Bernard. "Saga of a 'Compulsive Capitalist'": Fail, Fail, Fail, Fail 'til You Succeed." *New York Post,* 29 Sept. 1987.

Bowers, Brent. "Small Business." *Wall Street Journal,* 22 Nov. 1991, R4.

Byrne, John A. "The Saga of Tweezerman." *Forbes,* 13 Sept. 1982, 72.

Byrne, John A. et al. "Class Reunion: What a Long, Strange Trip It Has Been for the Harvard B-School's Class of 1970." *Business Week,* 18 June 1990, 160.

Burke, Rose Marie. "Small Business Winners and Losers." *Wall Street Journal,* 16 Oct. 1992.

Croke, Karen. "Profile: Dal LaMagna 'Tweezerman' Groomed for Success." *(New York) Daily News,* 5 July 1987, Business section, p. 4.

D'Antonio, Michael. "The Newsday Interview with Dal LaMagna: "It's Time to Take a Breath and Give Back." *Newsday,* 1 Oct. 1996, A41.

Fee, Gayle, and Laura Raposa. "Inside Track; Reunited Cowsills May Net a Global Comeback." *Boston Herald,* News section, p. 8.

Fresco, Robert, and Randi Feigenbaum. "Millionaires: Who Has Attained That Once-Elusive Goal? 15% of Nassau Households, 6% of Suffolk." *Newsday,* 7 July 1997, A4.

Hadrick, Celeste, and Ken Moritsugu. "Backroom." *Newsday,* 12 June 1997, A32.

Lombardi, Frank. "Name-Calling Battle in 3D C.D. Democrat LaMagna Seeks King's Throne." *(New York) Daily News,* 27 Oct. 1996, Suburban section, p. 1.

Long, Irving. "Around the Island/Politics & Power/It's Not Tweezerdum Against Tweezerdee/King and 'Tweezerman' Have Sharp Differences." *Newsday,* 5 June 1996, A25.

Skenazy, Lenore. "He's a Good Man in a Pinch." *(New York) Daily News,* 15 March 1999, 31.

"Tweezerman Revisited." *Forbes,* 23 Sept. 1985, 14.

Young, Monte R. "Campaign '96/Dems' LaMagna: Groomed to Lead." *Newsday,* 23 Oct. 1996, A6.

Chapter 10: Lisa G. Renshaw

Chiu, Yvonne. "Looking for a Place to Park in D.C.; Metro Contract Puts Baltimore-Based Penn on Road to Expansion," *Washington Post,* 14 Aug. 1995, F12.

Corey, Mary. "No Parking for Parking Executive." *Baltimore Sun,* 11 Aug. 1991, H1.

Davids, Meryl. "Making a Million Before You're Thirty." *Cosmopolitan,* 1 May 1996, 214.

Gulliver, Dave. "Park It Right Here, Buddy . . ." *The Capital* (Annapolis, MD), 22 March 1994, A8.

Kercheval, Nancy. "Parking Profits." *Warfield's,* February 1991, sec. 1, p. 49.

Mullaney, Timothy J. "Linthicum Parking Firm Gains $4.3 Million Pact." *Baltimore Sun,* 26 Feb. 1994, 16C.

Parker, Rich. "Lisa Renshaw/She Made Her Dream Come True." *Parking,* January 1993, 33.

"Renegades; Harassed and Scorned, They Did It Their Way—and Won; Innovators." *Success,* February 1990, 30.

Siegel, Micki. "Six Women Who Changed Their Lives . . ." *Good Housekeeping,* July 1992, 76.

Chapter 11: Marvin B. Roffman

Berg, Eric N. "If the News Is Bad, Silence the Messenger." *New York Times,* 15 May 1990, sec. D, p. 1.

Davis, Riccardo A. "Roffman: More Than Money Inspired Claims." *Philadelphia Business Journal,* 16 July 1990, sec. 1, p. 1.

———. "Roffman to Open New Firm Following Panel's Decision." *Philadelphia Business Journal,* 18 March 1991, sec. D, p. 1.

Hostetler, A. J. "Trump Settles Defamation Suit by Securities Analyst." *Associated Press,* 12 June 1991.

Noonan, Peggy J. "The Millionaire's Secret: Six Ordinary Guys Divulge the One Rule That Made Them Rich." *Men's Health,* 1 Oct. 1997, 160.

Roffman, Marvin B. *Take Charge of Your Financial Future.* Citadel Press, 1996.

"Statement by Janney Montgomery Scott." *PR Newswire,* 10 July 1990.

Weil, Dan, and Charles Keenan. "1st Union's Brash Sales Culture Repelled CoreStates Customers." *The American Banker,* 27 July 1999.

Chapter 12: David Copperfield

Ansley, Lesley. "Presto-Change-O! The Wizard of Awes." *USA Weekend,* 1 May 1994, 4.

Bagli, Charles V. "Poof! $34 Million Vanishes on Broadway." *New York Times,* 26 Sept. 1999, sec. 3, p. 1.

Biography, "David Copperfield." A&E Television Networks, 1998.

Braxton, Greg. "Sorcerer's apprentice no more; David Copperfield, at 37, comes into his own as a master of illusion; he has 15-year CBS retrospective Thursday and a new jet-set status with his engagement to model Claudia Schiffer. Now for his next trick . . ." *Los Angeles Times,* 8 May 1994, Calendar section, p. 8.

"Commencement; Fordham Class Hears Magician and Peacemaker." *New York Times,* 23 May 1999, 36.

David Copperfield's Web site: <*www.dcopperfield.com*>.

Dillon, Jennifer. "Magic of David Copperfield Enchants U. New Hampshire." *New Hampshire University Wire,* 23 April 1999.

Dominguez, Robert. "Q and A Magic Man David Copperfield." *(New York) Daily News,* 5 Nov. 1995, Spotlight section, p. 15.

Emling, Shelley. "Celebrities Flock to the Caribbean to See and Be Seen." *Dallas Morning News,* 11 July 1999, 13G.

"Forbes Celebrity Power 100." *Forbes,* 22 March 1999, 203.

Ford, Peter. "Poof! Where'd Tax Money Go? Russian Police Wonder." *Christian Science Monitor,* 24 Sept. 1997, 7.

Garbarino, Steve. "Breaking Up Is Hard to Do." *Detour,* May 1999, 76.

Graham, Jefferson. "The 'Honest Deceiver'; Copperfield Has New Tricks Up His Sleeve; His 'Passion' to Perform Is No Illusion." *USA Today,* 29 March 1993, 1D.

Gubernick, Lisa, and Peter Newcomb. "Now You See It, Now You Don't." *Forbes,* 27 Sept. 1993, 88.

Guttman, Monika. "Re-appearing Act: It Must Be Magic That Gets David Copperfield through 500 Shows a Year." *Chicago Tribune,* 29 March 1990, 19.

Harden, Mark. "Hocus Pocus Focus Copperfield's Audience a Part of New Illusions." *Denver Post,* 21 Feb. 1999, J-1.

Herman, Jan. "David Copperfield Dispels a Few Illusions About Magic." *Los Angeles Times,* 15 April 1988, part 6, p. 23.

Jaeger, Lauren. "David Copperfield's Latin America Tour Makes Millions 'Magically.' Magician's Show Pulls in $13.4 Million." *Amusement Business,* 14 July 1997, 7.

Jones, Chris. "The Master Manipulator: David Copperfield Is Up to New Tricks in His Search for Respect." *Chicago Tribune,* 7 March 1999, Arts & Entertainment section, p. 1.

Kelly, Charles. "Poof! Go Magic's Secrets: Tell-All Shows Destructive, Performer Says." *Arizona Republic,* 19 Aug. 1998, B1.

McTavish, Brian. "And Now for His Next Trick." *Kansas City Star,* 28 Feb. 1999.

Newcomb, Peter, and Jean Sherman Chatzky. "The Top 40." *Forbes,* 28 Sept. 1992, 87.

Paskevich, Michael. "Shedding Light: Copperfield Talks Candidly About His Profession." *Las Vegas Review-Journal,* 26 June 1998, 3J.

Robison, Ken. "It's No Illusion." *Fresno Bee* in the *Sacramento Bee,* 14 July 1996, EN12.

Sime, Tom. "Spellbound: Copperfield Ever-Dedicated to Sharing the Charmed Life." *Dallas Morning News,* 15 April 1998, 39A.

Spelling, Ian. "The Magic Touch." *Sacramento Bee,* 1 June 1994, SC1.

Witchel, Alex. "Theater: A Maestro of the Magic Arts Returns to His Roots." *New York Times,* 24 Nov. 1996, sec. 2, p. 4.

Zehme, Bill. "Shazam! David Copperfield and Claudia Schiffer Engaged." *Esquire,* April 1994, 90.

Zhito, Lisa. "Producers: There's More Than Magic Behind Success of Copperfield Tours." *Amusement Business,* 24 Jan. 1994, 7.

Chapter 13: Humberto Cruz

Cruz, Humberto. "Investing: Let's Get Real About Retirement Riches." Tribune Media Services, as published in *Newsday,* 22 Feb. 1998, F7.

Edgerton, Jerry. "Cover Story: How This Family Sets Aside 51% of Its Income." *Money,* 1 Sept. 1990, 73.

Noonan, Peggy J. "The Millionaire's Secret: Six Ordinary Guys Divulge the One Rule That Made Them Rich." *Men's Health*, 1 Oct. 1997, 160.

Chapter 14: Scott D. Oki

Buck, Richard. "Covering Market: Microsoft Executive Starts New Venture." *Seattle Times*, 29 Jan. 1992, E2.

"The Forbes 400." *Forbes*, 11 Oct. 1999, 174.

Kleiner, Adam. "Movers & Shapers." *Washington CEO*, May 1996, 14.

"Microsoft Invests $5M in Promo; Reseller Promotion Campaign." *Computer & Software News*, 6 Feb. 1989, 4.

"Microsoft Names Scott Oki as Senior Vice President of United States Sales and Marketing Reporting to Company President Jon Shirley." *Business Wire*, 2 Sept. 1986.

Moody, Fred. "Mr. Software." *New York Times*, 25 Aug. 1991, sec. 6, p. 26.

"Oki to Retire as Senior Vice President; Raikes Named Successor." *Business Wire*, 28 Jan. 1992.

Plummer, William. "Up Front: The Givers Microsoft Millionaires Prove There Is Such a Thing as the Nonprofit Motive." *People*, 27 Oct. 1997, 46.

Quinlan, Tom. "Microsoft President Shirley Sails into Retirement." *MIS Week*, 1 Jan. 1990, 4.

Ziegler, Bart. "Microsoft President Steps Down as Software Giant Reorganizes." *Associated Press*, 3 Feb. 1992.

Zuckerman, Ed. "William Gates III; at 34, the Software Satrap Is Working on His Third Billion." *People*, 20 Aug. 1990, 91.

Chapter 15: Dennis L. Lardon

Freiberg, Kevin and Jackie. *Nuts! Southwest Airlines' Crazy Recipe for Business and Personal Success.* New York: Broadway Books, 1996.

Hall, Cheryl. "Still Crazy After 20 Years: Original Employees to Retire as Millionaires." *Dallas Morning News*, 9 June 1996, 1H.

Jarman, Max. "Company Tries to Spur Loyalty Inside and Out." *Arizona Republic,* 26 April 1998, D1.

Labich, Kenneth. "Is Herb Kelleher America's Best CEO?" *Fortune,* 2 May 1994, 44.

Martin, Justin. "So You Want to Work for the Best; You'll Have to Sit through Multiple Interviews, Pass a Battery of Tests, Tell Your Life Story—Maybe Even Come Up with a Few Jokes." *Fortune,* 12 Jan. 1998, 77.

"Southwest Airlines' Extrovert-in-Chief Named CEO of the Year." *Business Wire,* 12 July 1999.

Chapter 16: Maya Angelou

Allen, Carl. "The Wars Behind the Black Experience." *Buffalo News,* 16 May 1999, Book reviews section, p. 6G.

Angelou, Maya. *Singin' and Swingin' and Gettin' Merry Like Christmas.* New York: Bantam Books, 1977.

———. *All God's Children Need Traveling Shoes.* New York: Vintage Books, 1991.

———. *Gather Together in My Name.* New York: Bantam Books, 1993.

———. *I Know Why the Caged Bird Sings.* New York: Bantam Books, 1997.

———. *The Heart of a Woman.* New York: Bantam Books, 1997.

"Ask the Globe." *Boston Globe,* 6 Feb. 1993, 58.

Associated Press. "From 'American Psycho' to 'Wrinkle,' Many Works Targeted for Censorship." *Los Angeles Times,* 25 Oct. 1992, part A, p. 24.

Associated Press. "Effort to Bank Book from Library Fails." *Boston Globe,* 14 May 1999, Metro/region section, p. E3.

Associated Press. "People in the News." 28 April 1999.

Aubry, Erin J. "The Oprah Effect: The TV Star Has Transformed the Publishing World." *LA Weekly,* 29 May 1998, Books section, p. 39.

Beyette, Beverly. "Angelou's 4-year Search for Grandson; Kidnaping Spurs Emotional Odyssey." *Los Angeles Times,* View section, part 5, p. 1.

REFERENCES

Blais, Jacqueline. "Make Yourself at Home at Maya's." *Asheville (NC) Citizen-Times,* 25 May 1997, F2.

Brozan, Nadine. "Chronicle." *New York Times,* 30 Jan. 1993, sec. 1, p. 22.

"A Caged Bird She's Not; Maya Angelou." *Washington Post Magazine,* 9 April 1978, 5.

Cataliotti, Robert H. "A Disappointing Debut by Maya Angelou's Son." *News & Record* (Greensboro, NC), 21 Feb. 1999, F5.

Crockett, Sandra. "The Many Lives of Maya." *The News and Observer* (Raleigh, NC), 23 Sept. 1997, E1.

Darling, Lynn. "A Woman's Heart: Inside the Raging Storm, Looking Out." *Washington Post,* 13 Oct. 1981, D1.

Dogar, Rana. "The Last Article You Will Ever Have to Read on Executive Pay? No Way!" *Forbes,* 20 May 1996, 176.

Donahue, Deirdre. "Has Oprah Saved Books? But Some Wonder If People Are Really Reading." *USA Today,* 12 Dec. 1996, 1D.

Dowd, Maureen, and Frank Rich. "The Inauguration: The Boomers' Ball; Picking Up the Perks of Presidential Power." *New York Times,* 21 Jan. 1993, sec. A, p. 11.

"Everybody's All-American Inaugural Ode Has Made Maya Angelou a Poet-Heroine." *Entertainment Weekly,* 26 Feb. 1993, 52.

Funderberg, Lisa. "Power Moves (a conversation with Maya Angelou and Eleanor Holmes Norton)." *Essence,* 1 Aug. 1998, 70.

Gallagher, Leigh. "Un-Free Speech." *Forbes,* 22 March 1999, 250.

Gavron, Darlene. "A Peek Inside a Powerhouse." *Chicago Tribune,* 7 Aug. 1988, Tempowoman section, p. 2.

Gillespie, Marcia Ann. "Maya Angelou; Lessons in Living." *Essence,* December 1992, 48.

Gowen, Annie. "Holy Hell; Fred Phelps, clergyman, is on a crusade. It's mean and cruel and filled with hate. Can he be stopped? Should he be? A matter of legal rights . . . and moral wrongs." *Washington Post,* 12 Nov. 1995, F1.

Guadan, Deborah G. "From Kudos to Lawsuit." *Sacramento Bee,* 26 June 1999, A2.

Haynes, Karima A. "Maya Angelou; Prime-Time Poet." *Ebony,* April 1993, 68.

Henderson, Shirley. "Phenomenal Poet; for Maya Angelou, Success Is Picking Up the Burden, Not Letting Pain Trip You Up." *Chicago Tribune,* 23 Oct. 1994, Womanews section, p. 8.

Himes, Geoffrey. "Ashfrod & Simpson: Versed in Angelou." *Washington Post,* 18 July 1997, N12.

Holmstrom, David. "Journey of a Poet Laureate." *Sacramento Bee,* 8 Nov. 1993, B5.

Houtchens, C.J. "Maya Angelou: 'You Must Not Be Defeated'; the Word According to Maya Angelou." *USA Weekend,* 10 Oct. 1993, 4.

"Induction of Albright, Angelou Tops Anniversary Celebration at National Women's Hall of Fame." *PR Newswire,* 1 July 1998.

"Just the Facts." *Journal of Business Strategy,* September/October 1998, Short Takes section.

Kelly, Dennis. "Poets Hope Inaugural Gives Verse Its Due." *USA Today,* 29 Dec. 1992, 1A.

Kennedy, Dana. "Holiday Films: A Poet at 70, Ventures into the Unknown." *New York Times,* 15 Nov. 1998, sec. 2A, p. 13.

Knight-Ridder/Tribune. "Fred Phelps' Latest Target Was Poet Maya Angelou." *Chicago Tribune,* 2 Dec. 1994, Tempo section, p. 1.

Lewis, Jean Battey. "A Revelation: Celebrating the Enduring Legacy of Alvin Ailey." *Washington Times,* 24 April 1999, part D, p. C1.

Lipson, Karin. "The Hidden Black Artists." *Newsday,* 16 Nov. 1994, B11.

Lorando, Mark. "Novel Development." *Times-Picayune,* 28 Oct. 1997, C1.

Maryles, Daisy. "Behind the Bestsellers." *Publishers Weekly,* 15 March 1993, 11.

———. "Behind the Bestsellers," *Publishers Weekly,* 12 May 1997, 23.

"Maya Angelou," in *Major 20th-Century Writers.* 2d ed. Gale Research Inc., 1998.

"Maya Angelou." *Writer's Directory.* 14th ed. Gale Research Inc., 1999.

"Maya Angelou Calls Off Poetry Reading." *Buffalo News,* 20 Nov. 1994, Local section, p. 3.

"Maya Angelou," in *Celebrity Biographies.* Baseline II Inc., 1999.

"Maya's Birthday: To Honor a Beloved Poet Turning 70, Oprah Winfrey Mixed Sweetness and Spirituality—and a Boatload of Wicked Excess." *Life,* July 1998.

Meroney, John. "The Real Maya Angelou." *The American Spectator,* March 1993, Clinton's America section.

Meyers, Caryn. "Want a Celeb? Save Up." *Successful Meetings,* Oct. 1998, 16.

Millner, Denene. "Maya Angelou: 'Delta Queen,' the Creator of Acclaimed Fiction and Poetry Tries Her Hand at Cinema." *(New York) Daily News,* 25 Dec. 1998, 56.

Molotsky, Irvin. "Poet of the South for the Inauguration." *New York Times,* 5 Dec. 1992, sec. 1, p. 8.

Musto, Michael. "La Dolce Musto." *Village Voice,* 22 Dec. 1998, 14.

Nappi, Rebecca. "Angelou's Words Could Save the Day. *Spokesman-Review* (Spokane, WA), 16 Aug. 1999, A12. For the editorial board.

The National Women's Hall of Fame Web page: *<www.greatwomen.org>.*

"Number of Challenges to Maya Angelou." Special customized request by the American Library Association on July 30, 1999.

Paglia, Camille. "Back to the Barricades." *New York Times,* 9 May 1999, sec. 7, p. 19.

"People." *Dallas Morning News,* 26 Oct. 1997, 2A. From Wire Reports.

Petrikin, Chris. "Lit Picks." *Daily Variety,* 12 May 1997.

Rozen, Leah. "Screen." *People,* 11 Jan. 1999, Picks & Pans section, p. 35.

Schofield, Matthew. "A Poet Is Left Speechless by Preacher's Harsh Words; Maya Angelou Cancels Visit to Emporia, Kan., After Phelps Tirade." *Kansas City Star,* 17 Nov. 1994, A1.

Stanley, Allessandra. "Whose Honor Is It, Anyway?" *New York Times,* 17 May 1992, sec. 9, p. 5.

Stein, Ruthe. "Maya Angelou and Her Sacred Places: New Poetry Faces the Pain of Aging." *San Francisco Chronicle,* 5 June 1990, People section, p. B3.

Sumner, Jane. "Simply Maya; . . . We Are Troubled. And Need to Have Some Idea if There Is Something Larger Than We Are, Says Professor and Author." *Dallas Morning News,* 25 Oct. 1993, 1C.

Thompson, Jean. "Fascinating but Bloody Epic Needs Tough Edit." *Baltimore Sun, The Plain Dealer,* 31 Jan. 1999, Books section, p. 12I.

Thorn, Patti. "Maya's Way: Maya Angelou's Zest for Life Continues to Fuel Her Creative Fire." *Rocky Mountain News,* 23 Nov. 1997, 1E.

Trescott, Jacqueline. "Poet to Read at Swearing-in; Maya Angelou Asked to Write New Work." *Washington Post,* 3 Dec. 1992, A1.

Turnbull, Barbara. "An Extraordinary Full Life." *Toronto Star,* 21 June 1998.

Unmacht, Eric. "Maya Angelou: From Creole Cook to Presidential Post." *Christian Science Monitor,* 17 Aug. 1999, 14.

Webb, Jack. "Despite Hoopla, Poetry Remains a Hard Sell." *San Diego Union-Tribune,* 1 Aug. 1999, E-1.

Wilson, Calvin. "The Luck and Talent of Maya Angelou: Here's Why Most Sing Praises of the Versatile Poet." *Kansas City Star,* 9 June 1999, sec. FYI, p. F1.

Winfrey, Oprah. "Mine Eyes Have Seen the Glory." *Los Angeles Times,* 15 Dec. 1996, Book review section, p. 1.

World-Herald News Service. "Poet Maya Angelou Cancels Iowa Event." *Omaha World Herald,* 4 Oct. 1994, 15.

"World's Largest Lesbian and Gay Performing Arts Festival Headed for Tampa; Maya Angelou to Keynote Opening Ceremonies." *PR Newswire,* 13 June 1996.

Chapter 17: Timothy B. and Karen Schmidt Faber

Davidson, Paul. "A Measly Million: So, How Much Money Does It Take to be Rich?" *USA Today,* 20 June 1997, 1A.

ABOUT THE AUTHORS

Husband and wife Alan Lavine and Gail Liberman are syndicated finance columnists and authors based in North Palm Beach, Florida.

Their joint columns run weekly in the *Boston Herald*, on America Online, and in numerous newspapers. Alan and Gail are also frequent guests on radio and television as well as columnists for Fundsinteractive.com and Quicken.com.

You may have heard or seen them on numerous financial talk shows on CNN, CNBC, and PBS as well as on NBC TV's *Nightside* and *Weekend Today in New York;* Fox's *Good Day New York; Fox and Friends,* WGN TV and radio in Chicago; Bloomberg television and radio networks; the *700 Club;* Business News Network; National Public Radio and TalkAmerica network. Individually or together, they have also been quoted in *The Wall Street Journal, Money* magazine, *USA Today,* the *New York Times, Business Week, Redbook* magazine, *First, Bride's, Elle, Investors Business Daily,* and the *Washington Post.*

The two have contributed to *Consumers Digest, Your Money,* and *Worth* magazine as well as the *Journal of the National Association of Personal Financial Advisors.*

Gail Liberman's column, "Managing Your Fortune," runs in the *Palm Beach Daily News.* She helped found Bank Rate Monitor in North Palm Beach, a publication that tracks bank interest rates and trends, and had been its editor for 15 years. An award-winning journalist, Gail began her career at the Associated Press, United Press International, and United Feature Syndicate. A graduate of Rutgers University, she also has appeared on *Good Morning America*.

Alan Lavine, former director of research at IBC, a publisher of mutual fund and financial planning advice, has his own personal finance column in the *Boston Herald*, the *American Lawyer* newspaper chain, and on CNBC.com. He is also a regular contributor to *Financial Planning and Accounting Today* and has written for the *New York Times, Financial World,* and *Individual Investor.* His family finance research was cited by the Joint Economic Committee of Congress in establishing economic policy in the 1980s. Alan has spoken before such groups as the American Psychology Association and the American Association for the Advancement of Science and Morningstar Inc.'s mutual fund conferences.

Prior to his postgraduate training in finance and economics at Clark University in Worcester, Massachusetts, he worked for ten years as a licensed clinical social worker in Massachusetts. He obtained his MA degree in psychology at the University of Akron and also trained at the Gestalt Institute of New England.

Gail and Alan are coauthors of *The Complete Idiot's Guide to Making Money with Mutual Funds; Love, Marriage, and Money;* and *Improving Your Credit and Reducing Your Debt.* Alan has also written *Diversify Your Way to Wealth; 50 Ways to Mutual Fund Profits; Getting Started in Mutual Funds;* and *Your Life Insurance Options.*

0-595-30091-X

LaVergne, TN USA
07 September 2010

196146LV00005B/4/A

9 780595 300914